KEVIN KOPELSON

Love's Litany

The Writing of Modern Homoerotics

STANFORD UNIVERSITY PRESS

STANFORD, CALIFORNIA

D1380421

Stanford University Press, Stanford, California
© 1994 by the Board of Trustees of the Leland Stanford Junior University
Printed in the United States of America

CIP data appear at the end of the book

Stanford University Press publications are distributed exclusively by
Stanford University Press within the United States, Canada, and Mexico;
they are distributed exclusively by Cambridge University Press
throughout the rest of the world.

Love's Litany

The Writing of Modern Homoerotics

FOR DOUG WINGO

Acknowledgments

Scholars fortunate enough to have gravitated toward lesbian and gay studies often find they have a problematic personal stake in their work. We tend to put ourselves on—and over—the line. We continually acknowledge our sexualities in contexts that are likely to be homophobic. We also continually question our ability to acknowledge our sexualities at all. I used to know what it meant to say, "I'm gay." I now realize how little I know what that means. I now realize it doesn't even mean what I once thought it did—for example, that I'm essentially effeminate or that I have an ascertainable "sensibility." I would like to acknowledge, and to thank, the many scholars, too many to name here, who have precipitated these realizations and who have proven them to be empowering, if not liberating.

I began this book three years ago as a doctoral dissertation at Brown University. I couldn't have conceived, and wouldn't have completed, that "unfashionable" project without the encouragement and guidance of Robert Scholes, Ellen Rooney, and William Keach. I cannot thank them enough. I would also like to thank my parents, Ida and Kenneth Kopelson, who have always supported me; Karen Bock, Eric Clarke, and Keith Green, who made my graduate school experience bearable and helped me write my way out of a number of corners; Henry Abelove, Amittai F. Aviram, Joseph Boone, George Chauncey, Lee Edelman, David Halperin, Richard Kaye, Wayne Koestenbaum, Robert K. Martin, Michael Moon, Larry Norman, and Helen Tartar, who read and critiqued the dissertation; Pierre Saint-Amand, Robert Kopelson, Michael West, and Brad Williams, who supplied translations; Eve Kosofsky Sedgwick, who brought my work to the attention of Stanford University Press; Ellen F. Smith, who edited the manuscript; and Doug Wingo, with whom I've learned *Love's Litany* and to whom it is dedicated.

K.K.

Contents

~

Love's Litany

The Writing of Modern Homoerotics

Introduction

What's love got to do with it?
Tina Turner

Could it be that the "it" to which this perspicuous lyric refers is
sexuality? Followers of Michel Foucault consider sexuality to be a
vexed and vexing cultural construction formed by, at the very
least, three powerful discourses: theology, medicine, and law. The
male homosexual, for example, is at once a sinner, an invert, and
a sodomite. Unfortunately, most Foucauldians fail to suspect, even
though common sense should tell them it must, that another
powerful (if nowadays undervalued) discourse inflects sexuality as
well: love, or more specifically, erotic philosophy. What does love
have to do with sexuality? Leave it to post-structuralists, Tina
Turner might snicker, to fail to ask this question—or to suggest
"nothing" as its answer.

Whence that failure and that answer? Why is "love" less fash-
ionable than "sex" or "desire"? Critical theorists tend to see love as
an outmoded and incoherent epistemological anomaly that has
no place among the discourses that construct sexuality as an epistemological field. According to Roland Barthes, the life of the lover is one of "'philosophical' solitude, love-as-passion being ac-
counted for today by no major system of thought (of discourse)"
(*Lover's Discourse* 210). Even though popular culture is obsessed
with love, love is "not contemporary," it is "left aside or disparaged
by the actuality of theoretical systems" (Heath 104). According to

Julia Kristeva, "today we have no love discourse" and "lack a code of love" because "social consensus gives *little* or *no* support to . . . amatory idealism" (*Tales of Love* 381, 6, 267). But even if conceptions of love are now passé and fragmentary, they are not necessarily inconsequential. They are active, if residual, cultural elements that have played and continue to play a crucial and underexamined role in the construction of sexuality. As Oscar Wilde, who had more to say about sexuality than he himself realized, once put it: "Do you wish to love? Use Love's Litany, and the words will create the yearning from which the world fancies that they spring" ("Critic as Artist" 399).

This book initiates an investigation of the role played by love in the construction, not of sexuality *per se*, but of *homo*sexuality. More specifically, it examines a number of erotic texts by lesbian and gay writers (Oscar Wilde, André Gide, Ronald Firbank, Virginia Woolf, Gertrude Stein, Marguerite Yourcenar, Mary Renault, and Roland Barthes)—texts that rewrite, and unwrite, romantic love in more or less coherent fashions—in order to describe ways in which these love stories have helped script lesbian and gay sexuality. But why focus on romantic, which is to say nineteenth-century, erotics?

One reason is that romantic erotics is rather amenable to an investigation of ways in which love inflects sexuality. Most nineteenth-century theorists saw love and sex as interrelated. They believed that "true love is the conjunction of concupiscence with affection," that it comprises both "sensual" and "tender" currents (Gay 45). The theorists did not, however, value sensuality as highly as tenderness, which they considered spiritual and therefore nobler—an all-too-familiar notion they cannot be said to have originated. Yet even if nineteenth-century erotics did not conflate love and sex, it would still be the focus of this study. To the extent that any one erotic discourse dominates current thought, it is romantic. The nineteenth century was "profoundly erotic" (Gay 422). It was characterized by a voluminous theorization and a widespread popularization of love that were almost unprecedented.[1] As one historian has observed of the preceding period: "despite the flood of poems, novels and plays on the themes of romantic and sexual love, they played little or no part in the daily lives of men and women of the late seventeenth and eighteenth centuries" (Stone 272). It is true, of course, that nineteenth-century erotic discourse is based upon earlier discourses (Platonic, Petrarchan, etc.). As Joseph Boone notes, many important nineteenth-century figures, and in particular "figures of total union, of desire and the obstructions engendering desire, and of sexual duality as a hierarchical balance," actually derive from medieval romance literature (38). However, the nineteenth-century bourgeoisie transfigured, or "reinvented," those earlier and predominantly aristocratic discourses—and it is the transfigurations that have survived into the present century (Polhemus 153). Lovers are simply more likely to croon "Isn't it romantic?" than "Isn't it courtly?" And if unadulterated pre-romantic discourses are now barely audible, more recent erotic discourse, as both Barthes and Kristeva note, has fallen on deaf ears. Lovers are simply more likely to croon "Isn't it romantic?" than "Isn't it psychoanalytic?" But what precisely is so "romantic" about love as most of us know it?

Romantic erotics deploys a dazzling array of figures, all of which deserve attention in this type of analysis. Some are celebratory: love as divine, as heroic, as eternal, as enchanting, as providential, as idolatrous, as transcendental. Some are somewhat negative: love as violent, as combative, as poisonous, as enthralling, as infectious, as tyrannical, as sacrificial. Some are relatively value-neutral: the idea that love is rational, that it is a vocation, that it is a potent energy, that it "conquers all."[2] This study, however, focuses on four features of romantic love—features that, as Irving Singer shows, are central to nineteenth-century erotic philosophy and that, as the following readings should suggest, are central to twentieth-century homoeroticism.[3]

First, romantic erotics conceives of love as the merging of two persons who complement one another, as an intersubjective dissolution of polar opposition, or obliteration of "the division between the 'I' and the 'not-I' . . . in a redemptive state of feeling" (Moglen 29). This complementarity is essentially heterosexual; it is the complementarity of sexual difference. For Schopenhauer, for example, lovers "feel the longing for an actual union and fusing together into a single being . . . and this longing receives its fulfillment in the child which is produced by them both" (3: 342). The English romantic poets are of like mind. Coleridge believes that "the blending of the similar with the dissimilar is the secret of all pure delight . . . more than all in the exclusive attachment of the sexes" (2: 107). Likewise, Shelley, in "A Discourse on the Manners of the Ancient Greeks Relative to the Subject of Love," claims that lovers seek beloveds who, being diacritically sexed, complement themselves. Keats's *Endymion* also represents the quest for "endless bliss" by a male and female who wish only to "melt into" one another (2.807, 815). And novelistic representations of "contrast" as the source of romantic attraction, such as Eliot's description of Maggie and Stephen in *The Mill on the Floss* as a "twofold consciousness that was mingled into one" (407), also "almost always reduce that 'contrast' to a simple binary opposition rooted in contemporary ideologies of sexual polarity" (Boone 11). This basic heterosexuality of the feature, or figure, is indicative of the extent to which nineteenth-century erotics subscribes to two countervailing and primarily novelistic ideals: marital and adulterous love.[4] It is also indicative, if not determinative, of a hierarchical and antagonistic quality with which, as this study will show, lesbian and gay writers have had to contend.[5] Because "the hierarchy of male and female roles [tends to transform a] love relationship into a battle for mastery and possession," the figure is perhaps best characterized as one "of irremediable division glossed over by surface unanimity," of "sexual dichotomization hidden under the unifying sign of marital harmony" (Boone 191, 196).

It is worth noting that the figure of complementary merger was itself complemented by the less pervasive figure of erotic identification, a figure often associated with *Wuthering Heights.* "Whatever our souls are made of," Catherine exclaims, "his and mine are the same. . . . Nelly, I *am* Heathcliff" (68, 70). The idea of falling in love with a duplicate image, as opposed to a contrasting one, formed a fairly conspicuous part of romantic ideology, and it created, as Robert Polhemus notes, a "contradictory logic of desire [as] both 'like with like' and 'opposites attract'" (99).[6] One might imagine that the concept of erotic identification was more likely to have been transfigured by lesbian and gay writers than was the concept of complementary merger, but in fact, and for reasons this study will touch upon, this does not appear to have been the case. It is also worth noting, if only to illustrate the workings of what Monique Wittig has called "the straight mind," that the figure of complementary merger was neither exclusively heterosexual nor oppressively hierarchical at its inception. It derives from a story recounted by Aristophanes in Plato's *Symposium* about the origin of desire:

In the beginning we were nothing like we are now. For one thing, the race was divided into three . . . besides the two sexes, male and female, which we have at present, there was a third which partook of the nature of both. . . . And secondly . . . each of these beings was globular in shape, with rounded back and sides, four arms and four legs, and two faces. . . . And such . . . were their strength and energy, and such their arrogance, that they actually tried . . . to scale the heights of heaven and set upon the gods.

At this Zeus took counsel with the other gods as to what was to be done. . . . At last . . . after racking his brains, Zeus offered a solution.

I think I can see my way, he said, to put an end to this disturbance. . . . What I propose to do is to cut them all in half, thus killing two birds with one stone, for each one will be only half as strong, and there'll be twice as many of them. . . . Now, when the work of bisection was complete it left each half with a desperate yearning for the other, and they ran together and flung their arms around each other's necks, and asked for nothing better than to be rolled into one. So much so, that they began to die. . . . Zeus felt so sorry for them that he devised another scheme. He moved their privates round to the front . . . and made them propagate among themselves. . . . So you see . . . how far back we can trace our innate love for one another, and how this love is always trying to reintegrate our former nature, to make two into one, and to bridge the gulf between one human being and another. (542–44)

As David Halperin notes, Aristophanes' myth clearly generates "three distinct 'sexualities'"—males attracted to males, females attracted to females, and, consigned to one classification, both males attracted to females and females attracted to males (19). Oddly enough, many critics, even ones who should know better, act as though it only generates heterosexuality. Peter Gay, for example, states that "Plato's engaging tale about the origins of amorous attraction, one half of the once-united *bisexual* creature desperately desiring the other half from which it had been torn, survived into the nineteenth century as an enduring metaphor for lonely, fragmented beings in search of love's healing power" (330; emphasis added). According to Barthes, "the two halves of the *androgyne* sigh for each other, as if each breath, being incomplete, sought to mingle with the other" (*Lover's Discourse* 15; emphasis added).[7] And Kaja Silverman credits Aristophanes with having portrayed a primordial "sexual *androgyny*" and with believing "that the *only* resolution to the loss suffered by the subject as the consequence of sexual division is heterosexual union and procreation" (152; emphasis added).

Like complementary merger, the three other features of romantic love with which this study is primarily concerned have heterosexual orientations. Unlike complementary merger, however, they are decidedly Continental. Love-death (*Liebestod*), the second feature, conflates the concept of love as metaphysical union, the concept of *death* as metaphysical union, and the concept of Petrarchan *acedia* (unhappy mutual love). Love-death is now commonly associated with Wagner's *Tristan and Isolde* (1865), but it appears in as early a text as Goethe's *The Elective Affinities* (1809). Wertherism, the third feature, can of course also be traced to Goethe. To the extent that we, like the romantics, associate love with sadness, solitude, and suicide, we have the hapless hero of *The Sorrows of Young Werther* (1774) to thank. The fourth feature of romantic erotics is known as "crystallization," a term coined by Stendhal in *De l'amour* (1822). The reference is to his famous "Salzburg Bough" metaphor, according to which a lover's penchant to imagine her or his beloved as perfect is analogous to the process by which a bare tree branch, if thrown into a salt mine, becomes encrusted with, and obscured by, beautiful salt crystals.

This Continental divide, while not, as this study will suggest, absolutely critical, should be borne in mind. Not every erotic death in Victorian fiction, for example, is a love-death (nor, or course, is every erotic death in nineteenth-century Continental fiction). The deaths of Maggie and Tom in *The Mill on the Floss* may be somewhat Wagnerian, but the death of Catherine in *Wuthering Heights* is not.[8] It is, as Boone states, "quite the opposite of the glorified and idealized *Liebestod*, or death-longing of Continental love literature; her death neither fulfills nor resolves anything" (161).

This study devotes one chapter, and in the case of complementary merger, two chapters, to each of these four features of romantic erotics. Chapter 1 deals with a number of fin-de-siècle deployments of the Liebestod trope. Chapters 2 and 3 concern contemporary and conflicted negotiations of the notion of complementary merger. Chapter 4 describes related rejections of the crystallization figure. And Chapter 5 analyzes a recent resurrection of Werther. This structure should not, however, suggest that these features are unrelated. As the readings themselves acknowledge, love-deaths can be Wertheresque, and crystallizations can involve the type of erotic domination that subtends complementary mergers.

But why focus on literary texts by modern, Western, lesbian and gay writers? First, why lesbian and gay texts? If the important question is "What has love to do with sexuality," why limit oneself to the question "What has love to do with *homo*sexuality"? To be frank, having been subjected to a number of them, I am simply more interested in constructions of homosexuality than in constructions of heterosexuality. A less idiosyncratic reason, however, is that a number of scholars, many of them feminist, have already begun to examine ways in which conceptions of love inflect literary texts that are either explicitly heterosexual or not explicitly homosexual.[9] Nancy K. Miller, for example, has demonstrated that erotic "rhetorics" compete with one another across gender lines in eighteenth-century novels written by men (*Heroine's Text* 150). Lee Edwards has argued that the late-nineteenth- and twentieth-century textualization of female characters as full-fledged "heroes" rewrote romantic erotics. Rachel Blau DuPlessis has described strategies (such as "reparenting" and "female bonding") that "delegitimate the specific narrative and cultural orders of nineteenth-century fiction—the emphasis on successful or failed romance, the subordination of quest to love, the death of the questing female, the insertion into family life" (34–35).[10] Joseph Boone has shown that "the undermining dialogue of uneasy wedlock, the male quest into a world of alternate possibilities, [and] the sustaining fiction of female community" transformed the history of the erotic novel (330). Although some of the deviations from romantic doxa noted by these scholars do, in fact, anticipate the deviations of lesbian and gay literature ("male quests" can be rather homoerotic, and "female bonds" rather lesbianic), the two sets of deviations are not coextensive.[11] Heterosexuality and homosexuality are not, it need hardly be said, identical constructions. For one thing, homosexuality, like femininity, is a problematic ("unnatural") and therefore marked (overtheorized) category, whereas heterosexuality, like masculinity, is a relatively unproblematic ("natural") and therefore unmarked (undertheorized) one. Of the two, that is, it is homosexuality that requires, and receives, an explanation—which could mean that love's role in the construction of homosexuality is more readily articulated than is its role in the construction of heterosexuality.

Why modern, and postmodern, texts? Homosexuality is a late-nineteenth-century construction. It is by now a commonplace of Foucauldian criticism that homosexual identities, as opposed to homosexual acts, arose only after a number of relatively recent, and primarily sexological, discourses breathed life into them. Men, for example, who from time to time had dabbled in sodomy eventually found themselves called, and called themselves, "inverts" and "homosexuals."[12] More or less insignificant sex acts now expressed discrete sexual essences. Hence, to ask "What's love got to do with homosexuality?" is to pose a question that has little or no meaning prior to the fin de siècle. "Love" may have meant something then (indeed, it meant more then than it means now), but "homosexuality" simply did not.

Why Western texts? Cultural constructions are culturally contingent. Sexuality as we know it is not a universal phenomenon. Our sense that one is either a homosexual or a heterosexual "personage" (to use Foucault's term), that one's essential identity is either "gay" or "straight" (a polar division that is disturbed both by its self-deconstructive tendencies and by the third term "bisexual"), as well as our complex and contradictory justifications (psychological, sexological, sociobiological, etc.) for this sense, are uniquely Western. The notion that gay men are Oedipal wrecks is quite foreign to cultures Freudian theory has not yet come to dominate. The by now outmoded notion, popularized in part by *The Well of Loneliness*, that lesbians have the psyches of "real" (i.e., heterosexual) men and only desire "real" (i.e., heterosexual) women (who, it goes without saying, never desire them in return) is quite foreign to cultures that have neither devised nor disseminated theories of sexual "inversion." Nor, it should be said, is what we mean by "love" universal. Even if love, as an emotion, makes the world go round (a dubious notion—feelings are also cultural constructions), love, as theorized by romantic writers, does not go round the world. Liebestod is at home in Bayreuth but not in Beirut. Crystallizations occur in Salzburg and not in Singapore. It may well be, of course, that non-Western cultures have constructed epistemological categories that to Westerners seem "sexual" and "erotic." It may even well be that non-Western "erotics" inflects non-Western "sexuality." However, it would be presumptuous, and imperialistic, to subsume those categories and that inflection, assuming they exist, within the context of this study. In other words, "What has love to do with homosexuality?" is a Western question posed and answered, howsoever incompletely, by a Western scholar for his Western readers. It may be *translatable* into, and have some relevance within, non-Western discourses, but there are many other scholars who are in better positions to do the translating and determine such relevance.

And why literary texts? All of the major texts analyzed here, including the theoretical ones by Barthes, are literary. On the one hand, this is due to an ever-weakening disciplinary constraint: literary scholars still tend, and are still expected, to study literature. On the other hand, it resists the blandishments of scholars who would limit lesbian and gay studies to analyses of popular culture. The reason for this somewhat unfashionable focus is that both romantic love and homosexuality are literary effects. Love is a literary effect insofar as a great deal of consequential erotic exposition is novelistic.[13] Modern perceptions of erotic desire are "very much formed and conditioned by the fact that the novel became such an influential art form" (Polhemus 2–3) and by the fact that love is the "governing preoccupation" of the novel (Gay 135). To put it bluntly, both Proust and Freud write on love, but who remembers what Freud says or where he says it?[14] Homosexuality is a literary effect insofar as it is structured by readings of "literary" texts. More "inverted" lesbians, it is safe to say, have read, and recognized themselves in, *The Well of Loneliness* than have read Richard von Krafft-Ebing's *Psychopathia Sexualis*. And more gay men have read *Dancer from the Dance* than Alfred Kinsey's *Sexual Behavior in the Human Male*. Which, of course, is not surprising. "Literature," for better or worse, has been a privileged site of cultural expression for so long that many modern subjects are predisposed to turn to it for what seems like self-articulation, self-validation, and self-explication. This is especially true of lesbian and gay subjects, who often find themselves represented unsympathetically—if, indeed, they find themselves represented at all—in non-literary cultural forms.

Of course, romantic love and homosexuality are not solely literary effects. Kristeva's claim that "love crosses the threshold of modern times *only* in literature" clearly overstates the case (*Tales of Love* 61; emphasis added). Popular culture (film, television, music) is as preoccupied with love as novels are. It is Tina Turner, after all, who asks "What's love got to do with it?" And if non-literary representations of homosexuality are, in fact, less plentiful and sympathetic than literary ones, they can hardly be described as negligible. "Divine," the shit-eating star of *Pink Flamingos*, made an indelible impression on thousands of avid fans, many of whom might be surprised to learn that he was named after a character in

Jean Genet's *Our Lady of the Flowers*. In other words, "What has love to do with homosexuality?" is a question that should be examined by looking at non-literary as well as literary texts. This particular examination does restrict itself to literature, but only in order that the literariness of homoeroticism not be lost sight of in an effort to popularize lesbian and gay studies.

The subtitle "The Writing of Modern Homoerotics" does not, however, signify the focus on literature; both literary and non-literary cultural forms can be read as "writing." Rather, it signifies a commitment to deconstructive modes of analysis—a commitment shared by a number of critics working in lesbian and gay studies. Lee Edelman, for example, has suggested that "a significant project for gay critics must be the study of the historically variable rhetorics, the discursive strategies and tropological formations, in which sexuality is not only embedded but conceived" (202). And Eve Kosofsky Sedgwick has proven just how significant such a project can be. *Epistemology of the Closet*, as Sedgwick herself describes the procedure, typically moves "through a deconstructive description of the instability of [a structuring binarism], usually couched as the simultaneous interiority and exteriority of a marginalized to a normative term, toward an examination of the resulting definitional incoherence: its functional potential and realization, its power effects, the affordances for its mobilization within a particular discursive context, and finally the distinctive entanglement with it of the newly crucial issues of homo/heterosexual definition" (92).

There are several reasons why a project of this nature should take its principal methodological cues from these and other similar directives. First, sexualities are structured like languages. Just as languages are complex equilibria of *terms* that mutually condition one another, sexualities are complex equilibria of *discourses* that mutually condition one another. To know a sexuality, in other words, is not simply to know the various discourses that constitute it. It is also to know the ways in which those discourses interact. The Wildean homosexual, as will be seen, recounts an "old" murderous story through a "new" suicidal story of "fatal gay love."

The Gidean/Firbankean pederast who unveils his true self forfeits his true power. Woolf and Stein have disjointed conceptions of erotic merger. Yourcenar and Renault mischaracterize pederastic relationships as heroic. Barthes mischaracterizes the Wertheresque lover as (in)significant. Second, as Sedgwick notes, sexualities are radically incoherent. The interactive discourses that constitute them are often contradictory. Lesbians and gays are subjected to both essentialist and constructionist discourses. They believe themselves to have been "born that way" *and* to have "become that way." But this is only one discursive contradiction among many. The Wildean homosexual is at once victimizer and victim. The Gidean pederast is a non-narcissistic narcissist. The Steinian "ontoeroticist" knows yet cannot know other others. Yourcenar's emperor oscillates between blindness and insight. Barthes's "cruiser" oscillates between masculinity and unisexuality. And finally, the discourses comprising these complex and incoherent equilibria are innumerable. Foucauldians know that theology, medicine, and law construct homosexuality. So, too, as this study argues, does romantic love. But the list of constitutive discourses does not stop there. It includes history (consider the problematic relationship between contemporary pederasty and classical pedagogy), folklore (consider the conflation of homosexuality and hairdressing), economics (consider the use and exchange values of "trade"), and political science (consider the connotations of sexual "liberation"). The list also includes a host of discursive formations that have no such disciplinary credentials. The undisciplined trope of "orgasmic death" has as much to do with Wilde's transfiguration of Liebestod as does the sexological notion of "degeneration." The undisciplined trope of "unveiling" has as much to do with Gidean/Firbankean pederasty as does the psychoanalytic notion of "narcissism."

Although the various modes of analysis used in this study are all deconstructive, they have markedly different emphases. The chapter on Wilde is "new historical" in the broadest sense of the term. It assumes, and argues, that literary texts are historically determined and determining elements of cultural systems, that they represent negotiations between writers with communal discursive repertoires and contemporaneous social institutions and practices, and that they are inseparable from other literary and non-literary "texts." Chapter 2, however, on Gide and Firbank, is not especially historical. Rather, it focuses on ways in which two related texts accommodate a number of irreconcilable discursive formations. Chapter 3, devoted to Woolf and Stein, is psychoanalytic—which is not to say that it *endorses* psychoanalysis. Like Barthes, it displays a decidedly undecided, and critical, attitude toward psychoanalytic theory, which it views not as the (or even *a*) discursive basis of textual and psychic truth, but as a dominant twentieth-century discourse that is only true to the extent that we credit its self-legitimating claims. Both Chapters 4 (on Yourcenar and Renault) and 5 (on Barthes) could be subtitled "Utopia and Its Discontents." They concern discursive, epistemological, and ideological constraints faced by writers who themselves would liberate eroticism from a number of other such restrictions. In other words, they deconstruct deconstructions and hence engage in the kind of critical work deconstructors are always claiming can, and should, be done. This methodological eclecticism is meant, in part, to suggest that a variety of deconstructive heuristics should be brought to bear on questions that arise in lesbian and gay studies. It is also meant to suggest specific heuristics that may be of some use to critics who would like to help answer those questions.

One final methodological strategy should also be mentioned. This study conjoins Gide and Firbank (Chapter 2), Woolf and Stein (Chapter 3), and Yourcenar and Renault (Chapter 4). Some readers may think these literary marriages rather unlikely. Woolf and . . . Stein? Gide and . . . *Firbank*? The readings themselves should justify these particular conjunctions. Gide and Firbank are both frustrated pederasts. Woolf and Stein are both "ontoerotic" Modernists. Yourcenar and Renault are both clear-sighted historical novelists. They should also suggest, more generally, the critical value of reading comparable writers against one another. This study does not, however, conjoin Wilde and Barthes. Instead, it gives them each a separate chapter. As the analyses in those chapters should demonstrate, the two writers have less in common than a number of critics, including the author of this study, seem to suppose.[15] Such are the hidden contradictions of one's erotic subjectivity.

CHAPTER I

Wilde's Love-Deaths

In the blessed abyss of the infinite ether,
in your sublime soul . . . I sink and am engulfed,
unconscious, O bliss!

> Richard Wagner, *Tristan and Isolde*

The man had killed the thing he loved,
  And so he had to die.

> Oscar Wilde, *The Ballad of Reading Gaol*

Isolde's Liebestod was the swan song of the "love-death" strain of romantic erotics. According to Denis de Rougemont, once Wagner "completed," and killed, the Tristan myth, the Western world entered "the era of its phantoms" (231). Indeed, one of the Liebestod trope's earliest and eeriest haunts is the field of fin-de-siècle gay literature. Why should this be? And how do these "decadent" texts deploy the trope? This chapter tries to answer these questions by analyzing a number of texts by, or attributed to, Oscar Wilde—texts that use Liebestod in more or less equivocal and subversive fashions and that demonstrate the extent to which homoerotic rhetoric is shaped by homophobia.

See the Gallows There

Nineteenth-century Britain was profoundly, and polyvocally, homophobic. A wide range of discourses (ethical, theological, medical, etc.) conspired to construct, constrict, and condemn "sodomites," "inverts," and "homosexuals." But of all the homophobic discourses that circumscribed writers like Wilde, one, the penal, was especially, literally, and notoriously noxious. Until 1816, when the pillory was abolished for most offenses, men pilloried for attempting to commit sodomy (that is, for soliciting) were often stoned to death by angry mobs. Until as late as 1861, when the death penalty for "buggery" was reduced to penal servitude for life, convicted sodomites could be, and often were, hanged. Even though a 1781 judicial decision requiring proof of both penetration and emission had made prosecution difficult, more than 50 sodomites were hanged during the first 35 years of the nineteenth century—a period during which the annual number of executions for all crimes dropped by 50 percent while the number for sodomy remained constant. Two statistics in particular attest to the murderous intensity of this form of British homophobia: more sodomites than murderers were executed in 1806, and four out of five convicted sodomites (as opposed to one out of thirty convicted felons in general) were executed in 1810. And in 1828, at a time when it was in the process of repealing the death penalty for dozens of nonviolent crimes, Parliament made sodomy convictions easier to obtain by passing a law requiring proof of penetration alone. As a result, more than 250 sodomites were sentenced to death (but not executed) between 1836 and 1859.[1]

Targets of lethal penal policies have long memories—so long as they feel persecuted, and so long as they comprise a community. In nineteenth-century Britain, middle- and upper-class "sodomites" (and, later, "inverts" and "homosexuals") belonged to a series of more or less self-conscious subcultures that saw this homophobic policy as truly persecutory. As early as the 1830's, one such subculture called for sodomy law reform in the opening lines of *Don Leon*, a spurious Byron "autobiography":[2]

> Thou ermined judge, pull off that sable cap!
> What! Can'st thou lie, and take thy morning nap?
> Peep thro' the casement; see the gallows there:
> Thy work hangs on it; could not mercy spare?
> What had he done? Ask crippled Talleyrand,
> Ask Beckford, Courtenay, all the motley band
> Of priests and laymen, who have shared his guilt

(If guilt it be) then slumber if thou wilt;
What bonds had he of social safety broke?
Found'st thou the dagger hid beneath his cloak?[3]

That particular sodomitical subculture saw itself as a "motley band" bound by a common sense of guiltless "guilt," a shared sense of an impending undeserved doom. But even the more clearly gay-identified homosexual subcultures of fin-de-siècle Britain that were lucky enough to face mere life imprisonment seemed to see gallows peeping through their closet casements.[4] At least, that is the phobic fantasy to which the protagonist of *Teleny* (1890), a pornographic novel Wilde underwrote for one of these subcultures, falls prey when an unidentified correspondent threatens to expose his homosexuality:[5]

Was I conscience-stricken? No, it was simply fear—abject fear, not remorse. Moreover is not a sodomite liable to be condemned to perpetual imprisonment?

You must think me a coward, but after all even the bravest man can only face an open foe. The thought that the occult hand of an unknown enemy is always uplifted against you, and ready to deal you a mortal blow, is unbearable. (123)

"Perpetual imprisonment" (the clear and present danger) is figured as a "mortal blow" (the "occult" and erstwhile danger) in this text because its gay authors knew themselves as incarcerable subjects who could not, or would not, forget that they were once exterminable. In other words, the dismal and diachronically outmoded image of the hanged sodomite was a staple (albeit "occult") feature of a gay fin-de-siècle image repertoire—even when that image repertoire was engaged in spinning blissful pornographic yarns.

Or should that be *especially* when that image repertoire was engaged in spinning blissful pornographic yarns? The spontaneous erections and ejaculations of hanged men may have made the executions of sodomites seem appallingly and scandalously pornographic to anyone who observed or imagined them. Appalling, because sodomites who had illicit orgasms were condemned to die having involuntary ones. Scandalous, because a society committed to eradicating sodomitical pleasure forced itself to witness sodomitical tumescence and excretion. In fact, this pornographic aspect of the hanging of a sodomite makes it easy to imagine *Teleny's* authors eroticizing the hanging itself. Barthes, after all, suggests that the pleasure of *any* text is analogous to "that untenable, impossible, purely *novelistic* instant so relished by Sade's libertine when he manages to be hanged and then to cut the rope at the very moment of his orgasm, his bliss" (*Pleasure of the Text* 7). *Lord Didcock is led to the scaffold. The muscular arms—arms in which I could die a happy man—are tightly bound. The prodigious phallus can be discerned beneath the coarse prison garb. I cannot help but decry the cruel law that claims this young life. Didcock, however, is calm. He is thinking only of the red rose-leaf lips of the ivory-gold boy, lips made for madness of kisses, and takes no notice of the clergyman, the crowd, and the executioner. The hood is lowered, the noose is tightened, and the prayers are said, but he is still thinking of the beautiful boy. Suddenly, the trap is pulled, the neck is broken. "The Adonis of Belgravia" has been launched into eternity. I turn to go, but steal one last look at the pendent corpse. The stiff dead cock is weeping huge ambrosial tears.*

Like the penal discourse, and like the theological discourse upon which that was based, many of the homophobic discourses that constituted nineteenth-century British "sodomites," "inverts," and "homosexuals" focused the greater part of their negative attention on sexual conduct.[6] Fin-de-siècle "inverts" and "homosexuals" who resisted the repressive force of and their negative self-construction by these discourses, who wanted to interrupt them with self-affirming reverse discourses, needed to dissolve, to make inapposite, this all-too-recently-lethal focus on sexual conduct. Gay self-articulation is a "reverse discourse" insofar as it contests conventional notions of sexual identity by appropriating and negotiating conventional ideology and discourse.[7] Although it cannot impose its own deviant language, it can interrupt dominant languages by "enter[ing] critically into existing linguistic configurations, and . . . re-open[ing] the closed structures into which they have ossified" (Silverman and Torode 6). Gay fin-de-siècle self-definitional discourse did just that. It critically refigured ossified linguistic structures, and it deployed "positive identifications usurped from the dominant culture" (Dollimore, "Dominant and Deviant" 182), in an attempt to persuade gays and nongays alike that homosexuality does not equal (transgressive, deviant, pathological, and criminal) homosexual sexual behavior. In other words, it seized upon readily available if slightly dated discourses that could help de-sexualize the male homosexual.[8]

One available discourse was that of "Platonic" love.[9] The early gay activists who conflated Victorian inversion/homosexuality and classical pederasty did so, in part, because their audiences construed Platonic love as chaste.[10] Another available discourse was that of romantic love. Romantic erotics, even though it sees "true love [as] the conjunction of concupiscence with affection," privileges the more transcendental and metaphysical component (Gay 45). For Kant, for example, two (complementary) lovers merge into "a unity of will" (167), while for Schopenhauer they long for "fusion into a single being" (2: 536). Gay deployments of "ossified" romantic erotics desexualized homosexuality quite as effectively, and quite as ineffectively, as did gay deployments of "ossified" Platonic erotics. In *Teleny*, for example, when the pseudonymous Camille Des Grieux and the eponymous René Teleny fall in love at first sight, the two do not come together physically (as the song goes, they see one another across a crowded room), but rather intermingle in a mutual envisioning of "the god-like corpse of Antinoüs, seen by the silvery light of the opaline moon, floating on the lurid waters of the Nile" (32). *Teleny* then inscribes this ideational union as the quintessence of gay love by repeatedly invoking images of Antinous and by describing both Des Grieux and Teleny as Antinous look-alikes, as physically mirroring their metaphysical mingling. However, unlike the Platonic deployment, which minoritizes homosexuality by inscribing it within an erotic discourse of the deviant (i.e., classical pederasty), the romantic deployment typified by *Teleny* universalizes homosexuality by inscribing it within an erotic discourse of the dominant.[11]

That is, even though romantic erotics deemphasizes sexual conduct, it is profoundly heterosexual. For Wagner, for example, "only as man and woman can human beings love most genuinely, all other love is derivative, having reference to this or artificially modelled upon it" (Mann 203). This fundamental heterocentrism is part of the gay sex appeal of romantic erotics. The gays who deployed this straight-laced idealist tradition aimed to, and perhaps to a certain extent did, compel "straight" minds to consider gay love (if not gay sex) as equivalent to, because bespoken by the same erotic discourse as, its nongay counterpart. It aimed to force the dominant to see, to speak, and thus to valorize the deviant in the dominant's own terms, in terms the dominant, if allowed, would have reserved for itself. Such force, however, was not unresisted. Straight minds are not easily bent. But even if straight minds resisted most gay deployments of the romantic conception of love as metaphysical union, they may well have been taken in by gay versions of Liebestod, which is a central figuration of that conception.

He Kissed the Happy Prince on the Lips

Liebestod, a figuration of love as "a fatal desire for mystical union" (Rougemont 322), as "a fusion [in which lovers] die together from loving each other" (Barthes, *Lover's Discourse* 11), combines the concept of love as metaphysical union, the concept of death as metaphysical union, and the concept of Petrarchan acedia. In its unadulterated romantic form, the trope enjoyed a long literary life (b. 1809 [*The Elective Affinities*], d. 1865 [*Tristan and Isolde*]) as well as considerable philosophic sanction (by Hegel [*Lectures on the Philosophy of Religion*], Schopenhauer [*The World as Will and Idea*], and Feuerbach [*Thoughts on Death*]). However, no dominant discursive system sanctioned the *type* of love Liebestod celebrated. As Rougemont has shown, romantic use of the trope was confined to adulterous love. Tristan and Isolde were not married to, and could not marry, each other. Nor would Isolde have died of love had they been married: the aesthetically crucial pathos of her Liebestod demanded that her relations with Tristan be unlawful and transgressive, and therefore figurable as misunderstood and wrongly persecuted. This adulterous essence of Liebestod made neoromantic gay deployments of the trope particularly viable. Gay love, like adulterous love, was unlawful, transgressive, misunderstood, and wrongly persecuted. (Note the uncanny gay overtones in Matthew Arnold's "Tristram and Iseult," written thirteen years before Wagner's treatment: "they feel the fatal bands / Of a love they dare not name" [*Poetry* 90–91].) Consequently, gay love-deaths were easily comprehended, if not embraced, by straight minds used to the adulterous likes of Isolde.[12]

Two of Wilde's nine fairy tales represent love-death in its unadulterated—if basically adulterous—romantic guise. (Unadulterated insofar as the stories still depict erotic annihilations, and not, as will be seen, murder/suicides.) One reads like a straightforward dominant discourse; the other reads like a straightforward "positive identification usurped from the dominant culture." In "The Fisherman and His Soul" (1891), the heterosexual version of the trope, a fisherman is duped by his soul, which he had forsaken in order to live with the mermaid he loves, into abandoning her. One day, upon discovering the mermaid's dead body washed ashore, the fisherman himself dies—as recounted in the following Malloryesque passage:

The sea came nearer, and sought to cover him with its waves, and when he knew that the end was at hand he kissed with mad lips the cold lips of the Mermaid, and the heart that was within him brake. And as through the fullness of his love his heart did break, the Soul found an entrance in, and was one with him even as before. (*Complete Stories* 308)

Although the reunion of the fisherman and his (male) soul can be seen as a homoerotic reflection of the fisherman's "fatal [and] mystical union" with his beloved mermaid, "The Happy Prince" (1888) is a less problematically homosexual version of the love-death trope. In it, a male swallow and a statue of a young prince fall in love, exhaust themselves trying to help the poor, and die love-deaths couched in the same terms as that of the fisherman:

He kissed the Happy Prince on the lips, and fell down dead at his feet.

At that moment a curious crack sounded inside the statue, as if something had broken. The fact is that the leaden heart had snapped right in two. (*Complete Stories* 161)

An angel collects the broken heart and the dead bird, "the two most precious things in the city," and gives them to God, thereby uniting the misunderstood and persecuted lovers (the heart and the carcass had been thrown together "on a dust-heap") in a vaguely erotic mutual apotheosis (162). Not that the erotic relationship of the fisherman and the mermaid is any less vague than that of the swallow and the statue. How, after all, could either pair have sex? Wilde's universalizing point seems to be that sex is *equally* irrelevant where both heterosexual and homosexual love are concerned. And yet, these two sexless love stories are not quite unsexy.

Wilde's fisherman, swallow, and statue all die of broken hearts upon kisses. But who can say what these fatal kisses connote? Just as a real kiss is either chaste (clean and dry), salacious (wet and sloppy), or somewhere in between, a literary kiss, as Catharine Stimpson points out, has "vast metonymic responsibilities"—especially when it occurs in lesbian or gay literature (366). Perhaps the heart-breaking kiss of the swallow and the statue is a metonym for their chaste "Uranian" love. Perhaps it is a metonym for homosexual sexual conduct (assuming that kissing is a prelude to and/or part of intercourse). Perhaps it is a metonym for both. It is hard to know for certain, because lesbian and gay literary kisses "embrace [such] contradictions" as "transgression [and] permissibility" (Stimpson 367). But so, albeit to a lesser extent, do heterosexual literary kisses (so too does the fisherman's heart-breaking kiss), which is why Wilde's "gay" use of the kiss trope in "The Happy Prince" is a subversive strategy that reopens the polyvalence of a discursive practice.[13]

This cursory analysis of two kisses (one in a fairy tale, one in a "fairy" tale) suggests one way in which the love-death trope offered analogous "protective/expressive camouflage . . . to distinctively gay content" (Sedgwick 161). A kiss that is just a kiss can also be a metonym for (gay) sex. Similarly, a (love-)death that is just a death can also be a metaphor for (gay) orgasm. And, to complete the circle, an orgasm that is just an orgasm can also be a metonym for (gay) sex. Love-death may be an admixture of Petrarchan acedia and idealist notions of love and death, but it is also an idealized, sublime, and profoundly sentimental metaphor for mutual orgasm and, by extension, sexual conduct. While this would seem to make love-death *tropus non gratus* for fin-de-siècle writers interested in desexualizing homosexuality, it was actually one of the figure's most attractive gay features. That is, gays could use love-death *both* to articulate homosexuality in a sublimely sentimental and ideal way (thereby satisfying the conventions of bourgeois self-representation and disarming conduct-focused homophobic discourse) *and* to articulate (for gay audiences, primarily) the otherwise inarticulable phenomenon of homosexual orgasm.[14] Of course, such tropological duplicity had been demanded of love-death even in its original heterosexual context. Only an imbecilic romantic auditor would not have realized that Isolde's "death" is, in one sense, purely lyrical. She "dies" singing the most orgasmic tonal music ever composed and climaxes on the words "höchste Lust!"[15] But if the Liebestod is just as sublimely sentimental and ideal *and* as sexy as "The Happy Prince"—no doubt it is more so—the point is not that Wilde merely reiterates a text Wagner has already "completed" (how, after all, can *Tristan and Isolde* be read as a gay text?), but that Wilde gives multiple gay meanings to an ossified discursive formation that was already known to be polyvalent.

Perhaps the claim that an innocuous little story like "The Happy Prince" is both an antihomophobic purification of gay love and a homophilic paean to gay sex seems a little extravagant. After all, the moral of the fable, in which the two protagonists die trying to help the poor, does seem to concern self-sacrifice. However, Wilde was notoriously unscrupulous about literary morality. And the kiss and love-death tropes were so thoroughly encoded within fin-de-siècle culture that even the most moralistic reader should have understood the double meaning of two male lovers' dying kiss—even if one was a bird and the other was a statue. This is especially true because the fable is an inherently allegorical genre. At the very least, any fin-de-siècle reader old enough to have known what gay love is might have learned from Wilde's story that such love is chaste, ideal, sublime, and sentimental, while a "perverse" one also might have learned that (gay) birds do, indeed, do it.

In spite of the facility with which "unadulterated" love-death performed this double duty of antihomophobic purification and homophilic eroticization, a facility attributable to its pronounced polyvalence, Wilde "adulterated" the trope. He changed the cause of death from heteroerotic annihilation to homoerotic murder/ suicide. In the Wilde canon, the number of homoerotic suicides just about equals the number of homoerotic murders. Where René Teleny, Cyril Graham (*The Portrait of Mr. W.H.* [1889/ 1893]), and Dorian Gray all kill themselves, Dorian Gray kills his lover Basil Hallward, Salomé kills her beloved Jokanaan, and Lord Arthur Savile murders his chiromantist Septimus R. Podgers ("Lord Arthur Savile's Crime" [1891]). While Teleny's is the only brazenly gay murder/suicide in the lot (it is the climax of a work of gay pornography), the others are undeniably homoerotic as well. Cyril Graham's relationship with Erskine, whose disbelief in his theory that the dedicatee of Shakespeare's sonnets was a beloved boy actor named Willie Hughes prompts the suicide, is quite as erotically charged as the Shakespeare/Hughes love affair itself.[16] Dorian Gray, who professes to be "in love with" his portrait, and Basil Hallward, who worships Dorian "with far more romance than a man usually gives a friend" (in the 1890 edition), certainly evoke homoerotic possibilities. Salomé is repeatedly called "Daughter of Sodom" (*Complete Stories* 544–46) by Jokanaan, whom she, in turn, addresses in decidedly lusty ("I am athirst for thy beauty; I am hungry for thy body" [566]) and priapic ("Thy mouth is like a band of scarlet on a tower of ivory" [546]) terms—terms that would have been construed as unladylike (i.e., as "inverted") in a period that wanted to believe "real" women to be essentially passionless.[17] The whole play, moreover, is suffused with a homoeroticism that can be traced to its obvious "aesthetic" tone, to the notorious "perversity" of both Wilde and Lord Alfred Douglas (who translated *Salomé* from Wilde's original French), and to the frequency with which purportedly heterosexual characters drop hairpins. (Herod, for example, upon seeing the dead body of The Young Syrian, complains: "I am sorry he has killed himself. . . . He had very languorous eyes" [549].) And in "Lord Arthur Savile's Crime," one of many fin-de-siècle bachelor narratives that thematize male homosexual panic, Septimus Podgers is the bewildering single man Lord Arthur Savile must do away with in order to marry Sybil Merton.[18] Even Savile's name is homoerotically charged: "Arthur Savile," as Wilde notes in *The Portrait of Mr. W.H.*, was a Carolingian boy actor who "took a girl's part in a comedy by Marmion" ([1893] 190).[19]

In spite of the evenhandedness with which Wilde fictionalizes homoerotic murder and suicide, his decided autobiographical emphasis is on murder. In *De Profundis*, the long prison letter originally titled "In Carcere et Vinculis," Wilde obsessively figures himself as Lord Alfred Douglas's victim. Douglas "sacrificed," "took," and "absolutely ruin[ed]" his "entire existence" (104, 107), was "fatal . . . to know even or to be with" (110), "had . . . drawn a bow at a venture [and] pierced a king between the joints of his harness" (134), was "fatal in bringing [Wilde] to utter destruction" (146), and "could do no better with [Wilde's] life than break it in pieces" (202). Even Wilde's attempts to portray himself as suicidal transfer murderous agency back onto Douglas. This transfer results in such syntactically tortuous "admissions" as: "I blame myself for having allowed you to bring me to utter and discreditable . . . ruin" (101); "I blame myself for the entire ethical degradation I allowed you to bring on me" (103); and "I cannot allow you to go through life bearing in your heart the burden of having ruined a man like me [and] must say to myself that I ruined myself, and that nobody great or small can be ruined except by his own hand" (150–51). It also results in the clear yet equivocal formulation, "the gods . . . bring us to ruin through what in us is loving," which refuses to accuse *either* Wilde or Douglas of doing the ruining (119). Of course, the murder emphasis and murder/

suicide confusion that characterize *De Profundis* make sense in light of Douglas's responsibility for Wilde's personal debacle (or at least in light of what Wilde believed that responsibility to be). However, the conflation of murder and suicide also occurs in the homoerotic fiction Wilde wrote (and cowrote) prior to his "gross indecency" conviction.

"Lord Arthur Savile's Crime," *Salomé, The Picture of Dorian Gray, The Portrait of Mr. W.H.*, and *Teleny* all cloud the issue of whether gay love-deaths are murders or suicides. Savile's connubial bliss requires that his homoerotic murder of Podgers be construed otherwise: "SUICIDE OF A CHIROMANTIST" reads the erroneous headline that saves Savile's conjugal life (*Complete Stories* 220). (Or was Podger's death really a suicide after all? Why was he loitering about a Thames embankment at two o'clock in the morning?) Salomé's lust destroys her as well as Jokanaan. Dorian Gray's murder of his portrait turns out to be a suicide, and his envisionings of Sybil Vane as Shakespearean heroines who are either murdered or driven to suicide by lovers (Juliet, Ophelia, and Desdemona) reflect his fears concerning what male lovers might do to him and/or make him do to himself.[20] (Note, too, that Dorian tells Allan Campbell that Basil Hallward, his murder victim, killed himself; that Lord Henry Wotton refuses to believe that Basil was murdered; and that Dorian feels as though he has slit Sybil's throat, even though she has poisoned herself.) When Erskine, following Cyril Graham's lead, commits suicide in order to make the narrator believe in Willie Hughes, his death turns out not to have been a suicide at all.[21] And *Teleny* thematizes the gay murder/suicide problem by not taking a position on the cause of Antinous's death, a notorious and historically indeterminable mystery that engaged the attention of many university-educated gay Victorians. On the one hand, the novel sides with J. A. Symonds, who, like most Victorian apologists for Antinous, considered the boy's death to be a Christlike voluntary sacrifice:[22] "Antinous . . . —like unto Christ—died for his master's sake" and "sacrifice[d himself] on the altar of love" (*Sketches and Studies* 26, 159). On the other hand, the novel treats Antinous as a murder victim in a turbid passage in which Teleny and Des Grieux contemplate drowning themselves:

"Thy will be done, but we shall die together, so that at least in death we may not be parted. . . . Let us bind ourselves closely together, and leap into the flood."

I looked at him, and shuddered. So young, so beautiful, and I was thus to *murder* him! The vision of Antinoüs as I had seen it the first time he played appeared before me. (103–4; emphasis added)

This incongruous fictional figuration of a suicidal love-death (note the metaphysically minded lovers' "fatal desire for mystical union") as a murder could be read as a metacommentary on incongruous historical figurations of Antinous's own death by drowning that refuse to settle the causation debate.[23] It is also an, if not the, archetypal instance of Wilde's gay transformation of heteroerotic annihilation into homoerotic murder-suicide, of his *equivocal adulteration* of love-death. The question remains, whence this adulteration and equivocation?

So Young, So Beautiful

One could scarcely pose a thornier question. Not only is the association of gay male sexuality with tragic early death grounded in heteroerotic intertexuality, it is also, as Eve Kosofsky Sedgwick points out, "densely grounded in centuries of homoerotic and homophobic intertextuality" (144). *Teleny*, for example, is a retelling of the Antinous tale, but it is also a tapestry woven with strands of the stories of Patroclus and Jonathan, a love lyric composed of strains of the elegiac poetry of Milton and Tennyson. Yet even though all textualizations of the fatality of gay love are abysmally intertextual, each such textualization is a unique cultural production. Each has distinctive features that are fixed by its constitutive ideological/epistemological regime. To solve the puzzle of Wilde's "equivocal adulteration" of love-death, then, is to suggest ways in which the transfiguration is both a function of the abysmal intertextuality of Wilde's fatal gay love scenarios and a function of the scenarios' culturally specific instantiation. In other words, it is to suggest that his version of homoerotic murder/suicide is an old story, a new story, and an old/new story.

The "old story" of fatal gay love has very little to do with suicide. With the notable exceptions of Antinous (who may have killed himself), Narcissus (who does not quite kill himself), and Ganymede (who does not quite die), nearly all of the nineteenth century's ancient gay icons are beautiful, young *murder* victims. The bisexual and hermaphroditic Dionysus, who figures prominently in the homoerotic fantasies of Wilde's beloved Walter Pater just as he does in those of Pater's beloved Johann Joachim Winckelmann, was torn to pieces by Titans.[24] The twice widowed and doubly misogynist Orpheus, who is esteemed (albeit furtively) by writers like Symonds for having introduced man-boy love into the Greek world, was dismembered by Thracian Maenads maddened by his pederastic proclivities in a murderous orgy that associates him with both Dionysus and, because his head and harp came to rest at Lesbos, Sappho.[25] Patroclus, whose love of Achilles Symonds hails as a "heroic" ideal, was speared by Hector before the walls of Troy (*Male Love* 4). Hercules's beloved Hylas was drowned by Mysian nymphs, a loss Symonds feels "supplied Greek poets with one of their most charming subjects" (*Male Love* 10). Apollo's beloved Hyacinth, whose death Pater recounts in the homoerotic portrait "Apollo in Picardy," was brained by a jealous Zephyrus. David's beloved Jonathan, who is the proverbial biblical counterpart of the pagan Ganymede, was slain by Philistines on Mount Gilboa. And Sebastian, the nineteenth century's favorite gay saint, was tortured and killed by Roman soldiers.

The power of this "old story" to produce, and reproduce itself in, nineteenth-century gay texts cannot be overestimated. The stereotype of the murdered minion constrained writers like Wilde to figure contemporaneous gay icons who were not murdered, or who were not even dead, as reincarnations of classical "victim" icons. Wilde himself, in a letter later used against him in court, likens the perfectly lively "Bosie" (Douglas) to the perfectly lifeless Hyacinth: "Your slim gilt soul walks between passion and poetry.

I know Hyacinthus, whom Apollo loved so madly, was you in Greek days" (*Letters* 326). He also likens Keats, who succumbed to consumption (and not, as some of his supporters muttered, to unkind criticism), to Sebastian, who succumbed to a fusillade of arrows, in "The Grave of Keats": "The youngest of the Martyrs here is lain, / Fair as Sebastian, and as foully slain" (*Complete Stories* 764). And Wilde's gloss on this sonnet shows just how unwitting, and uncontrollable, was the process by which such inappropriate images could suggest themselves to gay iconographers:

As I stood beside the mean grave of this divine boy, I thought of him as of a Priest of Beauty slain before his time; and the vision of [Guido Reni's] St. Sebastian came before my eyes as I saw him at Genoa, a lovely brown boy, with crisp, clustering hair and red lips, bound by his evil enemies to a tree and, though pierced by arrows, raising his eyes with divine, impassioned gaze towards the Eternal Beauty of the opening Heavens. (Mason 86)

But it is only we who find the images inappropriate. As Wilde's gloss makes clear, the iconographers themselves were perfectly content with them and do not seem to have felt at all constrained by the restrictive stereotype. Why might this be? Surely not because they knew of no ancient "nonvictim" icons. Classically minded fin-de-siècle gays could, if pressed, come up with a number of such pederastic pinups. Symonds, in *A Problem in Greek Ethics*, even provides a fairly exhaustive list of them:

Among the myths to which Greek lovers referred with pride, besides that of Achilles, were the legends of Theseus and Peirithous, of Orestes and Pylades, of Talos and Rhadamanthus, of Damon and Pythias. . . . Poseidon . . . loved Pelops; Zeus . . . was said to have carried off Chrysippus. Apollo . . . numbered among his favourites Branchos and Claros. Pan loved Cyparissus, and the spirit of the evening star loved Hymenæus. Hypnos, the God of slumber, loved Endymion, and sent him to sleep with open eyes, in order that he might always gaze upon their beauty. (*Male Love* 10)

Yet Pirithous, Pylades, and Pelops rarely appear in texts that would seem to welcome them. For example, in spite of Wilde's muzzy recollection in *De Profundis* that the incriminating "Hyacinth" letter compares the extraordinarily vain Bosie "to Hylas, or Hyacinth, Jonquil or Narcisse" (120), the missive does not, in fact, read "I know *Narcissus* was you in Greek days." And although Wilde would do well to compare Keats to the notoriously gay Alexander the Great, who also had a fatal illness, and not to Sebastian, who was healthy, the thought never occurs to him. The early Christian martyr looms too large in Wilde's image repertoire for there to be much room left over for the lusty Macedonian conqueror. Again, why might this be?

One reason that the old murder story produced, and reproduced itself in, nineteenth-century gay texts with such facility is that nineteenth-century gay writers were preoccupied with the murderous homophobia of the British state. As has been mentioned, the erotically outrageous, outrageously erotic specter of the hanged sodomite haunted these men long after Parliament abolished the death penalty for sodomy. It makes sense, then, that Orpheus, murdered by a hateful mob, and Hyacinth, murdered by a jealous god, came to mind when writers considered the unhappy fates of other, more modern, sodomites who also aroused a lethal kind of "homophobic enchantment."[26] However, it also makes sense that Orpheus and Hyacinth came to mind when the writers thought of contemporary heartthrobs who, like Lord Alfred Douglas, were in no particular danger of losing their lives. The threat Britain's repressive state apparatus posed to young gay lives was simply too recent to have seemed incapable of reconstruction.

Another reason for the persistence of the old murder story relates to a curious late-nineteenth-century conflation of sadism and homosexuality. It is tempting to trace this conflation to Richard von Krafft-Ebing's classic medical handbook on sexual deviance, *Psychopathia Sexualis*, which gave birth to both the sadist and the homosexual (qua "invert") in one great taxonomic spasm. (The text also constituted the masochist and the fetishist.) Perhaps lazy English readers of Charles Chaddock's 1892 translation ignored Krafft-Ebing's categorical distinctions and inferred that a perversion is a perversion is a perversion. But whether or not such mis-readings occurred, sadism and homosexuality were seen, in fact, as equivalent. This meant that the homosexual in general, and the pederast in particular, were often read as murderous victimizers, and that their young beloveds were often read as murder victims. (As Georges Bataille remarks, Sadean "objects of desire are invari-ably propelled towards torture and death" [*Literature and Evil* 95].) And it was Gilles de Rais, the fifteenth-century marshal of France executed for kidnapping, sodomizing, and murdering untold numbers of children (also often mistaken for the mythical wife-murderer "Bluebeard"), who, having stepped into a late-nineteenth-century spotlight, was a linchpin of the sado-homosexual confla-tion.

The first major biography of Rais (Abbot Eugène Bossard's *Gilles de Rais, Maréchal de France*) was published in 1886, the year in which *Psychopathia Sexualis* also first appeared. Although the gender of his young victims was a matter of little or no concern to the historical Rais, the Rais fantasized by many fin-de-siècle writ-ers was a confirmed pederast.[27] This fantasy is reflected, and per-haps critiqued, in Joris-Karl Huysmans's 1891 novel *Là-bas*, which is based on the Bossard biography. Durtal, Huysmans's protago-nist, is a writer working on a life of Rais that portrays him as a Sa-tanist who only sodomizes and murders young boys. His satanic research assistant (and lover), moreover, is a woman named "Hy-acinthe"—an appellation Huysmans, who calls it "a boy's name," wants read as pederastic (148). Huysmans also spells out the mur-derous connection between Rais the pederast and Rais the sadist. Indeed, Rais's "excesses of rape and murder," his "crimes of . . . murderous sadism," make him worse than Sade: "next to him, the Marquis de Sade is a timid bourgeois, a lame fantasist" (241, 72, 75–76). Like Huysmans, Wilde also cites, albeit disparagingly, the fin-de-siècle sado-homosexual conflation that Rais facilitates. In *De Profundis*, he complains to Bosie that "Clio [is] the least seri-ous of all the Muses, your father will always live among the kind pure-hearted parents of Sunday school literature; your place is with the infant Samuel; and in the lowest mire of Malebolge I sit between Gilles de Retz and the Marquis de Sade" (106).[28] But he knows that the conflation is inescapable and tries to make the best of it:

> I have said, and with some bitterness, I admit, in this letter that such was the irony of things that your father would live to be the hero of a Sunday school tract: that you would rank with the infant Samuel: and that my place would be between Gilles de Retz and the Marquis de Sade. I dare say it is best so. I have no desire to complain. One of the many lessons that one learns in prison is, that things are what they are and will be what they will be. Nor have I any doubt that the leper of medievalism and the author of *Justine* will prove better company than *Sandford and Merton*. (139)

This is a remarkable passage. It marks an epistemological slide that compelled homoeroticism to figure itself in terms of self-contained murderous energies. It shows how a homophobic culture that was killing Wilde forced him to imagine that he was killing Bosie. But the passage also registers Wilde's resistance to the slide. The "bitterness" and "irony" that temper the resignation ("I have no desire to complain") and the fact that the resignation itself may be both spurious (a sop offered to Wilde's captors) and satirical (a sop steeped in the venom of the vanquished) suggest that gay accounts of *inherently* fatal gay love should not always be read straight. Though some such accounts may indeed accede to the notion that gay love is murderously sadistic, others, like Wilde's, are more likely to be reverse discourses that attempt to upset the sado-homosexual conflation. To put it more conventionally, and perhaps less accurately, some may *be* "internally homophobic," while others may be *about* "internalized homophobia."

While this is not the proper context for an extended analysis of the sado-homosexual conflation and of Rais's pivotal role in it, such an analysis may be essential to a full understanding of modern homoerotic/homophobic intertextuality. The conflation and the Rais connection were not merely ephemeral fin-de-siècle phenomena. They have continued well into the twentieth century. They inflect, for example, Shaw's *Saint Joan* (1923), in which Rais is presented as a Wildean fop. The conflation and the connection inflect *The Thief's Journal* (1949), in which Jean Genet claims to "have roots in that French soil which is fed by the powdered bones of the children and youths buggered, massacred and burned by Gilles de Rais" (44–45). They also inflect Bataille's *The Trial of Gilles de Rais* (1965), which, although it acknowledges Rais victimized both "girls and boys" (125), presents him as a homosexual (he "lock[ed] himself up in the solitude . . . of homosexuality" [42]), as a pederast ("without a doubt Gilles preferred boys" [134]), and as a sadist *avant la lettre* ("who in the 15th century, before Sade . . . could have correctly depicted, without a false note, these horrible butcheries, which *would not be realistic in the absence of modern knowledge*" [141; emphasis original]). The conflation and the connection inflect Charles Ludlam's *Bluebeard* (1970), a camp classic in which the protagonist, a dapper vivisectionist bent on creating a third sex, is "an evil sadist" whose laboratory is repeatedly referred to as "the House of Pain" (133). They also inflect Edward Lucie-Smith's historical novel *The Dark Pageant* (1977), which portrays Rais as a gay sado-*masochist*. And the conflation and the connection may even inflect the sado-masochistic self-identifications of contemporary gays and lesbians who have never heard of Rais. This is not to say that lesbian and gay S/M subcultures are structurally murderous, but that the dominant discourses they negotiate and purportedly transvalue are. Of these instances—from Shaw's *Saint Joan* to lesbian and gay sado-masochism—only Ludlam's Bluebeard (who, like his mythical namesake, prefers female victims) and the S/M subcultures (which, ideally, limit themselves to consensual, mutually desired sexual activity) articulate critical reverse discourses akin to that of *De Profundis*. Ludlam, like Wilde, attempts to upset the sado-homosexual conflation—in Ludlam's case by de-gaying, if not de-camping, Gilles de Rais. (He also parodies the conflation by playfully collapsing other such categorical distinctions: "Open the door," one character screams at Bluebeard, "You pervert! You invert, you necrophiliac!" [135].) Lesbian and gay S/M subcultures attempt to demonstrate, *pace* Bataille, that Sadean objects of desire are not "invariably propelled towards torture and death."

What should be underscored here, what is important to an analysis of Wilde's love-deaths, is that the sado-homosexual conflation, coupled with vivid memories of lethal institutional homophobia, reinforced fin-de-siècle associations of male homoeroticism with murdered young men and helped pose a rather confounding question: Who were the murderers, their lovers or their governors? For Wilde, of course, the problem is more problematic yet. The question "their lovers or their governors?" becomes "their lovers, their governors, or themselves?" Whereas the "old story" of fatal gay love, which was modulated by the memory of hanged sodomites and complicated by the conflation of sadism and homosexuality, concerned murder, the "new story," which was a unique late-Victorian cultural production, concerned suicide. This can be attributed to three factors: suicide's topical, sensational, and phenomenological characteristics.

Suicide was very much on the minds of fin-de-siècle writers and readers. The British had always been troubled by the notion that suicide might be more frequent in England than elsewhere, and a highly publicized jump in official suicide and attempted suicide rates seemed to signal nothing less than pandemic suicidal mania.[29] "Gay" suicide was also in the air. There was a general perception that the 1885 passage and subsequent enforcement of the Labouchère Amendment, also known as the "Blackmailer's Charter," increased the number of self-murders committed by practicing and presumed homosexuals.[30] Because exposure by an extortionist, even if it did not result in incarceration, could mean social, professional, and economic ruin, many desperate gays saw suicide as their only escape. This position is articulated in *Teleny*. When Des Grieux receives the anonymous threat referred to above (a note from an acquaintance named Bryancourt that reads "If you do not give up your lover T . . . you shall be branded as an *enculé*" [121; ellipsis in original]), he considers his options and very nearly does himself in: "What was I to do? To be proclaimed a sodomite in the face of the world, dishonoured, pursued, perhaps sentenced in court, or to give up the man who was dearer to me than my life itself? No, death was preferable to either" (122).

If suicide was on the minds of fin-de-siècle gays because it was topical, it was on the minds of fin-de-siècle gay writers—gays, that is, who tried to interrupt homophobic discourses with affirmative reverse discourses—because it was sensational. By the end of the nineteenth century, it was hard not to read suicide in heroic and pathetic terms—terms in which it was not quite so easy to read murder. And, to a great extent, Goethe's *The Sorrows of Young Werther* was the source of these sensational registers.[31] The strand of Goethe that holds suicide to be heroic had threaded its way into the fabric of fin-de-siècle thought. In one colloquy, Werther suggests to Albert that self-murder can be courageous:

When a nation which has long groaned under the intolerable yoke of a tyrant rises at last and throws off its chains, do you call that weakness? The man who, to save his house from the flames, finds his physical strength redoubled, so that he can lift burdens with ease which normally he could scarcely move; he who under the rage of an insult attacks and overwhelms half a dozen of his enemies—are these to be called weak? My friend, if a display of energy be strength, how can the highest exertion of it be a weakness? (44)

In aesthetic and bohemian circles, the epicenters of the "new Wertherism," this gambit was a given, and it was standard form to extol "the courage to break away from the banquet of life."[32] Gay writers sensed they could profit from this premise, sensed they could heroicize gay love by depicting young, beautiful gay lovers as suicidal. Cyril Graham, who shoots himself in order to prove to his lover that Shakespeare loved "Willie Hughes," represents one such heroicization. According to the narrator of *The Portrait of Mr. W.H.*, Cyril's suicide makes him "the youngest and the most *splendid* of all the martyrs of literature" (166; emphasis added). Des Grieux, who contemplates drowning himself because he believes Teleny loves Bryancourt (the anonymous extortionist), represents another. According to Des Grieux, "In my case suicide was not only allowable, but laudable—nay, heroic" (101).

Werther, who killed himself because he was unlucky in love, is also central to the fin-de-siècle construction of suicide as pathetic. Victorians tended to sentimentalize lovelorn, and only lovelorn, suicides. But whereas Werther, the eighteenth-century prototype, was a young man, the nineteenth century's most highly senti-mentalized lovelorn suicides were young women. The figure of the seduced, abandoned woman who literally drowns her sorrows captivated the Victorian imagination. Innumerable melodramas snatched jilted women from the jaws of (watery) death, and in-numerable broadsheets sensationalized their plight.[33] Salons were studded with such works as George Frederic Watts's "Found Drowned" (ca. 1848–50), and John Everett Millais's "Ophelia" (1851–52). And Thomas Hood's pathetic poem "The Bridge of Sighs" (1844) enjoyed an unprecedented popularity:

> Take her up tenderly,
> Lift her with care;
> Fashion'd so slenderly,
> Young, and so fair!

Figures of lovelorn *male* suicides were forced to contend with this feminocentric ideology. As Victorians became increasingly wed-ded to the notion that suicide, like madness, is a "female malady," modern-day male Werthers found it increasingly difficult to elic-it purely sentimental responses.[34] Ko-Ko, the Lord High Execu-tioner in Gilbert and Sullivan's *The Mikado* (1885), milked "Tit-willow" for laughs as well as for tears. But if the feminization of self-murder made it hard to sentimentalize the suicides of "real" men, it made it relatively easy to sentimentalize the suicides of gay, that is to say of "inverted," men. "Female" men, "inverts" could be expected to contract, and to elicit sympathy for having contracted, "female maladies." Writers of gay reverse discourses could, and did, hope to validate gay love by sentimentalizing gay male suicide in the very same terms straight writers used to senti-mentalize straight female suicide. And they even enjoyed a mea-sure of success. *Teleny*, for example, manages to mimic "The Bridge of Sighs" without cracking a smile. Wilde's "so young, so beautiful" is a completely pathetic transposition of Hood's "young, and so fair!"

Homosexuality and suicide coincided phenomenologically as

well as sensationally. First, both were conceived of as degenerate. Late-nineteenth-century theorizations by eugenically minded physicians and intellectuals of both "inversion" and "true" (i.e., irrational) suicide as manifestations of hereditary degeneracy that ensured the survival of the fittest were both readily disseminated and readily credited.[35] Both homosexuality and suicide were also figured as demented and deliberate. In part, oppositional discourses polarized the two phenomena in these parallel terms. Radical medical discourse, which presumed homosexuality to be psychopathological and suicide to be insane, conflicted with conservative theology, which saw homosexual conduct as sinful, and conservative philosophy, which saw suicide as rational.[36] Individual discourses were also responsible for the parallel polarizations. Both jurists and eugenicists distinguished lunatic from volitional suicide. And most sexologists, including Krafft-Ebing, agreed that there were two basic types of homosexuals: "inverts," who were inherently, congenitally homosexual, and "perverts," who chose to engage in homosexual conduct out of lust.[37]

Whence, then, Wilde's adulteration and equivocation? While topical, sensational, and phenomenological factors urged him to create suicidal scenarios, penal and sadistic ones urged him to recreate murderous scenarios. The "new" story seemed culturally inevitable and aesthetically desirable, but so too did the "old" story. Both murder and suicide, that is, circumscribed gay love; both demanded the attention of gay writers. Hence the resurrection of an ambiguous figure like Antinous.

Kill That Woman!

Homoerotic murder-suicide, Wilde's gay version of love-death, is not, however, a simple synthesis of homoerotic murder (the "old" story) and homoerotic suicide (the "new" story). It is not a compromise formation. It is not the raucous sound of a gay organist who has pulled out all his stops. Rather, homoerotic murder-suicide is an intervention in, and modification of, the heteroerotic/homoerotic/homophobic intertext. It is a strategic de-

ployment of an available indeterminacy. It is a reverse discourse
that rewrites the pre-written. But what is the nature of the intervention? What strategies are served by the deployment? And how
are we to read Wilde's rewriting?

Many post-structural theorists tend to treat all subaltern discourse as equally subversive and nonsubversive. Like Jonathan
Dollimore, they often see evenhanded authentication of "both the
dominant and the subordinate" as "intrinsic . . . to the very idea of
a reverse discourse" ("Dominant and Deviant" 184). Or like Ga-
yatri Spivak, they often assume that the subaltern is, by definition, incapable of "speech." In part, this tendency reflects the mes-
merizing charm of such paradoxical (if indiscriminate) formulas as
"support yet subvert" and "reproduce yet resist." In part, it reflects
the deconstructive belief that no subordinate discourse can fully
displace its dominant discourse. It also reflects the difficulty of
theorizing, and demonstrating, one reverse discourse to be more
subversive than another. Some post-structuralists, however, do on
occasion resist this tendency and distinguish among various types
of reverse discourses. Dollimore, for example, finds that Wilde's
brand, which he labels "inversion as critique of authenticity," is
more subversive than Radclyffe Hall's, which he labels "from inversion to authenticity" ("Dominant and Deviant" 187, 181). But
the implication of such classifications is that all instances of one
particular variety of reverse discourse (say, the Wildean "inversion
as critique of authenticity" variety) are, for all practical purposes,
interchangeable. One homoerotic murder-suicide, in other words,
is as good (as subversive) as the next.

Wilde's homoerotic murder-suicides belie this equation. Although one may be as good/subversive as the next in some ideal
register, Wilde's gay love-deaths are never pure and simple. They
occur in, and are unreadable apart from, dissimilar texts and contexts, and were (and are) read by dissimilar readers. *The Picture of
Dorian Gray* is not a reproduction of *The Portrait of Mr. W.H.*
Gay readers who take the (unadulterated) love-death of "The
Happy Prince" to be orgasmic have little in common with nongay
readers who take it to desexualize homosexuality. Consequently,

any analysis of the subversiveness of Wilde's strategies, any analysis of the natures of his intertextual interventions, any analysis, that is, of a single "type" of reverse discourse, must proceed tentatively. It must discriminate among the various contexts in which the intervention (the reverse discourse) appears, and it must always ask itself: "Subversive for what readership(s)?" This particular analysis will conclude by examining four of Wilde's "gay love-death" contexts and by considering two readership coordinates (gay/straight and 1890's/1990's) in order to suggest, in a schematic fashion, how one such analysis might be done.

A fuller, finer analysis of Wilde's love-deaths would, no doubt, examine other relevant contexts and consider less reductive coordinates. It would also be more attentive to the historical record. Most of the following readings (of *Teleny, Dorian Gray, Salomé* [1894], and *Reading Gaol* [1898]) are fabulated. They represent conjectures, based upon a knowledge of operative hermeneutic protocols (i.e., upon reconstructions of fin-de-siècle intertexts and deconstructions of contemporary ones), about what typical gay and straight interpretations of these texts once were and now are.

It is fairly safe to say that *Teleny,* a work of gay pornography, had an exclusively gay fin-de-siècle readership. It is also fairly safe to say that it has a predominantly gay contemporary readership. Yet *Teleny* presents these two similar groups with two different texts. Fin-de-siècle readers were invested in reading Teleny's suicide as heroic and pathetic—as a positive identification usurped from the dominant culture. Contemporary readers are not, because erotic suicide is no longer seen as Wertheresque. Contemporary readers, on the other hand, are invested in reading *any* "fatal gay love" scenario as "politically incorrect"—as "internally" homophobic. Fin-de-siècle readers were not. In fact, they may even have read Teleny's suicide as a radical *indictment* of "internalized" homophobia. The death is pointedly pointless. Teleny faces neither social disgrace, nor criminal prosecution, nor, since the Des Grieuxes have paid his debts, bankruptcy.[38] He is not even lovelorn. The only proximate cause of the precipitous suicide is Des Grieux's discovery of an infidelity for which he ultimately forgives

Teleny. Gay readers, *Teleny* seems to have once said, have no good reason to kill themselves, even though, like Teleny, they may think they do, and even though they may find it pleasurable to read sensational gay texts about senseless gay suicides. The Victorian *Teleny* was also more subversive than the late-twentieth-century in that it presented a radical *analysis* of "internalized" homophobia that now reads as rudimentary. By figuring Teleny's suicide attempt as a murder ("So young, so beautiful, and I was thus to murder him!" [104]), and by repeatedly invoking Antinous (the beautiful suicide who may have been murdered), *Teleny* suggested to fin-de-siècle gays that suicidal agency is a displacement of murderous agency. It suggested, in other words, that "internal" homophobia is an epiphenomenon of "external" homophobia—a psychosocial insight that, to today's gays, seems commonplace. (In Barthesian terms, a bold paradoxa that has turned into a boring doxa.)

There is, however, one sense in which the late-twentieth-century *Teleny* is as subversive as the Victorian. Both deconstruct the love/lust binarism. Both show love and lust to be compatible—and possibly inextricable. Romances are rarely pornographic, and pornography rarely casts protagonists as romantic leads. *Teleny*, however, exceeds these generic limitations. It was, and is, as its subtitle asserts, "A Physiological Romance." *Teleny* shocked fin-de-siècle readers who did not expect a romance to figure gay love as sexy, and it continues to shock contemporary readers who do not expect pornography to figure gay sex as loving. In a sense, *Teleny* tries to displace what Foucault calls "the framework of established relationships" ("De l'amitié" 38). As Foucault suggests, it wants to "free ourselves and others from the two standard conceptions of the one-night stand on one hand, and the total fusion of identities in pure love on the other" (39). And the Liebestod of Wilde's two porn-pals (Des Grieux succumbs to consumption shortly after Teleny stabs himself), connoting and conflating as it does both mutual orgasm and mystical union, is the perfect trope for such a displacement.

The Picture of Dorian Gray has always had gay as well as nongay readers. And it has always been a gay as well as a nongay text. It has always, that is, refused to divulge the homoerotic nature of Dorian's deadly sins. But if for many readers Dorian's spec(tac)ular self-annihilation was not, and is not, especially homoerotic, for many other readers, gay and nongay, Dorian's death was, and is, the climax of a fatal (if obscure) "gay love" scenario. According to the unsubtle scheme of this analysis, there have been at least four takes on this climax. The gay fin-de-siècle gay take was not particularly subversive. Gay readers of Dorian Gray as gay, unlike gay readers of *Teleny*, did not find positive identifications usurped from the dominant culture. They did not see Dorian's suicide as especially heroic, because it was quite accidental. (Dorian meant to destroy his portrait, not to kill himself.) And they did not read it as especially pathetic, because Wilde's loveless libertine is more Don Juan than Werther. Gay readers also failed to find Dorian's demise to be an interdicted articulation of gay orgasm. None of the scene's metaphoric energy is invested in rapture, because all of it is invested in rupture (of Dorian's "exquisite youth and beauty" as well as of his portrait's "loathsomeness" [152, 149]).

The straight fin-de-siècle gay take, however, was truly subversive. As Ed Cohen has observed, *Dorian Gray*, taken as a whole, troubled "straight" readers by intimating the experience of homoerotic desire.[39] But as Sedgwick has argued, the novel's climax, in and of itself, was much more disruptive than Cohen suggests. According to Sedgwick, Dorian's death helped undermine the entire category of the sentimental. Not only did it defeminize suicide, it thoroughly and successfully de- and re-centered the "feminocentric Victorian version" of sentimentality (150). "Whereas in the nineteenth century it was images of women in relation to domestic suffering and death that occupied the most potent, symptomatic, and, perhaps, friable or volatile place in the sentimental *imaginaire* of middle-class culture, for the succeeding century— the century inaugurated by Wilde among others—it has been images of agonistic male self-constitution" (147). In other words, to cite two exemplary and analogous highway fatalities, *Dorian Gray* allowed James Dean's death to break hearts secretly gladdened by Jayne Mansfield's.

For gay readers of contemporary (nonpornographic) fiction, gay suicide is no longer figurable as heroic and pathetic, and gay orgasm is no longer unrepresentable. Consequently, such standards of subversiveness are now inapposite. But even though *Dorian Gray*, like *Teleny*, represents an "internally homophobic" fatal gay love scenario, today's gay readers find a text that, in at least one other respect, is somewhat subversive. Dorian's lurid death exposes and excoriates the endemic ageism of contemporary gay male sexuality. It is the last word in what now reads as a cautionary tale about the inherently self-destructive overvaluation of masculine youth and beauty—about subjecting oneself to a certain kind of iconography. In other words, Wilde's notorious chiasmatic climax (in which a decrepit portrait of an exquisite boy becomes an exquisite portrait of a decrepit boy) decenters gay subjectivities held in thrall by the likes of Dorian Gray (and James Dean). However, today's straight readers, unlike their fin-de-siècle counterparts, should not find Dorian's death subversive. If Sedgwick is right, they should read the novel's conclusion as a familiar manifestation of the phallocentrism of modern sentimentality. They should shed a tear and suppress a yawn. But they don't. Dorian is far too brutal (and, for young readers in particular, scary) for his suicide to be read (by any contemporary reader—gay or straight) as sentimental. Dorian is "pathetic," but only in the very worst sense of the word (as in the puerile put-down: "He's *pathetic*"). This is because Wilde's "modernist antisentimentality," which in the 1890's contested his own late-Victorian sentimentality, now contests our own antimodernist sentimentality (Sedgwick 132). In other words, *Dorian Gray* forces straight readers to take a dry-eyed look at one of the most fundamental "images of agonistic male self-constitution" and, in the process, subverts sentimentality as they, with Wilde's help, have come to know and feel it.

The late nineteenth century witnessed an unprecedented proliferation of Salomé texts. Mallarmé, Flaubert, Huysmans, Jules

Laforgue, Jean Lorrain, and Arthur Symons all wrote about her. Gustave Moreau, Edouard Toudouze, Ella Pell, Max Slevogt, Hugo von Habermann, Louis Corinth, and Juana Romani all painted her. But if Wilde's version drew upon many of these texts (notably, Moreau's, Flaubert's, Huysmans's, and Laforgue's), it also disrupted the Salomé tradition. One of Wilde's disruptive innovations was to have Herod annihilate Salomé, to give Herod the saga's final, murderous, say: "Kill that woman!" More specifically: to have Herod—the tetrarch, the patriarch, the state—*execute* Salomé because he finds her necrophilic love for Jokanaan perverse. However, Wilde's straight fin-de-siècle viewer was not particularly shocked by the innovative execution. (The comparison of fin-de-siècle "viewers" and contemporary "readers" is not meant to suggest that no one read *Salomé* in the 1890's or sees it performed today; rather, it is meant to expose the relative subversiveness of the two modes of reception.) What upset him was another one of Wilde's accretions to the liturgy: Salomé's hypererotic handling of Jokanaan's body. Unused to the uneasy pleasure of watching young women French-kiss severed heads, *Salomé*'s scandalized straight viewer tended to identify with the similarly scandalized Herod, and not with Wilde's perverse heroine. He tended, that is, to mimic Herod. He tended to mutter "Kill that woman!" and point his own accusing finger at Salomé. To the extent that he saw *Salomé* as homoerotic, he was thus successfully interpellated as a murderous homophobic subject. (The masculinization of this viewer is meant to suggest that his straight female counterparts may have been more likely to identify with Salomé, "perverse" as she was.)

Fortunately, *Salomé* had gay male viewers as well. The gay viewer, to the extent he saw the play as homoerotic, identified not with Herod but with Salomé, who, like him, formed "perverse" attachments to beautiful men and had a rather priapic image repertoire. And, unlike his straight counterpart, the gay viewer was shocked by the innovative execution. He was upset, not by the gory kiss, but by the representation of Salomé's love-death as a capital punishment. He was scandalized, in other words, by seeing

Salomé executed just as, and more importantly because, she experiences orgasmic bliss. The gay viewer knew that Wilde was pointing an accusing finger at Herod—that Wilde was making a gay spectacle of homophobic loathing as well as a straight spectacle of homoerotic lust—and pointed at Herod right along with him. The gay viewer, that is, was interpellated as an *anti*homophobic subject who understood Wilde to suggest an extremely subversive rejoinder to Herod's mandate. "Kill that woman?"—"Kill that governor!"

For today's gays, *Salomé* is a rarely performed work of classic camp. It is a familiar closet drama no gay can take seriously. And reading about Salomé's execution/love-death is simply not as upsetting as seeing it, especially when one knows to expect it, and especially when one's hermeneutic is comic. Consequently, *Salomé* is not as subversive as it once was. It no longer successfully interpellates antihomophobic gay subjects. However, camp readings make *Salomé* subversive in a new and different way. Gay readers who recast Herod as a buffoon take the play to label repressive state homophobia as ludicrous. They free themselves from abject fear by envisioning Salomé's death as too humorous to be horrible. (Ken Russell's recent film version of *Salomé*, with its horrifying "real" murder of the "actress" who plays Salomé, shows the extent to which this analysis is limited to *readings* of the play.) They liberate themselves from, by laughing at, their persecutors. For today's straights, *Salomé* is also not the shocker it once was. Like Salomé's love-death, the visually stunning necrophilic kiss has been reduced to a few naughty, and overly familiar, words on a page. Consequently, the play is now incapable of making a grotesque spectacle of perverse desire and of reproducing quite so much straight homophobia. And that is not the only good news. *Salomé* can now offer its straight readers the subversive service it once offered its gay viewers. It can now reveal and indict the murderous violence to which homophobia is prone by insisting that straight readers who no longer identify with Herod see Salomé as his victim—as a "woman" who is wrongfully killed for having flaunted "her" (homo)sexuality.

Like *Salomé, The Ballad of Reading Gaol* concerns a doomed, murderous lover. ("The man had killed the thing he loved, / And so he had to die" [*Complete Stories* 840].) However, the love-death inscribed within *Reading Gaol* is inflected by two factors none of the other contexts feature quite so prominently. It is a crucifixion, and it is a hanging. *Reading Gaol* accentuates, whereas *Teleny*, for example, merely alludes to, the homoeroticism of Christian iconography. Des Grieux understands "the love [Hadrian] felt for . . . Antinoüs, who—like unto Christ—died for his master's sake" (26), but Wilde's woman-murdering alter-ego *is* Christ:

> So never will wine-red rose or white,
> Petal by petal, fall
> On that stretch of mud and sand that lies
> By the hideous prison-wall,
> To tell the men who tramp the yard
> That God's Son died for all. (851)

And the execution of this Christlike convict replicates, whereas the execution of Salomé merely suggests, that of an early-nineteenth-century sodomite. A soldier's shield crushes Salomé to death, but a "hangman's snare [strangles the convict's prayer] into a scream" (849). This double inflection complicated gay as well as straight fin-de-siècle readings of *Reading Gaol*'s love-death. Gays read the hanged convict as gay because they were haunted by the specter of the hanged sodomite, and straights read him as gay because the notoriously gay Wilde identified with the man:

> A prison wall was round us both,
> Two outcast men we were:
> The world had thrust us from its heart,
> And God from out His care:
> And the iron gin that waits for Sin
> Had caught us in its snare. (844)

Both gays and straights, then, saw a "gay" prisoner hanged, like a sodomite, for having killed the woman he loves. Like Christ, however, this "gay" "murderer" is really guiltless. Like Christ, he is good—he is an innocent scapegoat. His crime is imaginary, his punishment murderous. And his death, like Christ's, could not be more pathetic. For these reasons, the ballad was subversive. It was a highly sentimental positive identification usurped from the dominant (Christocentric) culture, and like *Salomé*, it inculpated repressive state homophobia. However, like Christ, the prisoner is not really murdered by the state. Like Christ, he *allows* the state to murder him. His capital punishment is really a suicide. For this reason, the ballad was *not* subversive. Unlike *Salomé*, it *ex*culpated repressive state homophobia by implying that any self-destructive gay caught in its clutches has no one to blame but himself. On balance, one might say that this ambiguity (this inculpation/exculpation of homophobia) made *Reading Gaol* more subversive for straight readers, but less subversive for gay readers, than *Salomé*.

Gore Vidal recently asked: "Must one have a heart of stone to read *The Ballad of Reading Gaol* without laughing?" (1063). This sally suggests the nature of *Reading Gaol*'s radical recontextualization. But if Wilde's sob story has turned into a joke, it is not because, like *Salomé*, it is now camp. If it is a joke, it is a joke both gay and straight readers get. Sedgwick points out that Wilde set "in motion every conceivable mechanism by which most [fin-de-siècle readers knew] how to enter into the circuit of the sentimental" by toying with feminocentric as well as Christocentric feelings, by framing "his own image between, or even as, those of a woman-murdering man and the Crucified" (147). Unfortunately for Wilde, this strategy is now outdated. Most of today's readers, gay and straight, cannot be reduced to tears by weepy feminocentric and Christocentric scenarios, and attempts, like *Reading Gaol*, to so reduce them are quite futile, if not downright funny. (Christocentric sentimentality has become passé in an irreligious era that still clings to a phallocentric sentimentality based, in part, upon the Passion.) Even old-fashioned readers with soft spots for damsel-in-distress and lord-on-a-stick melodramas cannot take texts that combine the two varieties—their sentimental circuits become overloaded and burn out. But if *Reading Gaol* fails to move today's readers, it does educate them. It teaches them about ideology and textuality.

Contemporary readers, who are not successfully interpellated by Wilde's ideological apparatus, witness what used to be an invisible operation. They see his feminocentric and Christocentric text actually hail reading subjects other than themselves—ones who were already invested in both types of sentimentality. In other words, readers who are not the sentimental subjects of the enunciation see how the text once reconstituted readers' sentimental subjectivities. It is also emotional distance that enables contemporary readers to recognize that *Reading Gaol*'s vision, and version, of "fatal gay love" is a literary construction, and not a mirror held up to nature or life. Having dodged the text's reality effect by evading its sentimental snares, they are free to see that "and so he had to die" is nothing more than a figure of speech. And they are free to detect the artificiality, the cultural contingency, of *all* ("politically incorrect") textualizations concerning and constructing "fatal gay love"—even ones that are still movingly "real."

Reading Gaol's love-death also offers contemporary readers a valuable if veiled history lesson. It tells of the scores of sodomites who were hanged by their homophobic government. And it tells of the sexual bliss their executions aimed to eradicate. In other words, Wilde's last love-death serves as a figurative memento of men even homophobic history would now like to forget: the gay lovers who came as they were murdered by the state for having come together.

Foucault's conception of homosexuality as a "reverse discourse," as the foregoing analysis should suggest, lends itself two different, but equally valid, interpretations. On the one hand, homosexuality is a reverse discourse in that gays and lesbians occupy and transform subaltern ontological positions (e.g., that of sexual "inversion") that they have had little or no say in creating. On the other hand, homosexuality is a reverse discourse in that it misappropriates (i.e., subverts and adulterates) a wide range of discourses, including romantic erotics, that have little or no investment in articulating subaltern sexual identities. Chapter 2 continues this binocular focus. It records the responses of Gide and Firbank, two writers with close ties to Wilde, to the medical figuration of homosexuality as narcissistic—equivocal responses somewhat akin to Wilde's equivocal recollection of Bosie as "Hylas, or Hyacinth, Jonquil or Narcisse." It also describes their homoerotic misappropriation of the heteroerotic conception of love as complementary merger, one of the conceptions from which, as has been noted, Liebestod arose.

This move from Liebestod to complementary merger, although genealogically retrogressive, involves two critical complications. It requires concentration on the contradiction between essentialism and constructionism, which, like the contradiction between gender transitivity and gender separatism (e.g., "inversion" vs. "hom[m]osexuality"), is so central to modern homoerotics.[40] The move also demands that express attention be paid to erotic antagonism, polarization, and hierarchy. It demands, in other words, that attention be paid to power—a form of attention more or less implicit in any theorization of a subaltern sexuality as a reverse discourse. Homoerotic relationships can be marked by any number of power differentials—gender, race, class, ethnicity, age, and so on. When those relationships are figured as complementary mergers, however, those differential markings become key features. An age difference, for example, turns what might be described, incidentally, as a "May-December" romance into something that must be defined, fundamentally, as "pederastic"—an imperative that, as will be seen, can prove to be rather problematic.

CHAPTER 2

Pederastic Trappings: Gide and Firbank

> "I once," she said (resolutely refusing a stirring
> salmis of cocks'-combs *saignant* with *Béchamel* sauce),
> "I once peeped under a bishop's apron!"
>
> "Oh . . . ?"
>
> "And what ever did you see?" Mrs. Thoroughfare
> breathlessly asked.
>
> "Well . . . I saw," Lady Parvula replied (helping
> herself to a few *pointes d'asperges à la Laura Leslie*),
> "I saw . . . the dear Bishop!"
>
> Ronald Firbank, *Valmouth*

The ease with which Western culture conflates homosexuality and pederasty (older male–younger male eroticism), whether under the sign of sadism, narcissism, or otherwise, contrasts markedly with the rigor with which the two subcultures resist the conflations. Although many pederasts consider themselves homosexual, many do not. These men would rather be seen as lovers of youths (as Humbert Humberts), a dominant erotic construction, than as lovers of boys (as Gustave Aschenbachs), a deviant erotic construction. And although many nonpederastic homosexuals view pederasty as a form of homosexuality, many do not. Pederasty occupies an extremely marginal and problematic position within lesbian and gay culture in general and within lesbian and gay studies in particular. This should seem self-evident to readers who are involved in both.

For readers who are not, I would like, by way of introduction, to recount two personal, and I trust typical, experiences. The first occurred when I was thirteen, which is to say at about the time I was first beginning, howsoever cautiously, to think of myself as homosexual. (I was by no means yet gay.) I was in Greenwich Village, waiting on line to see Visconti's *Death in Venice*, when a man *d'un certain âge*, a member, as it turned out, of NAMBLA (the North American Man-Boy Love Association), an organization I had never heard of, handed me a flier extolling Thomas Mann's story as the greatest "affirmation" of man-boy love known to the Western world. Having already read the story, and knowing both that Aschenbach dies and that Tadzio (to whom, not incidentally, I was then close in age) never loved him, I deemed this claim to be rather dubious. I did not yet know that it was also pitiful. And having found the NAMBLA pamphleteer, like Aschenbach himself, to be decrepit in a sexually repulsive way, I decided that the whole idea of "man-boy love" was essentially disgusting. The second experience occurred in the more recent past. I was presenting an early draft of this chapter at an interdisciplinary seminar on sexuality, when one participant demanded to know what I thought pederasty, which she saw as predatory, if not sadistic, could possibly have to do with lesbian and gay studies. I was shocked and dismayed. How could man-boy love not concern the study of same-sex sexuality? And how could the lesbian/gay marginalization and problematization of pederasty, which were reproduced in the hostile question itself, not signal to people like my interlocutor (people, that is, who usually realize that what is socially peripheral is often symbolically central) that the serious study of homosexuality must encompass the serious study of this troubled and intrusive phenomenon?

Under such circumstances, it is not especially easy for pederasts—of whom, unlike André Gide, I feel compelled to confess I am *not* (yet?) one—to live out their love lives. They are seen as child molesters. They have—and perhaps take—Aschenbach as a role model. And they are spurned by squeamish boys who, unlike Gilbert and Sullivan's Ko-Ko, do not find "beauty in extreme old age." My focus here, however, is not on these very real problems.

Instead, it is on a number of other, less obvious discursive difficulties faced by two of this century's more notorious boy lovers.

Gide's autobiography *If It Die* (*Si le grain ne meurt*) and Ronald Firbank's novel *Concerning the Eccentricities of Cardinal Pirelli*, both published in 1926, concern the love of older men for young boys.[1] *If It Die* is an account of Gide's coming to terms with, and acting upon, his pederastic inclinations while traveling in Algiers (a French colony) in the winter of 1895—during which trip he happened to meet Oscar Wilde and Lord Alfred Douglas. In *Cardinal Pirelli*, the bare outline of which bears a striking resemblance to *Death in Venice* (1911), Don Alvaro Narciso Hernando Pirelli, the Cardinal-Archbishop of Clemenza, having been called to the Vatican to face charges arising from irregular ecclesiastic practices, chases a pretty acolyte through his cathedral on the eve of his departure, and, stripped "of everything but his fabulous mitre" (341), dies in the course of the pursuit. Given the opprobrium associated with both homosexuality and pederasty, these were not particularly easy texts to write and publish.[2] But even without such opprobrium, *If It Die* and *Cardinal Pirelli* would not have been easy to write.

Gide and Firbank were constrained by a number of irreconcilable discourses that made thinking and writing about pederastic love a highly precarious enterprise. They had to negotiate between the ideas that undressing is a metaphor for truth and that it is a metaphor for disempowerment. They had to negotiate between essentialist and constructionist conceptions of subjectivity. They had to negotiate between a conception of pederasty based on fixed polarities and a conception of love based on merged polarities. And they had to negotiate between the medical figuration of both homosexuality and pederasty as narcissistic and the philosophic figuration of love as object-oriented. The outcome of these seemingly futile negotiations, the textual strategies (compromises, forfeits, conflations, sublations) Gide and Firbank resort to as they wrest narrative coherence out of epistemological incoherence, is the subject of this chapter.

The organization of the chapter, the reader will note, is schematic. This is not, however, meant to suggest that *If It Die* and

Cardinal Pirelli are entrapped by only four sets of irreconcilable discourses. Like many literary texts, they are dialogic. They are constrained by and negotiate a multitude of contradictions. Nor is it meant to suggest that each textual strategy discussed accommodates only one set of irreconcilable discourses. Pirelli's retention of his "fabulous mitre," for example, has as much to do with the conflict between Firbank's conceptions of pederasty and love as with the conflict between essentialist and constructionist theories of subjectivity. The schematization is merely intended to make some sense of related texts that share a number of related incoherences. And just as there are more than four discursive contradictions to be found in the texts, there are other such senses to be made of them.

Revealing/Divesting

A naked truth about truth is that truth is often stark naked. Another, related truth about truth is that the removal of clothing is one of its central tropes. As Derrida has noted, "exhibiting, denuding, undressing [make up] the familiar acrobatics of the metaphor *of* the truth" (175). As Barthes has stated, "to denude [is] to know, to learn the origin and the end" (*Pleasure of the Text* 10). In order to reveal a truth, one must unveil it. On the other hand, clothing stands in so significant a metonymic relation to so many power differentials (gender, race, class, ethnicity, age, etc.) as to urge that its removal be read as disempowerment and that disempowerment be read as its removal. This poses a problem for pederastic writers, if not for pederastic practitioners, who would reveal themselves, or approximations of themselves, to beloved subalterns yet keep the alterns sub.

In order to reveal the bare truth of his "natural propensity" (*If It Die* 252), Gide is drawn, quite naturally, to the figure of shedding clothes. For example, when Ménalque, a character based on Wilde,[3] suggests a certain "evil" course of conduct to Michel, the character in *The Immoralist* with whom Gide is most closely aligned, it is as though "his phrases . . . suddenly laid bare my own mind: thoughts I had covered with so many veils I almost believed they were smothered" (*Immoralist* 112). And in textualizing his very first pederastic encounter (with a boy named Ali), Gide figures Michel's libidinal revelation as a literal unveiling of the beloved: "He didn't take long over the complicated knots in the laces that served him as a belt; pulling a little dagger out of his pocket, he sliced through the mess with a single blow. The garment fell; he threw his jacket far away and stood up naked as a god [*nu comme un dieu*]" (*Si le grain* 299).

Gide himself wishes to be naked—a desire he confesses to in the pederastic reveries of André Walter: "I saw again the thin torsos and sun-tanned limbs of the children . . . they were swimming and diving in these cold surroundings.—I became furious because I was not one of them, not one of the vagabonds who . . . dive, stark naked, into the refreshing coolness of streams. . . . I would have liked to bathe also, near them, and to have felt the softness of their brown skin" (*Notebooks* 123–24). Gide acknowledges in *If It Die* that this urge toward nudity is due in part to the fact that *dénuement* frees him of cultural inhibitions, that he feels able to lay aside with his garments "anxieties, constraints, solicitudes" (*If It Die* 267).[4] In fact, Gide, or at least Michel, often does strip—but only when certain he is alone:

One morning, stripping myself naked, I examined my body; the sight of my skinny arms, of my shoulders which the greatest efforts could not keep from slouching, but especially of the whiteness, or rather the colorlessness, of my skin, filled me with shame, and tears came to my eyes. I dressed again quickly, and . . . made for the rocks covered with lowgrowing grass and moss, far from houses or roads, where I knew I could not be seen. Here I slowly undressed. The air was quite cool, but the sun broiling. I offered the whole of my body to its flames. I sat, lay down, turned over. I felt the hard soil beneath me; the stirring grass brushed my body. Though sheltered from the wind, I trembled at each breath of air. Soon a delicious radiance enveloped me; my whole being brimmed to the surface of my skin.

We stayed two weeks in Ravello; each morning I would return to those rocks, resume my cure. Soon even the one garment I still wore became uncomfortable, superfluous . . . (*Immoralist* 55–56)

Gide seems to sense that disrobing in front of beloved boys, although disinhibitory, involves too great a risk of shame-faced disempowerment. Even Mohammed, the Arab youth, procured by Wilde, who figures as the erotic vortex of *If It Die*, is unable to uncover Gide's naked body—Gide flashes only his bare arms (*mes bras nus* [*Si le grain* 343]) before the reader's eyes. And when Daniel, the traveling companion Gide portrays as a colonial rapist,[5] takes his turn with and sodomizes Mohammed, Gide is careful to note that while the boy disrobes, the man does not:

While I stayed seated near our half-emptied glasses, Daniel took Mohammed in his arms and carried him to the bed which occupied the back of the room. He set him down on his back, right at the edge of the bed, across it; and soon I saw nothing but, on each side of Daniel, panting away, the slender legs hanging down. Daniel hadn't even taken off his coat. (*Si le grain* 345)

This tendency to keep the pederastic subject clothed cannot be attributed to mere accident, oversight, or modesty (*pudeur*) on Gide's part. Unlike William Beckwith, the pederastic protagonist of Alan Hollinghurst's *The Swimming-Pool Library*, who feels that "the naked person always has the social advantage over the clothed one" (20), Gide seems to feel that the disposition of the dominant and subordinate roles in a pederastic relationship depends, figuratively, upon which partner wears the pants, and even, literally, upon how much they cost. When, for example, young Ali dresses up for Lord Alfred Douglas "in brilliant garments with a silken sash and a golden turban" (*If It Die* 292–93), Gide infers that their proper roles have been reversed: "Douglas had found his master, and in spite of the elegance of his own clothes, he looked like an attendant, waiting on the orders of his gorgeous servant" (*If It Die* 292).

Cardinal Pirelli addresses in a more obvious way than does *If It Die* the tension between undress as erotic self-revelation and undress as disempowerment. The narrative itself is centered around two erotic unveilings. Pirelli progresses from one who is rumored by his female parishioners to be a heterosexual lover who "takes off his clothes" to "a little woman"[6] to one who is shown to be a pederastic lover who takes off his clothes to a little boy (the acolyte "Chicklet"). He also progresses from one who cross-dresses and is mistaken as a woman (Pirelli: "I remember it was the night I wore ringlets and was called 'my queen'" [295]) to one who undresses and reveals his phallus (Phoebe Poco, upon seeing Pirelli "dismantled": "I'm an honest widow; so I know what men are, bless them!" [341]). Yet *Cardinal Pirelli* is also the account of an eccentric prelate's clerical investiture and impending divestiture. The very first line—"Huddled up in a cope of gold wrought silk he peered around" (289)—signals the novel's obsession with what Pirelli is entitled to wear. By the third paragraph, Firbank has already noted that Pirelli is a party to "escapades [which], if continued, would certainly cost the Cardinal his hat" (289)—the one article of clothing he does not, in fact, forfeit. And Pirelli's final, fatal strip search is all the more spectacular for his having selected for the occasion an especially splendid outfit: "'I've a mind, do you know, to join you, boy; I declare I feel quite rompish!' he told himself, gathering up, with a jocund pounce, a heavy mantle of violet cloth-of-gold [and] setting a mitre . . . intended for Saint Peter's [upon his head]" (335).

Just as Gide wants to strip with, if not for, attractive boys but is too mindful of his power over them to do so, Firbank knows that, in stripping for Chicklet, Pirelli loses a sexual advantage attributable to their relative placement within an ecclesiastic hierarchy. Chicklet is not simply one of the choirboys about whom Pirelli is so solicitous and insinuating.[7] He is an acolyte. As a practical matter, the relationship of acolyte to cardinal is that of an attendant or assistant. As an etymological matter, however, an acolyte is a cardinal's follower. And although Pirelli is marked quite early in the text as one whose prerogative is to be followed, or sought—he is "as wooed and run after by the ladies as any *matador*" (290)—it is a prerogative he abnegates in running naked after an acolyte. For when the pederastic prelate undresses in pursuit of his love, one truth he unwittingly unveils is that the followed has become the follower, the cardinal the acolyte.

The strip-search scene also represents an attempt to conflate the two senses of undressing (metaphor for truth, metaphor for disempowerment). Having established that Pirelli is being pursued by clerical adversaries who wish to see him defrocked for his ecclesiastic transgressions (who feel there is "quite enough to condemn . . . this Pirelli for a *maleficus pastor* [and that] the earlier, the better, the unfrocking" [303]), Firbank has Pirelli defrocked in the course of a pederastic exposure. But pederastic exposure can be a form of ecclesiastic transgression, as in the case of "Don Fernando de la Cerde, Bishop of Barcelona, defrocked for putting young men to improper uses" (320). Does Pirelli strip off his garments himself, or is he being stripped of them? Is he, like Don Fernando, being defrocked for putting young men to improper uses, or is he disrobing to put a young man to improper uses? At first, Firbank seems to have no desire to settle these questions, and his sole reference to how Pirelli actually comes to be stripped of everything but his mitre refuses to resolve the matter: "Oblivious of sliding mantle the Primate swooped" (341). Has Pirelli himself removed the mantle? Or has someone or something taken it from him? The line suggests that we cannot know, that both explanations are equally viable.[8] Ultimately, however, Firbank does not, or cannot, sustain the conflation. He permits the discourse of disempowerment to triumph over the discourse of revelation: "Dispossessed of everything but his fabulous mitre, the Primate was nude and elementary now as Adam himself" (341). Pirelli, after all, has been "dispossessed," he is put out of possession of the authority—and of the trappings of that authority—with which his church had invested him. Or at least, that is, of nearly all the trappings. For reasons that remain to be explored, he still retains that "fabulous mitre."

Essentialism/Constructionism

The strip search Pirelli performs and the strips Michel performs alone are intended to reveal essential selves. Pirelli's dying words are "As you can perfectly see, I have nothing but myself to declare. . . . Only myself" (341),[9] and the nature of that self is signified both by Firbank's description of the nude Pirelli as "elementary . . . as Adam himself" and by the "novel, *Self-Essence*, on the Index, or about to be" that Pirelli has just packed for the trip to Rome (334).[10] Gide's aim in traveling to Algiers is to emerge from a "selve obscure"[11] period (*Si le grain* 280), and Algiers is indeed the colonized clearing in which he lights upon his true pederastic essence: "I was beginning to discover myself—and in myself the tables of my new law" (*Si le grain* 360). Gide felt at the time that he could uncover his authentic self only by following "nature—the unconscious, which is within myself and must be *true*" (letter to his mother, Feb. 2, 1895; quoted in Delay 396). As Michel puts it, underneath the false, social self lurks a true, natural one (an originary "Adam," as in *Cardinal Pirelli*):

The layers of acquired knowledge peel away from the mind like a cosmetic and reveal, in patches, the naked flesh beneath, the authentic being hidden there. . . . I sought to discover . . . "the old Adam" [*le "vieil homme"*] whom the Gospels no longer accepted; the man whom everything around me—books, teachers, family and I myself—had tried from the first to suppress. . . . I scorned henceforth that secondary, learned being whom education had pasted over him. Such husks must be stripped away. (*Immoralist* 51; *L'Immoraliste* 398)

However, both Gide and Firbank were aware of the countervailing position to their essentialism, a position made known to them by its most notorious champion, Oscar Wilde.[12] Wilde rejected outright the notion that an ego has an essence. Like Dorian Gray, he wondered "at the shallow psychology of those who conceived the Ego in man as a thing simple, permanent, reliable, and of one essence" and thought of man as "a being with myriad lives and myriad sensations, a complex multiform creature" (*Dorian Gray* 159). This, Wilde felt, was as true of erotic predilection, of the "yearnings" that derive from "Love's Litany," as of any other subjective attribute. When Gide first met Wilde in Paris (in 1891, the year of the publication of *The Picture of Dorian Gray*, and four years prior to their chance meeting in Algiers), he was terrified by this aggressive anti-essentialism and wrote to Paul Valéry: "Wilde is religiously contriving to kill what remains of my soul,

because he says that in order to know an essence, one must eliminate it: he wants me to miss my soul. The measure of a thing is
the effort made to destroy it. Each thing is made up only of its
emptiness" (Mallet 90).[13] Ultimately, however, Gide could not embrace the idea of such emptiness. By the time he wrote *If It Die*,
he had rejected Wildean anti-essentialism so thoroughly as to attempt to eliminate its trace even from its most self-evident construct—Wilde's own persona: "He would never cease from acting—could not, no doubt; but the character he acted was his
own; the role itself . . . was a sincere one" (*If It Die* 277–78).[14]

Firbank, who had an obsessive interest in Wilde's life and work,
was also familiar with his constructionist agenda.[15] His early novel
The Artificial Princess (originally entitled *Salomé, Or 'Tis A Pity
That She Would*), for example, is an exposition of Wilde's idea
that one need only repeat "Love's Litany" in order to love.[16] Princess Mary, struck by her family's uncanny resemblance to that of
Salomé, has Baroness Teresa Rudlied deliver to St. John Pellegrin,
a local prophet, an invitation to her debutante party, at which she
hopes to reenact the biblical scenario. Mary's hopes are frustrated
when the invitation goes undelivered (the oversexed Baroness having been waylaid by an admirer) and St. John fails to appear, but
at the last minute she mistakes a late arriver for her prophet and
proceeds to play the coquette with him. What makes Mary "artificial" is her belief that in all things concerning love, as in all
things concerning subjectivity in general, form precedes essence:
"'How I should care to be a new Salomé . . . all I need is to de-
velop my style'" (246). The Baroness shares this perspective: "All
you need, dear, is just the will to shut your eyes to everybody else
and tell yourself there is only *one* man, and that you have been
lucky enough to secure him all-to-yourself, and then, with a little
coaxing, Love is bound to come" (252). She also knows that the
essence of the Litany is its iterability:

"Dear Teresa," exclaimed the Princess. "You are so wonderful! But you
have had so many experiences. I feel I could never really love anyone
unless he was pale, but pale . . . with violet rippling hair, and had eyes,
blue, but blue, as skies in May, and could boast a big-big, Oh," she ab-

strusely broke-off, "have you ever loved anyone just like that, Teresa?"

"Several," answered the Baroness, recklessly. (252; ellipsis in original)

Yet if *The Artificial Princess* is an exposition of Wilde's "Love's Litany" theory, it is also a rejection of it. Firbank uses Princess Mary to demonstrate that life doesn't always fulfill the promises made by such litanies. Mary intends to kill a prophet ("she added mysteriously: 'You may play that [melancholy fugue] to me, if you like, after he is dead'" [244]) and merely "commence[s] a pious flirtation" (284) with a false prophet. She even has difficulty reiterating the one Salomean love litany she knows by heart: "It had been her intention to lead off with a little speech, previously prepared. But somehow (oh, why?) things seldom turn out as you suppose . . . " (282; ellipsis in original).

But even though both Gide and Firbank purport to reject the constructionist position, a Wildean worm of doubt gnaws at the heart of their essentialist texts—texts which unwarily reveal an awareness that there may be no authentic self to unveil. This nefarious worm is clearly gnawing away in André Walter's nightmare vision of Emmanuèle undressed:

She appeared to me, very beautiful, clothed in an unpleated rochet which fell to her feet like a stole; smiling faintly, she held herself erect, with only her head inclined. A monkey, hopping and skipping, drew nearer; he lifted her mantle, swinging the fringes to and fro. I was afraid to look; I wanted to turn my eyes away but, in spite of myself, I watched.

Under her dress there was nothing; it was black, black as a hole; I wept in despair. Then with both hands she grasped the hem of her dress and threw it over her face. She turned herself inside out like a sack. And I saw nothing more; darkness enveloped her . . . (*Notebooks* 133; ellipsis in original)[17]

Given his misogyny—given, for example, his claim in *Corydon* that whereas no one can resist naked boys, no one can desire naked women—one might take this dream to mean that, for Gide, *women* have no essence. The feminine other (but not the masculine other) unveiled reveals the void, the "emptiness," of which Wilde had spoken. (A more charitable interpretation might be that whereas Gide fetishizes female apparel, he would rather boys remove clothes than model them.) However, something similar to, if not quite so uncanny as, Emmanuèle's emptiness characterizes Gide's beloved boys, as when in *Amyntas* "the little Kabyle shepherd [who] exposes himself, stripping off his gandoura . . . seems a goat among his goats, and does not distinguish himself from the flock" ([1988] 73). Although, as Jonathan Dollimore argues, this kind of disappearing act is indicative of the exploitative side of Gide's erotic interactions with North African boys, particularly insofar as he tends to see in them "an image of [his] own despair" (*If It Die* 296), it is also indicative of Gide's antiessentialism. The Kabyle shepherd does not distinguish himself because, like Emmanuèle, he has nothing distinctive to expose. He simply fades into the natural world—a feat one might expect from Emmanuèle, were she the typically "natural" woman envisioned by so many other male writers. The worm of doubt gnaws away even at Firbank's princess, who is only ever artificial, who has no essence apart from her epigonism, who has no self apart from her desire to reenact a part already transcribed by Matthew (14: 3–6), Mark (6: 17–22), and Wilde (*Salomé*). And who, when unveiled, is inevitably discovered rehearsing the dance of the seven veils: "Far off, in the Palace, the Princess, who had obtained the King's word, that she might ask, during dessert, for anything she pleased, had risen from her bath, and was dancing a Tarantella before the Mirror, in just a bracelet and a rope of pearls" (267).

In other words, the strip search Pirelli performs, and the strips Michel performs alone, may well be intended to reveal essential selves, but they are essential selves the authors sense may not exist. Gide, trapped between rival tropes (revelation, disempowerment), does not have Michel undress in front of beloved boys who might notice that he has no pederastic essence to unveil, that underneath the trappings of his pederastic impulses there is only an unnamable emptiness. Pirelli, stripped of everything else, retains his mitre. But what is it that makes that mitre so "fabulous?"

The episcopal mitre is more than an incidental metonymy for a bishop's ecclesiastic status. It represents the cloven tongues of fire which descended on the apostles on the day of Pentecost (Acts 2: 1–12) and, consequently—for Firbank, if not for the Catholic Church, which prefers the pectoral cross—is the quintessential signifier of a bishop's election. Without his mitre, according to Firbank, Pirelli is simply not the Cardinal-Archbishop of Clemenza. The mitre is, or at least represents, his clerical essence. Yet if Pirelli has no clerical essence apart from his mitre, neither can he be parted from it. No matter that he is otherwise dis-mantled, no matter that he is otherwise defrocked, Pirelli dies a cardinal-archbishop, his mitre improbably in place. Perhaps what is "fabulous" about the mitre is this unlikely tenacity.[18] Perhaps what Firbank finds so fabulous is that a man who, alone, has no ecclesiastic essence is, nevertheless, never without it. But the mitre is fabulous in another sense as well. It is "fabulous" in the sense that, as an essence, it is a fiction, a construct. It is, moreover, anyone's fiction. While the Catholic Church may have determined that Pirelli's mitre reminds her of tongues of fire, Phoebe Poco thinks "it would make quite a striking toque" (312), and Firbank thinks it looks like a "wondrous mustard-pot" (335). In other words, Firbank uses Pirelli's "fabulous mitre" to hoodwink both essentialism and constructionism.

Pederasts in Love

The viability of the concept "pederasty," of pederasty as phenomenological figure, is contingent on the stability of a number of power differentials that enable the labels "subject" and "other," and "lover" and "beloved," to be assigned to two males engaged in erotic intercourse, as well as upon the stability of the differentials subject/other and lover/beloved themselves. These power differentials are fundamentally heteroerotic and include: age/youth, experience/innocence, domination/submission, masculinity/femininity, and aggressivity/passivity. In other words, the older, wiser pederastic lover should be socially superior to the younger, greener beloved whom he feminizes by fucking. Of course, power can be more evenly distributed between subjects and others in actual pederastic relationships than it is within this phenomenological figuration of one. In theory—theory that is somewhat homophobic—pederasty, like the type of heterosexuality after which it is patterned, is exploitative, predatory, and even sadistic. In practice, however, pederasty may be none of these. The North Africans Gide saw as boys were, in the eyes of their own culture, old enough to be married. And as Gide himself once noted, although "Rimbaud was ten years younger than Verlaine and was only sixteen when Verlaine called him to Paris," the youngster was also "furiously provocative, despotic, and authoritarian" (Pollard 229). The analysis I present here does situate power in the pederastic subject position alone, but it does so because the texts under consideration attempt to reinforce the figuration, not because power only ever resides there.

Gide is a pederast and even identifies himself as one: "Pederasts, of whom I am one (why can't I say that quite simply, without your immediately claiming to see a boast in my confession?)." He purports, however, to have far fewer differential criteria than are named above: "I call the person who falls in love with young boys a *pederast*, which is what the word means. I call the person whose desire is toward grown men a *sodomite*. . . . I call the person who in love making adopts the role of a woman and wants to be possessed an *invert*" (*Journal* 671). The only critical difference, for Gide, would appear to be age.[19] Neither the older male nor his younger partner is especially effeminate, and neither is especially sodomitical. In fact, Gide finds anal sex repulsive (Daniel, the colonial rapist, is a "huge vampire feeding upon a corpse" [*If It Die* 286]), preferring instead what one biographer characterizes as "reciprocal onanism with childish partners" (Delay 426): "For myself, who only understand pleasure face to face, reciprocal and without violence, and who am often satisfied, just like Whitman, by the most furtive of contacts, I was horrified both by Daniel's behavior and by Mohammed's complacent submission to it" (*Si le grain* 346).

This attempt to masculinize and, to coin a phrase, onanize pederasty is rather classical (see Chapter 4). It is also misogynist and apolitical. Gide is both repelled by the womanishness of sexual inversion and sodomitical submission, and drawn to a "pastoral" project, one engaged in by writers who would like to conceive of the sexual "apart from all relations of power," to see it as only "belatedly contaminated by power from elsewhere" (Bersani 221).[20] In other words, Gide would rather not acknowledge the colonial context of his sexual initiation. Unfortunately, as Michael Lucey notes, "a Frenchman and a North African boy can do all the free-floating imagining they want to—it won't affect their nationalities" (191 n.7). Nor would Gide, in reality, want it to. For all his pederastic pastoralizing, Gide—unlike, as will be seen, Yourcenar and Renault—is no erotic egalitarian. Age/youth is not, in fact, the only power differential that pertains to his private paradigm. Other, purportedly nongendered, nonsodomitical ones do as well—which is why, for example, Lord Alfred Douglas nearly forfeits his status as a pederast[21] when fifteen-year-old Ali is dressed so brilliantly as to look as though he might be his lordship's "master." (The importance of dressing for pederastic success is a lesson Gide may have learned at the age of nine when, at a fancy-dress ball held at Pascaud Gymnaseum, he fell in love with a more brilliantly costumed older boy who spurned his advances and broke his heart.)[22]

Like Gide, Firbank is a self-identified pederast. In fact, it was in 1920, the year of the private, noncommercial, publication of *If It Die*, that the "wonderful" boys of Algiers enabled him to succumb to his pederastic yearnings,[23] much as they had done so for Gide 25 years earlier.[24] And by 1923, the year he began work on *Cardinal Pirelli*, Firbank had so successfully overcome any reticence concerning the subject as to confide to one acquaintance that he was taking a taxi every morning at six to look at the "most beautiful creature about 16" with "eyes like a gazelle" whom he had found digging up a road in London.[25] Unlike Gide, however, Firbank takes pains to show that the concept of pederasty is contingent upon power differentials other than age/youth. In his play *The Princess Zoubaroff* (1920), which portrays Wilde and Douglas as the lovers "Lord Henry Orkish" and "Reggie Quintus," Orkish is described as a man of "a 'certain age'" and Quintus as "incredibly young" (716). Yet because it is the character based on Wilde who is dubbed "Lord," and not the character based on Lord Alfred Douglas, it appears that Firbank is making a point of inscribing what he perceives as a proper, and somewhat feudal, imbalance of power to their pederastic relationship—and of suggesting, perhaps, that the Wilde-Douglas affair would have been happier, or at least more appropriate, had the wit out-classed the peer. In *Cardinal Pirelli*, the *dén(o)uement* of which Firbank liked to describe as an "enfantment,"[26] the identification of Pirelli as a pederast is more circumspect, but no less campy. Pirelli, as described by Firbank in the novel, is one of those "men [who] in their natural lives, pursue the concrete no less than the ideal—qualities not seldom found combined in fairy childhood" (340). Any doubts concerning the pederastic character of Pirelli's pursuit of the "fairy" child Chicklet, who is feminized and disempowered by the punning predication, are put to rest, however, by "The Trial of Don Fernando de la Cerde, Bishop of Barcelona, defrocked for putting young men to improper uses" (320), the account Pirelli is found reading in preparation for his own related defense.

If Gide and Pirelli are pederasts, they are pederasts who *love* boys—a point the two texts insist upon. For Gide, the pederast is the man who "falls in love with young boys" (*s'éprend des jeunes garçons*), even, at times, against his will:[27] "My joy was immense, and such that I cannot imagine it any fuller even if love had entered into it [*si de l'amour s'y fut mêlé*]. How could it have been a question of love? . . . But how then should I name the rapture I felt as I clasped in my naked arms that perfect little body, savage, ardent, lascivious, and shadowy [*ténébreux*]?" (*Si le grain* 343).

Firbank has Pirelli confess his love for Chicklet in a less equivocal, and less conventionally exotic, passage:

> "Did I so wrong, my God, to punish him? Was I too hasty?" the Primate asked, repairing towards an ivory crucifix by Cano; "yet, Thou knowest, I adore the boy!"
>
> He paused a moment astonished by the revelation of his heart.
>
> "It must have been love that made me do it," he smiled, considering the incident in his mind. (334)

Yet the love Mohammed and Chicklet inspire is antithetical to Gide's and Firbank's conception of pederasty as contingent upon the stability of power differentials. Both writers subscribe to the romantic figuration of love as the *merging* of a subject with a complementary, or opposite, other—an apt subscription given that the figuration, like the pederastic power differentials, is fundamentally heteroerotic, hierarchic, and antagonistic. On the one hand, Firbank's position is that of Lady Rocktower in *The Princess Zoubaroff,* that lovers must be "sufficiently different . . . to be happy together" (715). He implies as much in *Cardinal Pirelli*: "Across the tranquil court a rose-red butterfly pursued a blue. 'I believe the world is all love, only no one understands,' [Pirelli] meditated" (322).[28] On the other hand, Firbank's position is also that there can be no love unless the "sufficient" difference signified by color complementarity is undifferentiated or unified. (Although red and blue are not true complementary colors, they are complementary enough for the purposes of this analysis.) Mrs. Blanche Negress, the lesbian author of *Love's Visé* (sic) ["Love's Aim"] in *The Princess Zoubaroff* (723), is a rather blatant embodiment of this position. By complementing herself, by uniting both white and black, she realizes love's aim alone. And by "joining" (335) Chicklet in the cathedral, which awaits "the quickening blush of day like a white-veiled negress" (340), Pirelli tries to eliminate the power differentials that separate them. To paraphrase the novel's final lines, he wishes that some "very great distinctions be commingled" (341–42).

Gide, too, is in Lady Rocktower's or, to be more precise, Schopenhauer's camp.[29] Unlike Firbank, however, he says so quite expressly: "Some people fall in love with what is like them; other with what is different. I am among the latter" (*If It Die* 256). Similar souls, he feels, such as those of Castor and Pollux, "remain parallel" and "cannot know each other" (*Cahiers* 70): "they find it impossible to meet because of the equal nature of their love" (Ms. of *Corydon,* quoted in Pollard 310). Gide, moreover, literalizes, and pastoralizes, Firbank's metaphorical red-blue color complementarity in justifying his taste for North African boys: "Strangeness solicits me as much as familiarity repels. Let me add besides,

and with much more particularity, that I am attracted by 'Phoe-
bus' amorous pinches' on a brown skin" (*If It Die* 256). Yet Gide,
like Firbank, conceives of love, and in particular pederastic love, as
the *dissolution* of the black/white (Blanche/Negress) complementarity upon which it is also based. The pastoral mode of *If It
Die*—the apolitical and nonpederastic egalitarianism, the *face à
face* sexual preference, the attempt to pass himself off as nonex-
ploitative, as something other than a sexual tourist—should, in
fact, be traced to this investment in erotic dissolution.[30] It is this
investment, moreover, that colors Gide's identification with Fabrice del Dongo, the hero of Stendhal's *The Charterhouse of Parma*,
when, at the age of 48, he writes of his love for young "M.": "For
long moments as he contemplated him, Fabrice [Gide] lost all
sense . . . of himself" (*Journal* 630).[31] Love, for Gide, is self-loss,
(white) subject / (black) other merger. After love, as he imagined
both Wilde and Verlaine realized, comes "self-recovery."[32]

It would not be surprising had the contradiction between the
conception of pederasty as contingent upon the stability of complementary differentials and the conception of love as the merging
of a subject with a complementary other led Gide and Firbank to
dissociate pederasty and love altogether. The position of the nonloving pederast, like the position of the nonpederastic lover, is,
within the epistemological universe of the two conceptions, unas-
sailable. Yet they do not dissociate the terms. The Gide of *If It
Die* and Firbank's Pirelli love the boys with whom they have, or
want to have, sex. By doing so, Gide fails to attain his ostensible
spiritual goal of severing love and sensuality—a goal alluded to
disparagingly in *If It Die*: "I had resigned myself to dissociating
pleasure and love; and even thought that this divorce was desirable, that pleasure would be purer and love more perfect if the
heart and senses were kept apart" (*If It Die* 240). And in Firbank's
case, the failure to dissociate love and pederasty in *Cardinal Pirelli*
is especially notable, and paradoxical, in light of his frequent attempts to dissociate love from nonpederastic erotic ventures in
his earlier novels. Whereas love is often portrayed as abhorrent
in these works, it is a sign of Pirelli's final pederastic apotheosis, in

which "distinction and sweetness . . . together with much nobility, and love [are] magnified and commingled" (341–42).[33]

The contradiction does, however, account for a significant lacuna common to *Si le grain ne meurt* and *Cardinal Pirelli*—that while the texts' pederastic protagonists can say "I love *him*," they cannot say "I love *you*." Gide acknowledges that no word other than *amour* adequately describes his feelings (343), and Pirelli readily declares "I adore the boy" (334)—nothing prevents them from telling themselves, God, or the reader, that they love Mohammed and Chicklet. Yet nowhere in these texts do Gide and Pirelli tell their beloved boys that they are loved. As far as Chicklet is concerned, the Cardinal truly has "nothing . . . to declare." The same might be said of Gide. Unlike Pirelli, however, Gide is clearly troubled by this incapacity and recalls that as a schoolboy he could not complete a poem after writing the stanza:

I wanted to tell him, but he didn't understand me.
When I said I was in love, he began to smile.
I should have chosen my words better before telling him,
Invented some kind of scorn to mask my secret love,
So as to not appear moved, perhaps I should have even laughed it off.

(*Si le grain* 223)[34]

This lacuna, this telling silence, bears an uncanny resemblance to Michel's inability to undress when in the presence of the boys he loves (and concomitant ability to undress when alone) and to an otherwise nude Pirelli's implausible retention of his "fabulous mitre." This resemblance is by no means accidental, for the sense of the lacuna is that while the power differentials upon which a pederastic relation depends might come undone were the pederastic subject to confess to the subaltern, beloved other that he desires their erasure, they remain firmly in place when the subject either merely fantasizes their erasure or relates his fantasy to a third party.[35] Gide and Pirelli want their boys to see them undress (unveil) and to hear them confess (reveal), yet they also want to retain their pederastic advantage. They want love, yet they want power. And although they consider disempowerment too high a

price to pay for pederastic love, they suggest that the canny pederast can steal love simply by refusing to say "I love you."

Unfortunately, the canny pederast who thinks he is stealing love
is really only paying a different price for it. By keeping his love, if
not to himself, then at least away from his beloved, he may be
that which according to his way of thinking is an impossibility—
a pederast in love. But he is not a pederastic lover. The lover must
say "I love you," and must say it to the beloved. As Barthes observes: "The one who does not say *I-love-you* (between whose lips
I-love-you is reluctant to pass) is condemned to emit the many
uncertain, doubting, greedy signs of love, its indices, its 'proofs':
gestures, looks, sighs, allusions, ellipses: he must let himself be *interpreted*" (*Lover's Discourse* 154). The beloved of the pederast who
will not say "I love you" is not likely to take him to mean "he
loves me, he is my lover." Like heartless Chicklet's purported
"fondness" for Pirelli, the love of a canny pederast will always risk
being interpreted by the one who matters most as "caring without
caring."[36]

Narcissists in Love

Contemporaneous medical discourse urged writers like Gide
and Firbank to conceive of both homosexuality and pederasty as
narcissistic—a conflation of the two (purportedly objectless) sexualities this section will also, to a certain extent, be compelled to
reproduce. Freud, for example, theorized narcissism as both a
stage of psychosexual development between autoeroticism and al-
loeroticism (object-relatedness) in which the libidinal object is the
ego itself and as a pathology in which libido is withdrawn from
external objects and invested in the ego.[37] He had also argued that
the homosexual object choice is more closely related to narcissism
than the heterosexual: "We have discovered, especially clearly in
people whose libidinal development has suffered some disturbance, such as perverts and homosexuals, that in their later choice
of love objects they have taken as a model not their mother but
their own selves" ("On Narcissism," *Standard Edition* 14: 88). Ped-

erasts, Freud felt, were no exception: "they proceed from a narcissistic basis, and look for a young man who resembles themselves" ("Three Essays on the Theory of Sexuality" [1914], *Standard Edition* 7: 145). This theorization, which was endorsed by many early psychoanalytic writers,[38] is, of course, heterosexist, if not homophobic. Narcissism, if one resists (as Gide and Firbank do) reading gender difference as difference per se, is more or less equally distributed between heterosexuality and homosexuality.[39] The theorization, moreover, is less concerned with conceptualizing homosexuality as a sexuality of sameness than it is with constituting heterosexuality as a sexuality of difference.[40]

If It Die and *Cardinal Pirelli* duplicate this figuration of the homosexual/pederast as Narcissus.[41] Firbank first presents "Don Alvaro *Narciso* Hernando Pirelli" at a baptismal font in which he is to perform "the act of Immersion" (290). Gide presents himself, at age eighteen or nineteen, gazing "unwearyingly" into a mirror at which, "like Narcissus, I hung over my own image" in order to find a facial expression that would "above all things . . . make myself loved" (*If It Die* 194). The two writers are drawn to the Narcissus trope for the same reason as are the early psychoanalytic theorists: they correlate the subject/other and male/female differentials, the primary correlation concerning both subjectivity and sexuality made by modern, masculinist epistemology,[42] and therefore view (male) attraction to the same sex as analogous to attraction to the same self. The correlation is implicit in their Adamic figurations of essential selfhood: for Firbank the real Pirelli seems like "Adam himself," while for Michel one's "authentic being" seems like "the old Adam." In other words, the primary self is the primary man. In Firbank's text, moreover, the revelation of Pirelli's self ("I have nothing but myself to declare. . . . Only myself") turns out to be indistinguishable from—it is one and the same act as—the unveiling of his phallus ("I know what men are, bless them!").

Unlike the psychoanalytic theorists, however, Gide and Firbank do not fully embrace the use of Narcissus as a trope for libidinal investment in the ego—they do not, that is, wholly endorse

Freud's contention that pederasts look for young men who resemble themselves. While they accept the idea that (male) attraction to the same sex is *analogous* to attraction to the same self, they resist the notion that the two are *identical*—a notion at odds with both their complementary-merger conception of love (a conception which presupposes that love is alloerotic) and their status as pederasts (i.e., as subjects completely differentiated from their beloved others).[43] This resistance accounts for Gide's deconstructive use of the Narcissus figure in his description of how at age thirteen he explored the tidal pools of Saint-Marghérite (an island off the coast of Cannes) while "leaning like Narcissus over the surface of the water" (*If It Die* 105)—a portrait of the subject looking *through* and not *at* a mirror-like surface. It also accounts for the fact that although the "little woman" to whom pederastic Pirelli is presumed to take off his clothes turns out to be a little boy, she does not turn out to be a mere reflection of Pirelli himself. It is instead heterosexual Princess Mary who is discovered dancing "before the Mirror, in just a bracelet and a rope of pearls."

All the same, Gide and Firbank do blur the boundaries between analogy and identity. They are seduced by, even if they do not fully embrace, the proposition that the pederast has a narcissistic investment in his own ego. This blurring of boundaries, this seduction, explains why Firbank's pederastic prelate dies trying to embrace an untouchable, unreachable other while uttering "only myself" to what may well be his own reflection: "some phantom image in the air" (341). It also explains why Gide's Narcissus figures tend to realize that the reflections they fall for are of themselves. André Walter, for example, gazes into a mirror, "senses the identity" of the "I" and "the other," and observes: "My eyes penetrate his, and in the depth of *his* pupils I search for *my* thought" (*Notebooks* 112–13). When Gide transcribes this observation in the corollary mirror scene of *If It Die*, he is certain of the identification Walter senses—"his pupils" become "my eyes:" "in order to become aware of my emotions, of my thoughts even, I must first, I fancied, read them in my eyes" (*If It Die* 195). And in *Le Traité du Narcisse*, Gide's Narcissus recognizes that his adored reflection is not a true other and thereby becomes what early psychoanalysts would have every homosexual be: "a self defined through the realization that it is enamored of itself" (Apter, *André Gide* 32): "He bends over and, suddenly, we see this illusion start to disappear; he sees in the stream nothing but two lips in front of his own extended lips, two eyes, his own, which look at him. He understands that it is he,—that he is alone—and that he has fallen in love with his own face [*qu'il s'éprend de son visage*]" (*Traité du Narcisse* 10). Like the Gide of *Amyntas*, Gide's Narcissus comes to understand himself as a lover with no object (*amoureux sans objet* [*Amyntas*/1925 187]).

Swayed to such an extent by medical blandishments, Gide and Firbank should disavow their contention that pederasty is a form of love. They should realize that if love is, but pederasty is not, object-oriented, then the two are incommensurable. They should, in other words, anticipate Julia Kristeva, who recognizes and subscribes to a related logic. Kristeva believes that "beneath homosexual libido . . . the chasms of narcissistic emptiness spread out" (*Tales of Love* 43), that "it is essential for the lover to maintain the existence of [an] ideal other," and that narcissistic (homosexual) desire is loveless: "The lover is a narcissist with an *object*. Love involves a sizable *Aufhebung* of narcissism; consequently, the relationship established by Freud between love and narcissism must not cause us to forget their essential difference. Is it not true that the narcissist, as such, is precisely someone incapable of love?" (*Tales of Love* 33). Yet Gide and Firbank never concede that the pederast lacks a proper love object and therefore does not love. Instead, they argue, or at least imply, that the very real otherness of his love object is merely *imperceptible* to those who believe that attraction to the same sex is identical to attraction to the same self. They show that what is distinct about this object is his indistinctness within a psychoanalytic epistemological universe, and not his purported nonalterity.

Gide and Firbank realize that the pederast's love object has no place within the conceptual borders of psychoanalytic theory and textualize this realization by portraying him as a liminal figure in that landscape. In *Amyntas*, he is literally erased from the (medicalized) field of vision—"the little Kabyle shepherd . . . seems a goat among his goats, and does not distinguish himself from the flock"—and, presumably, is still visible only to Gide, the pederastic voyeur/auteur who had discerned him in the first (nonmedicalized) instance. And Firbank's frequent declarations that heterosexual love is neither "ethereal" nor "elusive"[44] do not sound paradoxical (i.e., paradoxical because love is usually presumed to be both ethereal and elusive) to antipsychoanalytic readers who realize that only nonheterosexual love has come to be "ethereal" and "elusive," or, in other words, to be other-worldly and ungraspable. But perhaps the most felicitous expression of this liminality is Firbank's punning assertion that the pederastic love object is in his "fairy childhood." Not only are "fairy" children homosexual, they are fictitious and illusory as well. Firbank's phrase conflates all three senses. Chicklet is a "fairy" child in that he is Pirelli's homosexual/pederastic love object. He is also a "fairy" child in that, as Pirelli's other, his existence can only be imagined by, and his otherness seen as spurious by, those whose epistemological vision has been needlessly circumscribed. Chicklet, in other words, is a fairy's fairy whose home is a fairyland psychoanalytic thinkers can never hope to see.

Relations based on the complementary-merger conception of love are doubly vulnerable. Their investment in erotic opposition (complementarity) may confront ideologies of erotic identity (e.g., "narcissism"), and their investment in erotic identity (merger) may confront ideologies of erotic opposition (e.g., "pederasty"). Such relations are also, as Chapter 3 on Woolf and Stein will suggest, structurally unstable. The opposition of complementarity is at odds with the identity of merger. And the subject/other differential upon which the relations are based is easily upset by "jealous" intrusions of other others.

No doubt, many readers will resent this foray into lesbian erotics. Some may believe that gay critics should restrict themselves to gay texts, or that men cannot appreciate, because they do not experience, lesbian subjectivity. Other, more thoughtful readers may resist what they perceive as an unwarranted, and presumably phallocentric, conflation of lesbian and gay sexuality under the signs of "complementary merger" and "modern homoerotics." Although the insufferable separatism and essentialism of the former require no comment, the concerns of the latter do. Lesbians do, of course, differ from gay men in many respects, primarily insofar as they are constituted as women—something gay men, no matter how effeminate, never are. However, lesbian and gay sexualities are comparable insofar as they misappropriate the same dominant discourses—including, as it happens, the fundamentally heteroerotic conception of love as complementary merger. Which is not to say that lesbians and gays always misappropriate identical discourses identically. Nor is it to say that they always misappropriate them differently. Gender may well be the template of alterity, but it is a remarkably malleable one. In other words, gay critics should come to terms with lesbianism, with lesbian/gay similarity as well as lesbian/gay difference, and with the phallocentric figurations of female sexuality, lesbian or otherwise, for which, as men, they may well have some fondness. If they do not, they will know very little more about their female counterparts than did Gide, for whom, for example, lesbian jealousy was entirely unthinkable.[45]

CHAPTER 3

Another Other: Woolf and Stein

I like making you jealous, my darling, (and shall continue
to do so) but it is ridiculous that you should be.

Vita Sackville-West to Virginia Woolf, July 11, 1927

Speaking sober prose . . . I won't belong to the two of you,
or to the one of you, if the two of us belong to the one.
In short, if Dotty's yours, I'm not. A profound truth
is involved which I leave to you to discover.

Virginia Woolf to Vita Sackville-West, September 2, 1927

In some respects, the lesbian erotics of Virginia Woolf and Gertrude Stein and the pederastic erotics of André Gide and Ronald
Firbank are strikingly similar. All four writers subscribe to the
complementary-merger conception of love, and each pair comes
to divergent terms with the basic heterosexuality of that conception. For Stein, as for Firbank, complementarity is gendered,
whereas for Woolf, as for Gide, it is not. In other respects, the
erotics are markedly different. Woolf, for example, takes a decidedly nonhierarchic, nonphallocentric, nonphallocratic view of
erotic complementarity. And unlike Gide and Firbank, who find
their pederasty problematic enough as it is, both Woolf and Stein
explore the ontological dimensions, if not the epistemological limitations, of their lesbianism.

This chapter investigates these similarities and dissimilarities
by focusing on Woolf's *Orlando: A Biography* (1928) and Stein's
The Autobiography of Alice B. Toklas (1933). Other texts, as will be
seen, are relevant to this investigation, but none is quite so crucial.
The Autobiography of Alice B. Toklas is Stein's most extensive, and

accessible, textualization of lesbian love, as opposed to lesbian sex. And *Orlando* is Woolf's most important, and entertaining, textualization of lesbian erotics, as opposed to female bonding. Which is not to say that the thinking of either writer, and Woolf's in particular, is quite so oppositional.

Ontoeroticism

If *Orlando* and *The Autobiography of Alice B. Toklas* are closet dramas about lesbian love lives,[1] they are also closet dramas that *equate* loving and being.[2] Life and love, for Woolf and Stein, are identical. Both, that is, occupy the same vexed intersubjective yet contrasubjective conceptual space. According to feminist object-relations theorists, whereas male subjectivity is invested in maintaining firm ego boundaries, female subjectivity is invested in the desire for a symbiotic merger with the other. This longing, it is thought, is really a sublimated longing for the pre-Oedipal, or at least prenatal, oneness of mother and daughter. The wish "to rejoin the mother" is the basis for the wish "to merge with the other woman (lover, sister, friend) through whom we know ourselves [in] a union in which self and other often are indistinguishable" (Berry 4). However, the desire for merger with the other woman is seen as never fully realizable. As Nancy Chodorow has suggested, the trajectory of female identity is an unstable oscillation between the loss of self and the constitution of a separate self, between merger and differentiation.[3] It is marked by "the pre-oedipal mother-related concerns of fusion and separation" (Abel 417). It traces "a model of the self that permits both a saving maintenance of ego-boundaries and an exploration of the pleasures of intersubjectivity" (Yaeger 205). It "plays on the borders of identity and mergence with an other" (Chessman 56). It is what Julia Kristeva theorizes as a double motion of adhesion and distancing (*Desire in Language*, *passim*).

Such psychoanalytic pronouncements probably fail to theorize female subjectivity accurately. For one thing, like figurations of homosexuality as narcissistic, they are based upon the spurious heterosexist formula: same-sex equals same-self. They have, however, been readily credited, even before having been characterized as "psychoanalytic." Woolf, for example, sees herself as following the ontological double motion described by Kristeva. The kind of moment she records in her diary as "'I' rejected; 'We' substituted" (*Writer's Diary* 279) is a "moment of being" that marks an unfulfillable desire for unity that her "mother's death unveiled and intensified" (*Moments of Being* 93).[4] The female and feminized male subjects in Woolf's texts also tend to be traced along these proto-psychoanalytic guidelines and are often adduced in proof of them.[5] Clarissa Dalloway, Mrs. Ramsay, and Lily Briscoe, for example, all demonstrate the ego "boundary confusion" of which Chodorow writes (110): Clarissa sensing herself as "part of people she never met" (*Mrs. Dalloway* 14), Mrs. Ramsay entering trances in which she "became the thing she looked at," and Lily longing to merge with Mrs. Ramsay, to become "like waters poured into one jar, inextricably the same, one with the object one adored" (*To the Lighthouse* 97, 79). Such mergings attempt to compensate for what Bernard in *The Waves* calls "severance from the body of our mother" (261)—Bernard, too, conceives of identity as interpenetrative: "we are not single, we are one" (221)—and are associated with what Woolf calls "embryo lives," selves that existed "before 'I' suppressed them" ("On Being Ill" 199). But where there is merger there is always already differentiation. The diegesis of *To the Lighthouse* reflects Chodorow's problematic trajectory of female identity, moving from Mrs. Ramsay's desire for self-diffusion in Part I to the realization of self-diffusion in Part II (with her death) to the emergence of Lily's desire for self-articulation in Part III.[6] And in *Night and Day*, Katharine Hilbery's sense of oneness with Ralph Denham is necessarily compromised by her sense of isolation: when they are "alone together" she feels that "someone shared her loneliness" (398, 492).

Stein, like Woolf, sees herself as following Kristeva's double motion.[7] She both emblazons the figuration of her own identity as intersubjective across the famous title page of "*The Autobiography of Alice B. Toklas* by Gertrude Stein" and embeds it within such lesser known texts as "A Sonatina Followed by Another," in which she prays "God bless me which is she." Yet Stein also figures her identity as contrasubjective. When she concludes *The Autobiography* with the lines "Gertrude Stein said, . . . I am going to write it for you. . . . And she has and this is it" (252), she is declaring her independence from Toklas and asserting that, ultimately, fundamentally, a Stein is a Stein and a Toklas is a Toklas. But it is Stein's figuration of *Toklas*'s identity that associates ontological intersubjectivity with the originary oneness of mother and daughter. In the portrait "Ada," the young Alice B. is indistinguishable from Emilie Toklas: "She and her mother had told very pretty stories to each other . . . really mostly altogether the mother and the daughter had told each other stories very happily together" (15). And in *The Autobiography*, Emilie's death, quite inexplicably, jeopardizes her daughter's existence: "my mother had died and there was no unconquerable sadness, but there was no real interest that led me on" (4). (Toklas quickly revives when Stein enters her life, her autobiography, one paragraph later.)

Woolf's erotics, like her ontology, is rooted, in part, in a conception of subject/other merger. Like Lily in *To the Lighthouse*, Woolf's lovers often long to become "one with the object one adored" (79). In *Orlando*, this is true for Orlando and his first true love, Sasha, although they never express this longing directly. Rather, the idea of erotic merger forms the basis of their interpenetrative tropes for one another. For Orlando, Sasha seems like "the green flame . . . hidden in the emerald" (45), while for Sasha, Orlando looks "as if he were burning with his own radiance, from a lamp lit within" (52). These two luminous tropes are interpenetrative in that both *concern* a merger (they both image a solid body infused by a flame) and *constitute* one (the figurative identity of their vehicles unites their tenors, the lovers Orlando and Sasha). But Woolf's erotics encompasses the notion of differentiation as well as the notion of dissolution. It involves opposition and complementarity as well as identity and merger. When Rachel Vinrace, in *The Voyage Out*, realizes she and Terence Hewet are in love, she thinks: "drawn so close together, . . . there seemed no division between them, and the next moment separate and far away again" (282). Indeed, when Orlando (now female) watches a procession of heterosexual couples "indissolubly linked together" in "indissoluble alliance," she finds the matter of "this indissolubility of bodies . . . repugnant to her sense of decency and sanitation" (218, 219). Nonetheless, in spite of her repugnance and in a truly Kristevan double motion, Orlando also feels a "tingling" urge to "take a husband" herself (219). This intrasubjective/contrasubjective erotic oscillation is also inscribed in Orlando's two nicknames for the lover she eventually takes as her husband, Marmaduke Bonthrop Shelmerdine: "Mar," "meaning hot baths and evening fires" and signifying her "amorous" mood (278, 231), and "Bonthrop," "meaning the death we die daily" and "signif[ying], mystically, separation and isolation" (278, 234).

For Woolf, moreover, contrasubjectivity is characteristic of lesbian as well as nonlesbian love. Although she may well be tempted to believe that lesbian love transcends subject/other differentiation because it transcends gender differentiation, Woolf does not yield to the heterosexist temptation. Like Gide and Firbank, Woolf does not believe that two homosexual lovers are the same person, even though they are both female, or both male, and, hence, not diacritically sexed. As she wrote to Vita Sackville-West six days before her suicide: "No, I'm not you" (*Letters* 6: 484 [Mar. 22, 1941]).[8] Nor does Woolf deploy a figuration of the homosexual as "androgyne" in order to show that lesbian love, by erasing male/female difference, also erases subject/other difference. Some critics who, following Carolyn Heilbrun's lead, read *Orlando* as androgynous dispute this. Kari Weil, for example, who detects in *Orlando* "a hermaphroditic . . . aesthetic of unstable bounds," finds that the text challenges the process by which "sexual identity structures relationships between self and other [because it makes terms] such as 'man' and 'woman' appear only as conventional masks which conceal the other in the same and the same in the other, as we discover . . . through Orlando's love for Marmaduke Bonthrop Shelmerdine" (17, 11).[9] Rachel Blau DuPlessis argues that *Orlando* is a "drama of androgyny" in which Orlando and Shelmerdine "are not polarized, but fuse and interpenetrate"

(61, 63). Similarly, Barbara Fassler sees "the whole of *Orlando* [as] built upon a series of ever more *integrative* combinations of [gender] role playing versus reality" (244; emphasis added).

Such assertions might seem warranted, especially inasmuch as Woolf herself asserts that "different though the sexes are, they intermix. In every human being a vacillation from one sex to the other takes place" (171). But what Woolf proceeds to say—"and often it is only the clothes that keep the male or female likeness, while underneath the sex is the very opposite of what it is above" (171–72)—implies that although the *essential* self might be either male or female, it cannot be both. (Essential, that is, insofar as Woolf, like Gide and Firbank, associates the removal of clothing with the revelation of truth.) And such "vacillation" as Woolf describes is not, as Fassler claims, only the beginning of an "ever more integrative" androgynous project. It is only a temporary phase that precedes sex-gender restabilization: it is only "*for the time being* [that Orlando] seemed to vacillate; she was man; she was woman" (145; emphasis added). Ultimately, Orlando becomes and is all woman, in a sex-gender transposition certified both by a juridical finding that her sex "indisputably, and beyond the shadow of a doubt [is] female" (229) and by the birth of a son. Woolf believes in neither stable (androgynous) male/female mergers nor in stable (same-sex) subject/other mergers.

Like Woolf's, Stein's erotics involves a Kristevan double motion. Post-structuralist analyses of *The Autobiography* have not ignored the virtuosic sleight-of-speech I have associated with a feminist psychoanalytic ontology. Philippe Lejeune, for example, takes Stein's "Toklas" to be a "fictive witness" who "is ultimately no more than an alibi for the presentation of [Stein herself]" (43), whereas Domna Stanton reads Stein as "openly reject[ing] the 'autobiographical pact' of identity between a real person, the subject, and the object of enunciation" (18), and Cynthia Merrill sees in *The Autobiography* a Lacanian dismantling of the "*méconnaissance*, misrecognition, [and] mistaken identity" built into the conventional autobiographical "I" (15). But no matter how reticent the text may be on the subject, theorizations of Stein's uncanny

ventriloquial skill in *The Autobiography* should address the fact
that Stein and Toklas are lovers. They should examine ways in
which the enunciative apparatus of *The Autobiography*, a discursive
construction of a mutual love-life, speaks to Stein's conception of
love.

Speaking on behalf of Toklas is itself a kind of romantic congress. As Kristeva notes:

> When the object that I incorporate is the speech of the other—precisely
> a nonobject, a pattern, a model—I bind myself to him in a primary fu-
> sion, communion, unification. An identification. . . . In being able to
> receive the other's words, to assimilate, repeat, and reproduce them, I be-
> come like him: One. A subject of enunciation. Through psychic osmo-
> sis/identification. Through love. (*Tales of Love* 26)

But if Stein incorporates the speech of Toklas *through* love, she
does so, in part, in order that she might speak *of* love. Stein, in
speaking as and for Toklas in a primary fusion, communion, and
unification, yet declaring her independence from Toklas in the
text's final lines, bespeaks her own conception of love as complementary merger, as subject/other adhesion/distancing. And if this
conception of love is attested to by *The Autobiography's* enunciative apparatus, it is also confirmed by the text's two enunciations
concerning love. (There are only two direct references in *The Autobiography* to romantic love, although there is a related reference
to "making love," discussed below.) When "Alice Princet met [An-
dré] Derain and Derain met her," Stein writes, "[i]t was what the
french call un coup de foudre, or love at first sight. They went
quite mad about each other" (24). For Stein, although there is no
telling who met, or went mad about whom, and although Princet
and Derain "have never separated since" (24), there is no evidence
that the two lovers are the same person (no erotic identification,
no "Nelly, I *am* Heathcliff" claim). In fact, *The Autobiography's*
own Nelly—Nellie Jacott—tells a similar love story, a "story
which Gertrude Stein loved to quote, of a young man who once
said to her, I love you Nellie, Nellie is your name, isn't it" (150).
Perhaps what amuses Stein so about Nellie's anecdote is not that
her ardent admirer is a shameless liar, but that although Nellie

(quite wisely, she thinks) chooses to keep her distance from this fool for love, he is quite oblivious of even the most obvious signifier of Nellie's severable subjectivity—her name.[10] For Stein, the funny truth of love lies in between, or perhaps at both of these two poles—the pole of Nellie's distancing and the pole of her young man's adhesion.

Woolf and Stein themselves make the somewhat obvious connection between their ontologies and their erotics. Woolf describes the desire for unity as both a moment of "being" and as an "ecstasy," as an *amorous* dissolution.[11] In *Orlando*, being and loving are often linked, especially after Orlando's sex change. When still male, the phrase "Jour de ma vie" (the Sackville motto) is his coded symbol for elopement with Sasha (54, 58).[12] When newly female, Orlando sails home from Constantinople on board the "Enamoured Lady" (140) and soon commences a deliberate quest for "life and a lover" (168, 173). And when her female "identity" becomes "an open question," the moment is marked by Orlando's vision of the equally open-ended motto "Amor Vin—" (276). But Woolf mocks "the male novelists" who subscribe to the sexist, materialist notion that, for women, love "is slipping off one's petticoat and—" and who hold that such "Love . . . is woman's whole existence" (241–42). Rather, the only "love" Woolf equates with "existence" is the love she conceives of, idealistically, as complementary merger. When Orlando feels one with Sasha, it is not when they are together, when he might perceive their conjunction as physical; it is when they are apart, when their conjunction could only be metaphysical. Orlando feels the absent Sasha "scampering up and down within her, like some derisive ghost" (148) in an intersubjective intermingling he failed to experience during their actual lovemaking.

The interpenetration for Woolf of ontology and erotics is played out more explicitly in the letter she wrote to Sackville-West upon completing *Orlando*: "Did you feel a sort of tug, as if your neck was being broken on Saturday last at 5 minutes to one? . . . The question now is, will my feelings for you be changed? I've lived in you all these months—coming out, what are you really like? Do you exist? Have I made you up?" (*Letters* 3: 474 [Mar. 20, 1928]). That she sees herself as enclosed within, or enwombed by, Sackville-West (much as she has Orlando imagine Sasha "scampering up and down within her") and as "coming out" of her after "all these months" is, of course, further evidence that Woolf, like Chodorow, conceives of existence, of identity, as an inter-yet-contra-subjectivity grounded in, or at least figured by, a maternal paradigm. The letter is also notable for its figuration of Woolf's textualized *erotic* merger with her beloved ("will my feelings for you be changed?") both as an ontological merger ("I've *lived* in you") and as coterminous with her beloved's very viability ("Did you feel . . . as if your neck was being broken . . . ? . . . Do you exist?"). But the query "Have I made you up?" is not incidental to Woolf's musings in this passage, because it raises the vital issue of the discursivity of ontoeroticism, an issue Stein was to address as well.

In *The Autobiography*, as in *Orlando*, being and loving are expressly linked. Toklas is said to have begun a "new full life" (5) when she met her life-long lover (Stein), Manolo (the sculptor Manuel Hugué) to have "always loved and . . . always lived under the protection of the saints" (97), and René Crevel to have "lived and loved" in "confused negation" (227). But the coupling of living and loving is contingent upon words being uttered and understood, upon the related coupling of telling and listening. (Stein has taken the interlocutionary place of Toklas's ["Ada's"] mother: "mostly altogether the mother and the daughter had told each other stories very happily together.") For Stein, erotic existence is discursive.[13] (This might explain why, according to Hemingway at least, "[s]he talked all the time" [14]). The final lines of "Ada," co-authored by Toklas and Stein[14] and incorporated by reference in *The Autobiography* as Toklas's other "autobiography" (114) (although it is not written in the first-person), offer a clue to the interdependence of the two couplings:

She [Ada/Toklas] was telling some one, who was loving every story that was charming. Some one who was living was almost always listening. Some one who was loving was almost always listening. That one who was loving was almost always listening. That one who was loving was telling about being one then listening. That one being loving was then telling stories having a beginning and a middle and an ending. That one was then one always completely listening. Ada was then one and all her living then one completely telling stories that were charming, completely listening to stories having a beginning and a middle and an ending. Trembling was all living, living was all loving, some one was then the other one. Certainly this one was loving this Ada then. And certainly Ada all her living then was happier in living than any one else who ever could, who was, who is, who ever will be living. (16)

Clearly, the interdependence of living/loving and telling/listening is somewhat problematic for Stein. The desired full presence, the present fullness of all four terms at once ("always completely listening," "one completely telling," "all living," "all loving"), she hints, is impossible. For not only might one, for example, be only "almost always listening," but it is simply inconceivable that one can both "tell" and "listen" simultaneously—that one can, as Stein puts it, be "telling about being one then listening." But the paradigm is unstable for other reasons as well. If the one "completely telling" is not heard, she does not completely exist: "Jeanne told endless stories of french village life and Gertrude Stein could listen a long time and then all of a sudden she could not listen any more" (*Autobiography* 166). And one might, after all, be loving without telling: "[Andrew Green] said to Gertrude Stein, if I could talk french, I would make love to [Fernande] and take her away from that little Picasso. Do you make love with words, laughed Gertrude Stein" (48).

Power

Woolf would not have been amused. Less sexually active than Stein, Woolf believed that one *does* make love with words. "The intercourse of lovers," she writes in *Orlando*, is a dialogue, "a voice answering a voice" (292). It is, moreover, a true dialogue. "A voice answering a voice," unlike "telling" and "listening," is thoroughly nonhierarchic and nonantagonistic. Several critics who have no-

ticed this egalitarian aspect of Woolf's ontoerotics, but who see
opposition as inherently dominative, fail to appreciate Woolf's
purchase on erotic complementarity. Equals, for them, are alike.
Elizabeth Abel, for example, finds that "serious novels [about] the
actual friendships of women," like *To the Lighthouse,* "suggest that
identification replaces complementarity as the psychological
mechanism that draws women together" (415), and that "the intensity of identification increases as erotic feelings enter the relationship" (416 n. 5). Joseph Boone claims that *To the Lighthouse*
"dismantles the Victorian marital ideal embodied in the Ramsays'
union of complementary opposition" (201). Woolf does, in fact,
reject the heterosexist notion that the subject and other who
merge in loving union must complement one another as male and
female. Orlando and Shelmerdine, for example, affirm that the
beloved other must be the *same* gender as the loving subject
("'You're a woman, Shel!' she cried. 'You're a man, Orlando!'
he cried." [227]). However, she does not reject the idea that the
other must complement the subject in some fashion:

One has a profound, if irrational, instinct in favour of the theory that the
union of man and woman makes for the greatest satisfaction, the most
complete happiness. But the sight of the two people getting into the taxi
and the satisfaction it gave me also ask whether there are two sexes in the
mind corresponding to the two sexes in the body, and whether they also
require to be united in order to get complete satisfaction and happiness.
(*Room of One's Own* 98)

As DuPlessis notes, Woolf "separates *eros* from any forced or conventional bonds, especially such institutions as heterosexuality and
marriage" (48), in order to render it noncombative, not in order to
figure it as noncomplementary. She would rid love in general, and
lesbian love in particular, of repression, but not of differentiation.
Shelmerdine neither controls nor resembles Orlando. And in *Mrs.
Dalloway* Clarissa and Sally neither dominate nor replicate one
another, whereas poor old Miss Kilman alienates young Elizabeth
by attempting to manhandle her.[15]

     Had Stein written *Mrs. Dalloway,* however, Miss Kilman might
be its heroine. Unlike Woolf, but quite like Gide and Firbank,

Stein is inured to, if not fond of, ontoerotic domination. She sees the double motion of adhesion and distancing as a power struggle. This is due, in part, to her realization that the paradigmatic mother-daughter bond is hierarchic. She knows, in other words, that mothers tend to "suppress . . . daughters' stories through their domination and alliance with fathers" (Chessman 75). It is also due to her acceptance of the heterosexist notion that erotic opposition is gendered and, therefore, antagonistic. Unlike the Woolf of *Orlando*, the Stein of *The Autobiography* believes that subjects and others in love complement one another as male and female. Stein swears, Toklas cries. Stein drives, Toklas rides. Stein likes cars and dogs, Toklas likes "needlework and gardening" (3). The gender and power differentiations go on and on. This is not, of course, to say that Stein really managed to control Toklas. On the contrary, just as Gide found Rimbaud to be unduly "provocative, despotic, and authoritarian" (Pollard 229), many of Stein's admirers found Toklas unbearably manipulative.[16] It is, however, to say that Stein imagined she controlled Toklas.

Some feminist critics would rather not see Stein as power-crazed and, in order not to, claim she transcends both matriarchy and patriarchy. According to Harriet Chessman, for example, although Jane's pedagogic power over Melanctha in *Three Lives* does represent a "version of matriarchal . . . control" (47), Stein "does not conceive of intimacy in mother-infant terms" (55) and ultimately "transform[s] the mother into a loving 'other'" (60–61). The mother simply "disappears from the picture, to be replaced by a more equal figure" (57)—a disappearance that "allows the possibility for a democratic, nonhierarchic mutuality in which the I and the you can participate in an unlimited exchange" (76). Even the mother-daughter relation in "Ada," Chessman claims, represents one such transformation. "At least some mutuality of relation exists here," she writes: "Each figure, mother and daughter, tells stories to the other, instead of one telling and the other listening in silence" (67). Stein's transmatriarchal "leap beyond hierarchy" is also, albeit for reasons Chessman fails to articulate, a transpatriarchal "leap beyond gender" (76). Neither leap, however, occurs in *The Autobiography*. If, as Chessman argues, Stein has an equivocal attitude toward ontoerotic power, it is one over which hierarchic gender inscriptions and assertions of authorial control ("I am going to write it for you. . . . and she has and this is it"), and not an "impulse toward equality and a sharing of narrative power" (29), triumph. Just as Orlando, in the final analysis, is all woman, Stein, when all is said and done, is all "man"—a "man," moreover, who, like Gide, has her "pastoral" proclivities under contol.

Jealousy

The epistemological field of ontoeroticism, which is mapped along the coordinates "subject" and "other," is not very spacious. It has room for one subject and one other. If a third party enters it, the trajectory traced by a love life following a double motion of erasing and inscribing the diacritical divide in the binarism subject/other leaves the field altogether. Yet third parties often do wander into love lives. They wandered into the love life of Woolf and Sackville-West as well as that of Stein and Toklas. They wander into love lives textualized in *Orlando* and *The Autobiography*. This section will try to describe the disrupted trajectories of these interrupted love lives.

As a preliminary matter, such a third party should be denominated an "other." She is conceptually indissociable from the "other" who belongs to an ontoerotic subject/other dyad. She is not what René Girard calls an "object," because although his nomenclature for triangulated desire—"subject," "Other," and "object"— is amenable to his thesis that desire is imitative, his term "object" obscures the essentially binary nature of an epistemology of the self that knows only subjects and others.[17] And she is not a "subject" within an ontoerotic discourse in which she is neither a speaking subject nor a subject of the enunciation—that is, the type of discourse analyzed here. A speaking (ontoerotic) subject knows only herself as a subject; all other individuals bespoken by her discourse are individual "others."[18] (In order to maintain orthographic consistency, and in order to distance myself from Girard, I will not replicate his capitalization of terms like "subject" and "other"—nor will I replicate Lacan's.)

Sackville-West was, by her own admission, "incapable of fidelity" (Nicolson 34),[19] and although Woolf claimed to be only one "half, or 10th, part, jealous" of Sackville-West's other lovers (*Letters* 3: 435 [Nov. 11, 1927]), she always resented this faithlessness.[20] She could never, however, quite comprehend her resentment: "And then I'm cross with Vita: she never told me she was going abroad for a fortnight—didn't dare; till the last moment, when she said it was a sudden plan. Lord Lord! I am half amused, though; why do I mind? what do I mind? how much do I mind? . . . And why do I write this down?" (*Diary* 3: 239 [Aug. 5, 1929]). Woolf was particularly perturbed while writing *Orlando*, a sensitive period during which the promiscuous Sackville-West, a reckless "dolphin," often found her "soft crevices lined with hooks" (*Letters* 3: 395 [July 4, 1927]). When, for example, Woolf believed that Sackville-West's friend Dorothy Wellesley was her chief erotic rival, she threatened: "I won't belong to the two of you, or to the one of you, if the two of us belong to the one. . . . if Dotty's yours, I'm not" (*Letters* 3: 415 [Sept. 2, 1927]). And when she learned that Mary Campbell was the real interloper, Woolf chided Sackville-West that although *Orlando* might be "all about you and the lusts of your flesh and the lure of your mind," it could not be about her heart, for "heart you have none, who go gallivanting down the lanes with Campbell" (*Letters* 3: 429 [Oct. 9, 1927]), and reiterated the threat with a vengeance: "If you've given yourself to Campbell, I'll have no more to do with you, and it shall be written, plainly, for all the world to read in Orlando" (*Letters* 3: 431 [Oct. 14, 1927]). After publication, Woolf took a final swipe at her fickle friend: "For Promiscuous you are, and that's all there is to be said of you. Look in the Index to Orlando—after Pippin and see what comes next—Promiscuity *passim!*" (*Letters* 3: 514 [July 25, 1928]).

Although "promiscuity" is not one of *Orlando's* actual index headings, it could be. As Jean Love points out, the text grants

Sackville-West "the license . . . to lead whatever sexual life she pleased and to have the best of both sexes" (214). "Jealousy," too, would be a helpful indexical guide, because the text also presents, in rapid succession, five dramatic variations on the theme. The first scene is an amorous subject's blinding and fatal vision of her betrayal: an aged Queen Elizabeth, who "loved him" (26), becomes undone upon seeing "in the mirror . . . Orlando . . . kissing a girl" (27). She breaks the mirror, is knocked out of her chair, and is so "stricken" that, bemoaning "man's treachery," she expires shortly thereafter (27). The second scene is a juridical misprision of an amorous trespass: the Earl of Cumberland stumbles upon Orlando and Sukey enjoying their "active" (30) and "illicit love" (31) in the hold of his treasure ship, but, "his conscience laden with many a crime, the Earl [takes] the couple . . . for a phantom sprung from the graves of drowned soldiers to upbraid him" (30). The third scene is an amorous subject's reluctant realization of her betrayal: Orlando's fiancée, Lady Margaret, having recognized his involvement with Sasha for what it is, comes "at last to suspect that something [is] brewing against her peace of mind" (41). The fourth scene, like the first, is an amorous subject's blinding and nearly fatal vision of his betrayal: Orlando sees Sasha and a sailor embracing in the hold of a Russian ship, whereupon "the light [is] blotted out in a red cloud by his rage," a "deadly sickness [comes] over him," and "he [comes] to doubt what he saw" (49). And the final scene is an amorous subject's paranoid fantasy: Orlando identifies with Shakespeare's Othello, seeing in "[t]he frenzy of the Moor . . . his own frenzy" and imagining "Sasha . . . killed with his own hands" (54).

Toklas may have had similar fantasies of her own. In fact, during the summer of 1932, when Stein was writing *The Autobiography*, Toklas became quite "paranoid about the name May" (Dydo 13).[21] "May" is May Bookstaver, a woman with whom Stein had had a triangulated love affair 30 years earlier, and about whom Stein had not told Toklas prior to their joint "discovery" of the manuscript of *Q.E.D.*, Stein's early roman à clef about the affair, on or about May Day 1932.[22] Stein suggests in "Here. Actualities"

(May 1932), that she had "hidden [*Q.E.D.*] with intention," inasmuch as "[t]here is no blindness in memory" (quoted in Dydo 12), but makes the dubious claim in *The Autobiography* that she "must have forgotten about" writing it (85). Toklas, however, could not forget about May. In her "fierce and jealous rage," she destroyed, or had Stein destroy, May's letters, and even went so far as to urge the deletion of the words "may" and "May" from *Stanzas in Meditation*, which Stein was also writing that unhappy summer (Dydo 17, 13). Years later, Toklas tried to suppress the publication of *Q.E.D.*, which she felt concerned "a subject I haven't known how to handle nor known from what point to act upon" (Souhami 255).

If Toklas wished to engrave a Stein text with her jealous paranoia by gouging out the name of her rival, Stein had no desire to make their private erotic discord a matter of public literary record. In fact, not only does *The Autobiography* occlude the "May" mishap (by depicting the Stein-Toklas relationship as placid, happy, and monogamous, if hierarchic, and by containing no reference to Bookstaver), it also occludes lesbian promiscuity and jealousy in general. And these are not isolated public occlusions. According to Hemingway, Stein told him that lesbians, unlike male "perverts," who "are always changing partners and cannot be really happy," "do nothing that they are disgusted by and nothing that is repulsive and afterwards they are happy and they can lead happy lives together," except for the few "truly vicious" ones who "can never be happy except with new people" (20).[23] The [Willie] Uhde of *The Autobiography*, who "used often to come Saturday evening accompanied by very tall blond good-looking young men," is one such "pervert" (96). But, by and large, such instances of promiscuity and jealousy as do occur in *The Autobiography* are displaced squarely within the heterosexual field: Alice Princet's husband is "angry for the first time in his life" when she and André Derain fall "in love at first sight" (24); when Picasso sees a photograph of a skyscraper for the first time, he thinks only of "the pangs of jealousy a lover would have while his beloved came up all those flights of stairs to his top floor studio" (50); there are "some redoubtable battles" when Picasso leaves Fernande Olivier for Eve Humbert (111); and although "Clive Bell [goes] along with" Vanessa Bell and Roger Fry, he is "rather complainful" (122). Even the Book-staver imbroglio itself seems to be recontextualized as Picasso's heterosexual bid to make Stein renounce all "intimacy" with Juan Gris (211). Much as Toklas wished to erase all traces of "May," Picasso "wishe[s Gris] away." Much as Bookstaver, unlike Toklas, was not erotically exclusionary, Gris, unlike Picasso, is not artistically exclusionary. And much as Toklas reacted to the *Q.E.D.* revelation with "paranoid" jealous rage, Picasso responds to Stein's interest in Gris "with violen[t]" demands: "tell me why you stand up for his work, you know you do not like it" (212). Stein, however, ignores his demands, "and [does] not answer him" (212).

Although they might sound like similar discursive defaults, Stein's resolute refusal to "answer" Picasso designates a far more serious ontoerotic disturbance than does her intermittent inability to "tell" Toklas anything. The difference between the two is that, with the intervention of another "other," the extremely coercive and hierarchic coupling of demanding and responding has replaced the somewhat less coercive and hierarchic coupling of telling and listening as the discursive basis of Stein's ontoerotic paradigm. Yet Stein's refusal to "answer" is still an inadequate sign of the disturbance other "others" create. It does answer to the logocentric conception of ontoerotic discourse as *speech* to which Woolf and Stein, to a certain extent, adhere—for Woolf, erotic intercourse is "a voice answering a voice"; for Stein, it is telling, listening, asking, and answering. However, it does not answer to the nonlogocentric conception of ontoerotic discourse as *writing* to which, as writers, they also subscribe. As the jealous scenarios cited above indicate, Woolf and Stein almost always describe the crisis of the intervening "other" as a crisis of writing, not as a crisis of speech. "Why . . . write this down," Woolf asks herself, not "why talk about it?"

If *Orlando* is about a writer (Sackville-West/"Orlando"), it is also about writing. It is about the voluminous quantity of inferior poetry Orlando is perpetually writing, rewriting, and unwriting, as well as about the virtuosic quality of the superior prose Woolf herself is writing (i.e., *Orlando*—Woolf may be egalitarian, but she has her pride). It is also about writing that claims to be speech, that purports to be vocal, present, original, and immediate. Woolf repeatedly insists that her writing is a current utterance, that "writing" is a verb, not a gerund. When Woolf concludes *Orlando* with the knell "And the twelfth stroke of midnight sounded; the twelfth stroke of midnight, Thursday, the eleventh of October, Nineteen hundred and Twenty Eight" (295), she is not inscribing some imaginary *temps perdu*. She is inscribing the hour of publication. She is inscribing her desire to stop time, to anchor *signifiance*, with a full stop, a desire that comes across loud and clear in the earlier knell: "In fact it was ten o'clock in the morning. It was the eleventh of October. It was 1928. *It was the present moment*" (268; emphasis added). Woolf also ascribes to script an essentially vocal metaphysics of presence in describing "writing" poetry, like "the intercourse of lovers," as "a voice answering a voice" and as the "stammering answer" one makes to nature (292). Apart from "It *was* the *present* moment" (emphasis added), which deconstructs the idea of presence, these examples, drawn from *Orlando*, do point more toward Woolf's conception of ontoerotic discourse as *speech* than toward her conception of it as *writing*. However, texts that circumscribe *Orlando* clearly figure the intervening-"other" crisis as a writing crisis. They attest, that is, to the nonlogocentric aspect of Woolf's conception of ontoerotic discourse. And they do so by signifying the metaphysical nonpresence of the written sign through the physical nonpresence of the referent. Woolf threatens Sackville-West: "If you've given yourself to Campbell, . . ." it shall be written, plainly, for all the world to read in Orlando," yet the Campbell/Sackville-West affair is not, in fact, plainly written there. Woolf suggests that Sackville-West "[l]ook in the Index to Orlando—after Pippin and see what comes next—Promiscuity *passim!*" yet "Promiscuity" can not be found there. Woolf even signals the nonpresence of the referent when she chides Sackville-West that her "heart," unlike her "flesh" and her "mind," is not in *Orlando*, for "heart you have none, who go gallivanting down the lanes with Campbell."

This oscillation of ontoerotic discourse between a vocal metaphysics of presence and a literal metaphysics of absence duplicates the oscillation or double motion of ontoerotic epistemology between a metaphysics of adhesion and a metaphysics of distancing. The conjunction/disjunction of author and text mirrors the conjunction/disjunction of subject and other. As Claire Kahane theorizes, writing, for Woolf, seems to be "a *tentative* re-union of self and (m)other accomplished through objects rendered, possessed and mastered in the act of writing" (75; emphasis added). But the absent referents ("Campbell," "Promiscuity," "heart") in Woolf's jealous writing crises are not exactly "objects"; they are themselves signs, or at least would be were they present in *Orlando*. Woolf literally obliterates the scripted sign in writing of Sackville-West's other "others." This placing of the jealous sign under erasure consigns it to a permanent nonpresence, to a perpetual separation from both author and referent. (Orlando, too, places his/her writing under erasure by destroying all but one of his/her poems, "The Oak Tree.") And, given the coincidental oscillations of ontoerotic discourse and epistemology, Woolf's jealous erasure of the jealous sign also marks an erasure of the possibility of ontoerotic adhesion. That is, the permanent separation of sign from author and referent correlates to the permanent separation of subject and other, a correlation that can be taken as the allegorical significance of Woolf's gift to Sackville-West of the *Orlando* manuscript. This transfer of the written record of a lover's jealousy and a beloved's promiscuity was an alienation in both senses of the word, because if it was a conveyance, it was also a separation. In one and the same act, Woolf relinquished her writing and her lover-as-writing (i.e., Sackville-West as *Orlando*) to someone who was not especially likely to ever give them back to her. In one and the same act, the jealous lover divorced herself from the sign of her love[24] and from the faithless other she loves.

With Stein, the crisis of the intervening other is not simply a crisis of speech. It does not simply provoke the discursive, hierarchic shift from telling to responding. As with Woolf, it is also a crisis of writing. As with Woolf, it also provokes the erasure of writing. Toklas destroys Bookstaver's correspondence and expunges "May" from *Stanzas in Meditation*, and Stein bans Bookstaver from *The Autobiography* and obliterates the existence of *Q.E.D.*, the "forgotten" book of May. However, the Stein erasures of the intervening "other" (as word, as book), unlike the Woolf erasures, are not altogether successful. Traces of "May" remain in *Stanzas in Meditation*,[25] and *Q.E.D.* emerges from the oblivion to which Stein had consigned it to tell Toklas who "May" had been. The tense differential between May Bookstaver's "having been" and Mary Campbell's "being" is not inconsequential, as it suggests why Stein's erasures need not be as successful as Woolf's. Campbell is a current, and Bookstaver a foregone, rival. Campbell upsets the epistemological field of ontoeroticism in a way that Bookstaver, whose involvement with Stein ended years before Toklas even met her, simply does not. Whereas Bookstaver says to Stein, "I *could* come back into your love life, there *could* be more than one 'other' here," Campbell says to Woolf, "I *am* in your love life, there *is* more than one 'other' here." Campbell, and not Bookstaver, represents the clear and present danger that must be eliminated both discursively and epistemologically.

Ordinarily, questions concerning discourse and epistemology arise concurrently because only that which is writable is knowable. In the context of the crisis of the intervening "other," however, the questions arise concurrently because what must not be known (that other "others" have destabilized the ontoerotic paradigm) must not be written (must be erased). Woolf and Stein are not unaware of the interdependence of the questions. They treat the intervening "other" crisis as a discursive crisis because they perceive it as an epistemological crisis, a perception to which *Orlando* and *The Autobiography* attest.[26] Stein "forgets" about, that is, has no knowlege of, having written *Q.E.D.*, her discourse on Bookstaver. Queen Elizabeth shatters the mirror in which she sees Orlando betraying her with another—a trope for how ruinous the scene is for the ontoerotic field of vision. Lady Margaret's "peace of mind" is shattered by the knowledge that Sasha is Orlando's lover. And Orlando refuses to acknowledge that he saw Sasha embracing the Russian sailor. Unfortunately, if these citations represent a certain perceptivity, they also represent a point beyond which Woolf and Stein hesitate to venture. They are reluctant, that is, to investigate fully the *nature* of the epistemological crises posed by Campbell and Bookstaver. Fortunately, their texts bespeak the nature of the crises despite that reluctance.

Epistemological Crises

Tony Tanner has described one way in which the crisis of the intervening "other" is an epistemological crisis. Cultures that police the difference between licit and illicit intercourse, he notes, often find that the two are identical. *Madame Bovary*, for example, "enacts a loss of category distinctions, thus a loss of meaning, that in experiential terms reaches its climax when Emma discovers that adultery and marriage are effectively the same thing" (326). Emma Bovary's categorical confusion is, of course, quite disturbing. But it is not unique. All culturally constructed binarisms, including, as Eve Kosofsky Sedgwick and others have shown, the binarism homosexual/heterosexual, tend to self-deconstruct. Tanner's insight has no real bearing on the crises Woolf and Stein confront, however. Emma Bovary's confusion is that of someone who is legally married. And while some lesbian love affairs may seem marital, they are all illicit. No lesbian, in other words, is likely to be shocked by the recognition that the marital unit, as Tanner puts it, "contains potentially antagonistic and disruptive elements that make it a center that cannot hold, an illusory center, or perhaps not a center at all" (373).

According to Lacan, whose own epistemological field is onto-erotic insofar as it encompasses only one subject and one other, "there is no Other of the Other" (311). The imaginary beloved other, he argues, is perfectly whole and therefore requires no other to compensate for the lack that affects the subject. The other who does have an other, who is inscribed by lack, is the symbolic "m-other" who looks to the father or the child for her missing phallus. (For Lacan, this phallocentric and, to my mind, dubious scenario represents the only sense our phallocentric epistemology allows us to make of the other of the other.) To a certain extent, Woolf sees her other's others in similar terms. However, whereas Lacan cannot conceive of a m-other's other who does not have (or who is not taken to have) the phallus, Woolf, as a lesbian, is forced to conceive of just such an other. Woolf, who loves Sackville-West, must acknowledge that Sackville-West loves an other (a Campbell or a Wellesley) who, like Woolf and Sackville-West, has no phallus. (Like me, Woolf does not subscribe to Lacanian Phallus/phallus/penis distinctions.) But if *Orlando* is an ontoerotic discourse on the lesbian other's lesbian other, it is still a discourse rigidly constrained by the same phallocentric epistemology that constrains Lacan. So it should come as no surprise that *Orlando*'s diegesis anticipates Lacan's phallocentric other/m-other/father/ child scenario: Orlando is born male (a wholly perfect other), but becomes female (a m-other who lacks the phallus), and marries a man (a phallic father) by whom she has a son (a phallic child). And it should come as no surprise that the female Orlando's only female lover, the Archduchess Harriet, turns out to be a man in disguise, to be the phallus masquerading as lack. (It is only when Orlando thinks of the Archduchess as a "Maypole" that she reveals herself to be the Archduke [162].) However, Woolf strains against the epistemological constraints that force her to figure "Orlando's" female others as male. She strains to suggest both that the phallus might signify absence and emptiness as readily as it signifies presence and plenitude, and that the phallus is not what the m-other really lacks.

Orlando's husband, Archduke, and son, who retain and proffer the phallus Orlando lost in her transition from male other to female m-other, also personify Woolf's radical conception of the phallus-as-absence. The unnamed son, once delivered, disappears from Orlando's life. The Archduke, once spurned, flees to Rumania. And the husband, once married, sails to (and, until *Orlando*'s last page, remains at) the end of the earth where, "always sailing round Cape Horn" (238), he performs a perpetual priapic rite about which his wife does not concern herself. In fact, Orlando is remarkably content without Shelmerdine: "she had never felt bet-

ter in her life" (238). These absent phallic others must not have
what Orlando (what m-other) wants, because she can hardly be
said to miss them when they are gone. But if not the phallus, the
male sexual organ, what *does* an other-loving m-other like Sackville-West want? According to Woolf, a nonsexed and nonsexual
organ—a "heart." "Heart you have none," she writes Sackville-
West.

Why a "heart?" Woolf is accusing her heartless paramour of
more than mere cruelty. She is accusing her of lacking the organ
of love.[27] Woolf believes what Lacan, blinded by phallocentrism,
cannot—that maternal love (the heart), and not patriarchal power (the phallus), is all the desiring subject really wants.[28] She rewrites the Lacanian other/m-other scenario in nonphallocentric
terms: the perfect loving other (Sackville-West) becomes the
m-other who seeks from an other (Campbell) the love the subject
(Woolf) once sought from her. The other, in other words, is imagined to have the "heart" the m-other was once imagined to have
had. Unfortunately, this psychoanalytic scenario is not especially
coherent. Like Sackville-West, the nonloving m-other, Woolf herself, the loving subject, lacks a heart. This is reflected in Woolf's
self-consciously futile fantasy that Sackville-West might remove
her "core": "Please come, and bathe me in serenity again. Yes, I
was wholly and entirely happy. If you could have *uncored* me—
you would have seen every nerve running fire—intense, but calm"
(*Letters* 3: 306–7 [Dec. 8, 1926]; emphasis added). The impossible
image of Sackville-West expropriating Woolf's vibrant "core" is
somewhat gruesome, but very much to the point. The other cannot, in fact, "uncore" a subject who has no "core" to remove. But
if the subject has no heart, or core, she should neither love the
other nor look to her to love her (to have a heart) in return. And
even if the subject were to have a heart—if she were, that is, to
truly love the other—why would she want another one from the
other? Woolf does not attempt to resolve these contradictions.

One can understand why Woolf figures this primordial, if incoherent, erotic crisis (of disheartenment, not castration) as a *writing* crisis (of absent scripted signifiers) by comparing the signifiers

"heart" and "phallus." The phallus is the signifier of patriarchal power just as the heart is the signifier of maternal love. However, the actual phallus is visible in a way that the actual heart simply is not. The phallus (the penis) is readable on the body. The heart is not. The heart is hidden beneath the surface of the body, behind the writing surface of the skin. It is an imperceptible signifier. Like Julia Stephen, Woolf's first m-other, it is a wholly imaginary "invisible presence" (*Moments of Being* 80). So how better to figure the crisis of learning that the imaginarily whole loving other loves an other (i.e., has no heart) than by (mis)representing to the new m-other herself that her textual body conceals (nonexistent) signs she will never uncover there? That is, when Woolf enjoins Sackville-West to look in the index to *Orlando* (the m-other's textual body) for the imaginary reference to "Promiscuity," when she lies that Sackville-West's having given herself to Campbell "shall be written, plainly, for all the world to read in *Orlando*," she is doing more than just signaling the impossibility of further ontoerotic adhesion. She is trying to show the m-other just how unloving, how heartless, one amorous subject has discovered her to be.

If, however, the crisis of the intervening other marks the demise of ontoerotic adhesion as well as the birth of the heartless m-other, what bearing has the m-other's heartlessness on Woolf's onto-eroticism? Why, in other words, does Sackville-West, who turns to Campbell not for the phallus but for love, lose her place in Woolf's love life, lose her place in the ontoerotic equation subject-other / merger-differentiation? Because she is no longer imagined to have what Woolf lacks. Because she no longer *complements* Woolf. The ontoerotic other who seems to offer the subject the love, the "heart," she craves seems to complement her in the most fundamental way possible. However, when she is discovered not to have a heart to offer the subject (whether because she has given it to an other or because she herself, like the subject, is looking to an other for one), she no longer qualifies as a complementary onto-erotic other. She is now an un-complementary m-other who does not have what it takes to be an other.

Woolf confronts her other's other in Campbell. Stein, however, confronts her *own* other other in Bookstaver. Woolf creates writerly figures of significant invisibility and nonpresence that mimic the m-other's lack of the complementary "heart" within a non-phallocentric and ontoerotic symbolic order. Stein, on the other hand, creates figures that reflect the difference between the epistemological crisis presented by an *other's* multiple beloveds and the crisis presented by a *subject's* multiple beloveds. Whereas Woolf, for example, claims that the other's textual body has no heart, Stein claims that the other has no textual body at all. For Stein, that is, *Q.E.D.* is "forgotten," there is no book of Bookstaver. Or is there? What is Stein really saying about her all-too-dubious memory lapse?

Stein's account of her accidental discovery of the *Q.E.D.* manuscript virtually self-deconstructs before the attentive reader's eyes. Stein writes:

The funny thing about this short novel is that she *completely forgot* about it for many years. She remembered herself beginning a little later writing the Three Lives but this first piece of writing was *completely forgotten*, she had never mentioned it to me, even when I first knew her. She must have forgotten about it almost immediately. This spring just two days before our leaving for the country she was looking for some manuscript of The Making of Americans that she wanted to show Bernard Faÿ and she came across these two carefully written volumes of this *completely forgotten* first novel. She was very bashful and hesitant about it, did not really want to read it. Louis Bromfield was at the house that evening and she handed him the manuscript and said to him, you read it. (84–85; emphasis added)

In this short passage Stein insists upon her "complete" forgetting of *Q.E.D.* no fewer than three times. Yet she also subverts this triple claim of total amnesia. She makes the absurd deduction that she had no recollection of the novel as soon as she finished writing it ("She must have forgotten about it almost immediately"). She notes that *Q.E.D.* was "carefully written" and thereby implies that it could not have been carelessly forgotten. And she insinuates that she recalled at least enough of the erotically incriminating work to be "very bashful and hesitant about it," to have no need to reread it, and to want to prevent Toklas from reading it (both "when [Toklas] first knew her" and nearly 25 years later, when Stein tells Bromfield, and not Toklas, to read the manuscript).[29] Of course, one interpretation of all this equivocation is that Stein's "discovery" of her "forgotten" novel is merely a fiction necessitated by Toklas's discovery of Stein's epistemological scam. That is, having kept Toklas in the dark about her other other, about *Q.E.D.*, Stein must now pretend to the nearly inconceivable: she must pretend to have been, yet not quite pretend to be, in the dark herself. However, Stein's account of the *Q.E.D.* "discovery" is also an unwitting indication of the nature of her epistemological crisis.

Stein knows yet does not know about *Q.E.D.* because her masculinity is at odds with her ontoeroticism. As noted above, unlike Woolf, Stein is quite partial to patriarchal power. She likes having a wife. And one important aspect of Stein's phallocratic conception of erotic complementarity is epistemological. Stein, a knowing male subject, is complemented by Toklas, her unknowing, and known, female other. Stein "talks" to geniuses while Toklas "sits" with their wives (87). Stein writes works of genius that Toklas types and proofreads. Stein even denies Toklas any derivative knowledge she might glean from these works, both by claiming to write only "for [her]self and strangers" (240) works for which Toklas was often as not her sole audience, and by claiming that Toklas was not exactly reading them: "I always say that you cannot tell what a picture really is or what an object really is until you dust it every day and you cannot tell what a book is until you type it or proof-read it. It then does something to you that only reading never can do" (113). As befits an unknowing other, the "something" Stein's drafts do to Toklas appears to involve subliminal suggestion, not conscious comprehension.[30]

If Stein knows about Bookstaver (about *Q.E.D.*) as a knowledgeable male subject, she also knows about Bookstaver/*Q.E.D.* as a naturally promiscuous male lover. Patriarchy entitles men both to know and, Biblically speaking, to "know" multiple beloveds, and Stein's patrimony includes the double standard as well as the epistemological mandate. This explains, in part, why Stein can conceive of gay-male more readily than nonbutch-lesbian promiscuity. However, the knowledge of the other other endorsed if not demanded by the double-standard and by the epistemological mandate must contend with ontoeroticism. Because ontoeroticism knows only one subject and one other, an ontoerotic subject like Stein must eliminate all other others from her epistemological field, must forget them "completely." In other words, where her other others are concerned, Stein's ontoeroticism exerts an amnestic pressure that her masculinity resists. This pressure, moreover, creates putative memory lapses even as to the identity of *other* subjects' other others. It is instructive, in this regard, to compare how Stein and Toklas recall Stein's realization that Picasso had left Fernande Olivier for Eve Humbert. (Toklas's account appears in her own autobiography, aptly entitled *What Is Remembered*.)

Toklas recalls Stein guessing that Humbert was Picasso's new lover when Stein first met her:

Picasso and Fernande had by this time separated definitively. Shortly before the separation Picasso and Fernande and Fernande's new friend Eve came to see us one evening. They brought with them the painter Marcoussis, with whom Eve had been living. Gertrude said to me after they left, Is Picasso leaving Fernande for this young thing? He was. (66)

Stein, however, recalls being oblivious at that meeting of Humbert's intervention in the Picasso-Olivier love life:

Fernande had at this time a new friend of whom she often spoke to me. This was Eve who was living with Marcoussis. And one evening all four of them came to the rue de Fleurus, Pablo, Fernande, Marcoussis, and Eve. It was the only time we ever saw Marcoussis until many many years later. (111)

Stein even claims that this obliviousness continued for some time:

Not long after this Picasso came one day and told Gertrude Stein that he had decided to take an atelier in the rue Ravignan. . . . One day we went to see him there. He was not in and Gertrude Stein as a joke left her visiting card. In a few days we went again and Picasso was at work on a picture on which was written ma jolie and at the lower corner painted in was Gertrude Stein's visiting card. As we went away Gertude Stein said, Fernande is certainly not ma jolie, I wonder who it is. (111)

We cannot know, of course, whether it is Stein or Toklas who is telling the truth. As far as we can tell, neither has any reason to lie.[31] Stein's obliviousness, for example, cannot be said to mask an epistemological scam, the light in which a cynic would construe her *Q.E.D.* memory lapse. And it is because these two incompatible accounts are equally credible that the tension between the masculine intuition of (the Toklas) Stein's "Is Picasso leaving Fernande for this young thing?" and the ontoerotic opacity of (the Stein) Stein's "I wonder who it is" cannot be resolved. As a composite figure, "Stein" can neither acknowledge nor ignore the other other. She is at an epistemological impasse.

Although Woolf's and Stein's crises are epistemologically distinct, although the other other means very different things to these very different ontoerotic writers, there is one sense in which they face the same epistemological crisis. They are both forced to imagine the demise of the binarism upon which ontoeroticism itself depends, the binarism subject/other. The other other is the Barthesian "third term" that overwhelms and surpasses this binarism.[32] She is the interloper who extinguishes exclusive erotic dyads, the meddler who muddles polarized ontoerotic thinking. She reveals the binarism subject/other to be a classification that may be "both necessary and transitory: [one that is essentially] a metalanguage, a particular taxonomy meant to be swept away by history, after having been true to it for a moment" (Barthes, *Elements of Semiology* 82). Woolf, even though she claims to be "half amused," finds this prospect somewhat bleak: "Speaking sober prose, I won't belong to the two of you, or to the one of you, if the two of us belong to the one. . . . A profound truth is involved which I leave to you to discover." She clings desperately to dyads that no longer signify, to "ones" and "twos" that no longer cohere. Who exactly is "the one"—Sackville-West or Wellesley? Who are "the two"—Sackville-West and Wellesley, Wellesley and Woolf, or Woolf and Sackville-West? Woolf cannot say, despite the purported sobriety of her text. Indeed, the utterly unwritable "profound truth" she wants Sackville-West to discover may well be that another other has intoxicated her "sober prose." Stein, however, finds the prospect liberating, or at least, like Sackville-West, ridiculous. For Stein, Bookstaver's troublesome intrusion into her love life is no grim threat. As epistemological disruptions go, it *is* amusing. It *is* a "funny thing" (84). Of course, Stein takes a perverse pleasure in most epistemological crises. Even her dying declaration ("What is the answer? In that case, what is the question?") is a ludic celebration of radical uncertainty. Stein, unlike Woolf, is a devoted lover who can laugh at love as she knows it.

Wilde, Gide, Firbank, Woolf, and Stein all subscribe to nineteenth-century conceptions of love. Wilde may complicate Liebestod, and Gide and Woolf may de-sex complementarity, but none goes so far as to reject romantic erotics. Homoeroticism is not, however, essentially affirmative. Many lesbian and gay writers find romantic erotics reprehensible. The following chapter, on Marguerite Yourcenar and Mary Renault, considers two such writers. Like Woolf, Yourcenar and Renault are erotic egalitarians who would rid love of phallic domination. Unlike Woolf, however, they concern themselves not with the hierarchic basis of erotic complementarity, but with the cognitive disadvantage of erotic blindness. It is, of course, somewhat surprising that two writers so averse to abjection should fail to tackle complementary merger, a figure that celebrates the power imbalance constitutive of both patriarchy and heterosexuality. What, then, accounts for this failure? Yourcenar and Renault attack "crystallization" and not complementarity because, like Foucault, they see knowledge and power as coterminous. They believe that lovers who know one another cannot control one another. But they also fail to challenge the heterosexuality of erotic opposition because, like many gays and lesbians, they find pederasty, with its heteroerotic subtext, equally dominative and, therefore, objectionable. This bias also accounts for one other surprising, indeed disturbing, failure. Yourcenar and Renault are lesbians who almost always write about, because they resent the pederastic inclinations of, male homosexuals. Which is not to say that they see gay men as *hopelessly* invested in phallic power. Unlike Luce Irigaray, Yourcenar and Renault can imagine hom(m)osexuality disburdened of that purportedly pederastic investment.

CHAPTER 4

Friends and Lovers: Yourcenar and Renault

In the matter of love, too, I hold for perfection unadorned.

Marguerite Yourcenar, *Coup de Grâce*

"Reverse discourse" is usually taken to mean subaltern speech that transfigures—but not speech that disfigures—dominant ideology. Discursive appropriations, negotiations, adulterations, and transvaluations are subversive reversals, but discursive contestations, it would appear, are not. This construction, resulting in part from a literal reading of the term "subversion," is far too narrow. Subaltern contestations can be as subversive as subaltern appropriations—which, to repeat a point made in Chapter 1, is not to say that all reverse discourses are equally subversive. Subaltern contestations, like subaltern appropriations, have dissimilar contextual and critical features. Both Gide and Woolf reject the hierarchical basis of erotic complementarity, but Woolf's utopian egalitarianism, as the reader will have inferred, is far more radical. This chapter delineates an analogous comparison. Marguerite Yourcenar and Mary Renault, like Gide and Woolf, are utopian egalitarians who would liberate sexual love in general, and homosexual love in particular, from erotic domination, from the lover's subjection of, or by, the beloved. Unlike Gide and Woolf, however, Yourcenar and Renault would also liberate love from another related constraint: erotic blindness (the lover's misperception of the beloved). Although this double contestation is found in much of their fiction, my comparison will focus on two somewhat complementary historical novels: Yourcenar's *Memoirs of Hadrian* (*Mémoires d'Hadrien*, 1951), the story of an emperor who loved a beautiful boy, and Renault's *The Persian Boy* (1972), the story of a beautiful boy who loved an emperor.[1] It will also suggest that the subversiveness of these "reverse" contestations depends upon the ways in which they confront the discursive, epistemological, and ideological obstacles with which any such utopian project is fraught.

A Picture of My Life as I Should Have Wished It to Be

Yourcenar and Renault believe that lovers should be equals who know one another very well. With Renault, one infers this belief from her fiction. In *The Charioteer* (1959), for example, Renault faults one protagonist for being "attracted to people [he] can push around" (342) and praises another for falling in love with "a clear kind of person, about whom one has to think clearly" (58). Yourcenar, however, articulates this position in nonfictional as well as fictional terms. "True love," she asserts in one interview, is nonhierarchical: "Some people think they can possess another through domination. This obviously is not true love. . . . We bestow the name of love on something that stands in its place and even claims some of its privileges but that is not love, not in essence at any rate" (*Open Eyes* 207). Unlike "passion," love is a form of abnegation. "In passion there is a desire to satisfy oneself, to slake one's thirst, in some cases coupled with a desire to control, to dominate another person. By contrast, in love there is abnegation" (*Open Eyes* 71). It may be difficult to distinguish between the two (*il est difficile dans notre optique de différencier un grand amour d'une grande passion* [*Yeux ouvertes* 99]), but it is necessary to do so. "Most people see no difference, viewing passion simply as love pitched one degree higher. But it would be more accurate to say that the two emotions are close to being opposites" (*Open Eyes* 71). This theorization of "true love" as egalitarian is part of an extensive antipatriarchal project. According to Yourcenar, *all* interpersonal relationships should be nonhierarchical and nondominative. "The Italians have a wonderful way of saying I love you: *Ti voglio bene*. We must try to approach everything we do with this same 'good will' toward others" (*Open Eyes* 235). But not only does Yourcenar believe that interpersonal relationships *should* be egalitarian, she also believes, naively, that they often *are*. She finds, for example, that we "are constantly transcending" class barriers we "incorrectly assume divide us from one another" (*Open Eyes* 192, 193). And she is sure of her own transcendental aptitude. Yourcenar has, she claims, "no class feeling whatsoever" and never pays "any attention to differences of age" (*Open Eyes* 6, 10).

True love, for Yourcenar, is also a matter of epistemological confidence, of knowing the other full well.

The first thing is to know what one means by love. If love means to adore another person, if it means the conviction that two people are made for one another, that they complement one another by virtue of their unique qualities, then a thoughtful person is likely to see it all as a mirage and to say to himself, Look, [there's nothing that exceptional about me and] there's [probably] nothing that exceptional about my beloved either. Let's take a good look at what we are, and love each other for that. (*Open Eyes* 52)[2]

Love requires, above all else, "a feeling for the other person's freedom and dignity coupled with clear-sighted acceptance of that person as he or she really is" (*Open Eyes* 254). It requires, as Yourcenar puts it in "Reflections on the Composition of *Memoirs of Hadrian*," a sense that one's beloved "is neither our shadow nor our reflection, nor even our complement, but simply himself" (*Hadrian* 343; citations are to the English translation unless otherwise noted).

This utopian conjunction of egalitarianism and clear-sightedness is both somewhat counterintuitive and radically unconventional. It is counterintuitive insofar as we, like Stein, conceive of perception in phallic, unilateral terms. To know, after all, is to control. As Foucault has observed, "power and knowledge directly imply one another, . . . there is no power relation without the correlative constitution of a field of knowledge, nor any knowledge that does not presuppose and constitute at the same time power relations" (*Discipline and Punish* 27). Yourcenar and Renault, however, see erotic understanding as reciprocal. Equal partners know one another equally well. Lover and beloved enjoy identical epistemological advantages and mutual cognitive empowerments. But there is no getting around the fact that the conjunction is unconventional, and both writers know it.

Yourcenar is quite certain, as one amorous boulevardier was not, that fifty million Frenchmen *can* be wrong.

The clichéd French notion of love [does] not ring true. The French have in a sense stylized love, created a certain style of love, a certain form. And having done that, they proceeded to believe in what they had invented, they forced themselves to love in a particular way when they would have experienced it in an entirely different way had there not been all that literature behind them. In my view, it's only in France that La Rochefoucauld could have said "there are many people who, had they never heard of love, would never have felt it." I don't think that such a statement makes any sense here [in the United States] and perhaps in many other parts of the world. It's different in France because there everyone is exposed to the notion of love à la française, which runs through our literature from *Andromaque* to *L'Education sentimentale*. Convention plays a large part. (*Open Eyes* 51–52)

This particular contestation places Yourcenar in a series of French novelists, most of whom are women, who reject a wide range of heteroerotic ideologies.[3] It is also far more indiscriminate than Yourcenar need be. For although Yourcenar would like to displace three centuries of French literature, she, like Renault, concentrates on one writer in particular—Stendhal.

For Stendhal, "passion-love" [*l'amour-passion*] is a matter of domination and misperception. Heteroerotic antagonism—the figuration of love as a battle women almost always lose—subtends every one of his novels. As Julia Kristeva notes in *Tales of Love*, the Stendhalian novel is "a narrative of war . . . in other words, of 'modern' love" (343). It associates love with "the cold and calculating, ambitious and underhanded logic that [goes] with conquest" (342) and shows love to be "anchored . . . in the quest of phallic power" (363). And even though "love's lightning bolts [can] tear to pieces this game of mastery," the "disturbing abyss of passion nevertheless opens up only on the surface of calculated politics" (345). Erotic misperception also subtends Stendhal's novels, but is more clearly articulated and more thoroughly theorized in *De l'amour* (1822). The lover falls prey to what Stendhal's treatise extols as "a pattern of exquisite illusion" [*ensemble d'illusions charmantes*] (*Love* 128; *De l'amour* 143). He believes his beloved to be beautiful and endows her with thousands of qualities—qualities, as Denis de Rougemont points out, "she does not in the least possess" (225). Although this theorization is subverted by the idea of masculine cognition, it is supported by a central tenet of romanticism, the creativity of the imagination.[4] It is also supported by the notion of feminine mystique, which even Woolf and Yourcenar seem to credit.[5] Stendhal calls the phenomenon "crystallization"—a reference to his famous "Salzburg bough" metaphor:

At the salt mines of Salzburg, they throw a leafless wintry bough into one of the abandoned workings. Two or three months later they haul it out covered with a shining deposit of crystals. The smallest twig, no bigger than a tom-tit's claw, is studded with a galaxy of scintillating diamonds. The original branch is no longer recognizable. (45)

The lover, according to Stendhal, crystallizes his beloved with imaginary perfections.

Yourcenar and Renault find this combination of heteroerotic antagonism and crystallization objectionable.[6] They doubt that Stendhalian love provides "man with the greatest pleasures the species can know on earth" (49n). Like Kristeva, who has a more sophisticated understanding of feminine mystique, they regret that Stendhal's domineering "lover concocts an image of his beloved [that] hardly allow[s her] to be seen" (*Tales of Love* 347). Yourcenar, in *Coup de Grâce* (1957), condemns Sophie's conventional "subservience" (49) to Erick von Lhomond, who yields to "the temptation of playing God to [his] adorer" (32). Renault, in *The Friendly Young Ladies* (1944), decries the conventional marriage of Maude and Arthur Lane, who "had never loved one another, only images of their own devising, built up from books and the romantic conventions of their young day; no moment of pitiful, of humorous, of self-forgetting light had ever revealed either of them to the other" (22–23). Yet, if "convention plays a large part" in both Stendhal and the spurious erotic tradition to which he belongs, it also plays a large part in the countervailing tradition Yourcenar and Renault would establish.

Yourcenar and Renault want to convince readers that the type of love they envision is both desirable *and* possible, and in order to do so they invoke the conventional relationship that most closely approximates their erotic ideal: friendship. In *Coup de Grâce*, for example, Erick describes his erotic relationship with Conrad, Sophie's brother, as an "ardent friendship" (14). In *The Charioteer*, Laurie Odell says of Ralph Lanyon, his lover: "He's a friend of mine. It's a good old English word and I'm using it in the literal sense" (226). Western culture views friendship, unlike Stendhalian love, as a nonhierarchical, nondominative affective experience. It thinks of, and designates, friends as equals: they are mates, partners, colleagues, comrades, and companions. Western culture also conceives of friendship as cognizant. Friends have no secrets from one another. One reads a friend as one reads an open book. To cite Bussy-Rabutin's *Histoire amoureuse des Gaules* (1665), "Love comes from blindness, / Friendship from knowledge." To cite *Coup de Grâce*, "Friendship affords certitude above all, and that is what distinguishes it from love" (19). Yourcenar and Renault would have readers see and treat lovers much as they see and treat friends—as familiar equals. Yet they know that this is hard to do. They know that we, like Byron, who felt that "lovers . . . can never be friends" (50), tend to conceive of love and friendship as distinct, if not oppositional, categories. Yourcenar, for example, knows that we would probably disbelieve her deconstructive *ipse dixit* "friendship . . . is a particular kind [of love]" even if she had not also asserted that passion-love and friendship-love "are close to being opposites" (*Open Eyes* 254, 71). They know, in other words, that they are trying to effect an epistemological slide. And they realize that this slide is easier to effect in two interrelated epistemological fields that do not, or that many people *think* do not, draw rigid distinctions between love and friendship—fields known as "homosexuality" and "classicism."

Some critics would argue that any such slide involves a substitution of homoerotic identity for heteroerotic complementarity.[7] This was not, however, the case with Woolf. Nor is it true of Yourcenar and Renault. Renault scorns conventional heterosexuality and butch/queen male homosexuality in *The Charioteer*, but approves of unconventional heterosexuality and butch/femme lesbianism in *The Friendly Young Ladies*. And although Yourcenar rejects the notion that lovers "complement one another by virtue of their unique qualities" (*Open Eyes* 52), Alexis, her first gay character, claims: "one does not lose one's heart to what resembles oneself—and it was not women I was most different from" (*Alexis* 23). The two writers have an equivocal attitude toward both complementarity and identity and, as a result, gravitate toward the idea of nonoppositional erotic difference, of noncomplementary nonidentity. As Yourcenar puts it, "there was a subtle but absolute difference between Conrad and [Erick], like that between alabaster and marble" (*Coup de Grâce* 13).

Friendship, even cross-sex friendship, is generally conceived of as a same-sex institution. As Renault's Joe Flint tells Leo (Leonora) Lane, his butch girlfriend: "There are two people in you. One of them I have known much longer than the other. I am missing him [Leo] already, as much as I ever missed a friend. I should like him back—sometimes. But you know, now, how much he counted for when he came between my woman [Leonora] and me" (*Friendly Young Ladies* 274). This same-sex conception is due, in part, to the fact that men tend to know one another better than they know women and to the fact that women are not as put-upon by one another as they are by men. Men are conditioned to see women as mysterious, to believe in feminine mystique, and both men and women are implicated in sex-gender systems that inscribe phallocentric power differentials in *all* cross-sex relations, including ones that purport to be friendly, and therefore equal.[8] And just as friendship is generally conceived of as a same-sex institution, many same-sex institutions are generally, if somewhat incorrectly, conceived of as friendly. Homosexuality is one such institution. Gays and lesbians are both encouraged and inclined to think of lovers as friends. However, there is one important respect in which homoerotic love fails to conform to the dominant paradigm of friendship, a paradigm primarily promulgated by panicky, straight-minded, and male-bonded men. Unlike conventional friends, homosexual lovers have sex, or *want* to have sex, with one another.[9]

Notwithstanding this dominant paradigm, and notwithstanding our tendency to distinguish between love and friendship, the boundaries that separate friendship, love, and sex are actually difficult to draw. These conceptual and behavioral categories vary within individual cultures as well as from one culture and one historical era to another. Where Wordsworth, for example, saw love as "a compound of Lust with . . . Friendship," Coleridge took the remark to mean that Wordsworth was "incapable of love" (quoted in Gay 57). Consequently, we cannot understand these categories if we insist on segregating them. Any anxiety, homosocial or otherwise, about categorization will skew our vision. It may be that contemporary lesbians and gays, whose love relationships can be both friendly and sexy, have little such anxiety. Yourcenar, at least, believes as much. Witness her explanation of the homosexual proclivities of the bisexual protagonist of *L'Oeuvre au noir* (1968):

> Zeno was not what we would today call a homosexual but a man who from time to time had adventures with other men. . . . He prefers someone who resembles him, whom he can approach as it were on a footing of equality, a lover who is also a traveling companion and a comrade in time of danger. Many men would make the same argument even today, and in Zeno's time [the sixteenth century] the position of women made it even more difficult to treat a woman as anything other than a wife or a mistress, never as a companion. (*Open Eyes* 142)[10]

"Many men today," like Zeno, are frustrated by heterosexual politics. And "many men today," like Zeno, want "a lover who is also a . . . companion and a comrade," who is, in other words, a friend. But do they really want a "comrade in time of danger"? Do they, that is, really want someone like Achilles' Patroclus? Both Yourcenar and Renault suggest that the answer to these questions is "yes." In *Coup de Grâce*, for example, Erick describes Conrad, who, like him, is busy battling Bolshevism, as "the ideal companion in war, just as he had been the ideal childhood friend" (19). In *The Charioteer*, Laurie and Ralph, both of whom were wounded at Dunkirk, like to think of themselves as members of "the Sacred Band" (217), as men who "fighting at each other's side might well conquer the world" (329).

Yourcenar knows that the lines that divide friendship, love, and sex vary within individual cultures, as well as from one culture or historical era to another. She knows, in particular, that classical culture, even though it distinguished between the two categories, viewed some same-sex lovers as friends, and some same-sex friends as lovers. However, Yourcenar does not limit her historical fiction to what she knows to have been true. She projects back onto previous cultures fantasies of her own that might well have been true. As Yourcenar indicates in the Preface to *Feux* (1936), her readers should expect to find that "a very deliberate bias of superimpression mingles the past to a present that has, in turn, become the past" [*Fires* xii]. In *Memoirs of Hadrian*, the retrofitted fantasy is that lovers should have wanted, and in fact did want, to be more like friends. Yourcenar's Hadrian is a man who, above all else and against all odds, wants to believe that his beloved Antinous had been his friend.

Hadrian's problem is a familiar one. He is constricted by conventional limits. He can make sense of his relationship with Antinous only in terms of two classical paradigms: pederasty and heroic comradeship. A pederastic relationship, as classical convention would have it, occurs between an adult male, who is either married or accustomed to contact with adult women, and a youth between the ages of twelve and eighteen. It does not extend beyond the youth of the junior partner, and, if the junior partner is a citizen, is supposed to be restricted to intercrural copulation, which spares him the effeminizing humiliation of bodily penetration.[11] Hadrian's relationship with Antinous would seem to fall within this paradigm. Antinous is a young boy when he first meets Hadrian, who is forty-seven and married. The boy is a foreigner, a Bithynian, and therefore sexually penetrable. And he dies at nineteen. As Royston Lambert points out, Hadrian should see "himself as re-creating an *erastes-eromenos* relationship in the great classical tradition" (96).[12] But Yourcenar's Hadrian has the same reservations concerning classical pederasty as Yourcenar herself has concerning Stendhalian erotics, both of which are structures in domination and misperception. Hadrian, who regrets that he and his women lovers "knew almost nothing" of one another (62), wants to believe that he has shared Antinous's "secrets" (133). He imagines that "a system of human knowledge" (14) might be based on same-sex eroticism, that homoerotic pleasure might be a means of knowing the other. Like Yourcenar, however, he feels that rank and position "restrict [one's] field of vision" (22). And he knows that pederasts maintain distinctions of rank and position. Hadrian knows, to use David Halperin's definition, that classical pederasty is a "hierarchical relation of structured inequality between a free adult male and an adolescent youth of citizen status—or a foreigner or slave (the latter combination being considerably less glamorous)" (47) and believes that one cannot really know a subaltern.

Hadrian turns to his one conventional alternative: heroic comradeship. He sees Antinous as "an emulator of Achilles' friend" (177). He characterizes a dangerous lion hunt as a crucial rite of passage that takes the two of them "back into that heroic world where lovers die for each other" (187). He compares the tragic early death of Antinous to that of Hephaestion. And he is quite taken by the suggestion that Achilles's "ardent love for his young companion" (277) was not unlike his own love for Antinous.

Arrian [an admiral in Hadrian's navy] . . . offers me a gift which I need if I am to die in peace; he sends me a picture of my life as I should have wished it to be. . . . As seen by him the adventure of my existence takes on meaning and achieves a form, as in a poem; that unique affection frees itself from remorse, impatience, and vain obsessions as from so much smoke, or so much dust; sorrow is decanted and despair runs pure. Arrian opens to me the vast empyrean of heroes and friends, judging me not too unworthy of it. . . . [T]he isle of Achilles . . . is becoming my secret abode, my innermost haven. I shall doubtless be there at the moment of my death. (277–78)

Renault's classical deployment of these classical paradigms is similar to Yourcenar's. In *The Persian Boy*, Bagoas, a castrated Persian slave, recounts his life with Alexander the Great. Renault's *The Nature of Alexander* (1975) is a nonfiction account that covers much of the material treated in the historical novel. It also covers material fictionalized in *Fire from Heaven* (1969). Renault, like Yourcenar, plays two roles in these texts: factual historian and erotic fantasist. And of the two, it is the fantasist who makes the more interesting, if unverifiable, assertions. In *The Nature of Alexander* she imagines, for example, that "the real loves of [Alexander's] life were friendships, including his sexual loves" (32). She is certain that Alexander had sex with his best friend: Hephaestion was his "lover" (165), and not "simply the beloved confidant" (171). She claims that Alexander looked upon Hephaestion as an equal: "Theories that this was some mere bedmate or boon companion prized for his doglike devotion are hardly tenable" (46). And she believes that they knew one another well: Hephaestion was "the one man who would understand" (181). These fantasies, which reflect Renault's utopian erotics, are prefigured in *The Persian Boy*. Bagoas, who "never crave[s] for power, as some eunuchs do, only for love" (223), finds that Alexander both treats him as a "lover," not a "master" (237), and sees him as "a companion . . . , not an entertainer" (157). But Bagoas does not really *know* Alexander. It is only Hephaestion, the one man who is Alexander's true equal (the one man of whom Alexander can say "He too is Alexander" [114]), who can make such a claim. When Bagoas begs the dead Hephaestion to "leave [Alexander] to me, who love him more," he receives, and believes, the reply: "Ah, but I knew him" (398).

Bagoas wishes he had been as lucky in love as he, and Renault, imagine Alexander and Hephaestion to have been. Bagoas, like Hephaestion, is a real historical figure. And the one thing the historical record makes clear about the boy is that his relationship with Alexander was pederastic. As Renault puts it in her "Author's Note" to *The Persian Boy*, Bagoas "is the only person explicitly named in the sources as Alexander's *eromenos*" (413).[13] Renault's Bagoas, however, is dissatisfied with this role. He is murderously envious of Hephaestion's relationship with Alexander—a relationship he reads as heroic:

Alexander, of whom men tell many legends, lived by his own. Achilles [Alexander] must have Patroklos [Hephaestion]. He might love his Briseis [Bagoas]; but Patroklos was the friend till death. (366)

Somewhere, perhaps up in the mountains riding alone, they [Alexander and Hephaestion] had broken the wall, cast themselves into each other's arms, were once again Achilles and Patroklos. (373)

Bagoas too, for example, wants to fight alongside Alexander: "I asked him to take me with him; saying my father had been a warrior, and if I could not fight at his side, I would be ashamed to live" (182). But having been castrated—which, to Renault, means, in part, having never outgrown his childhood ("I am a little better than small, and all my life have kept the shape of a boy" [11])—he is never given the chance. As Renault states in *The Nature of Alexander*, "years later Bagoas was *still* his recognized *eromenos*" (160; emphasis added).

However, Renault does not wish to discourage readers. She, like Yourcenar, wants them to learn that the diacritical divide between these two paradigms is not unbridgeable, and in particular that pederastic relationships can evolve into heroic ones. In *The Nature of Alexander*, not only does Renault fantasize that Alexander must have treated Bagoas "as his friend" (117), a term she associates with Hephaestion, she also surmises that Bagoas's "influence [over Alexander] did not grow less as he passed out of adolescence" (141). The jarring notion of this eunuch's "adolescence" is justified, it would seem, by the idea that the "friendship" should no longer be read, after a certain, if indeterminate, point, as pederastic. And in *The Persian Boy*, Bagoas comes to read the Alexander/Hephaestion relationship as heroic only after having first read it as pederastic—after having first found Alexander to have been "made a boy of" by Hephaestion (139). This unproblematic evolution of Hephaestion from *erastes* (and not, it should be noted, from *eromenos*) to heroic comrade clearly represents a fairly optimistic attitude toward the possible realization of the author's erotic ideal. Yourcenar implies that such a change is revolutionary, that it can happen quite suddenly at a lion hunt. Renault, however, implies that the change happens gradually over time. And Bagoas never stops seeing Hephaestion as Patroclus. He has no reason, as he puts it, to "deface the legend" (373).

Renault's sense that pederastic relationships evolve into heroic ones is hinted at in *The Charioteer*, which, unlike *The Persian Boy*, is set in the twentieth century. She notes there that a three-year age difference, such as that between Laurie and Ralph, although "significant in the teens, can become almost meaningless in the twenties" (320). However, neither Yourcenar nor Renault deploys both paradigms in her nonhistorical fiction. They invoke heroic comradeship contemporaneously, but not classical pederasty. In *Coup de Grâce*, Yourcenar sets heterosexuality (as embodied by Sophie), and not pederasty, against Erick's heroic love for Conrad. In *The Charioteer*, Renault contrasts Laurie's heroic love for Ralph with both heterosexuality and butch/queen homosexuality (Ralph and Bunny, Alec and Sandy), but fails to describe Laurie's love for Andrew, who is "quite a bit" younger (243), as at all pederastic. These contemporary, nonpederastic paradigms would appear to be sufficiently hierarchical, if not delusionary, for their purposes. Why, then, compare these paradigms with classical comradeship, as opposed to modern homosexuality? Because both Yourcenar and Renault are less disturbed by differences between heroic comradeship and homosexuality than they are by differences between classical and contemporary pederasty, which they probably do not consider to be homosexual at all. But heroic comradeship and modern homosexuality are, in fact, quite distinct.

The classical paradigm, of which the Achilles/Patroclus and Orestes/Pylades relationships are proverbial instances and of which Hadrian is so enamored, differs from both classical pederasty and modern homosexuality.[14] A hero and his "pal," to use Halperin's term, are valiant friends who have no erotic rivals of either sex. Their friendship takes place in a militaristic or political sphere.

And the tragic early death of the weaker friend is the climax of the relationship.[15] A glance at the historical record shows why, for example, Yourcenar's Hadrian is, without too much difficulty, able to conceive of his relationship with Antinous in heroic terms. They did act valiantly at the lion hunt. They did enact their love in a militaristic and political setting. And Antinous's death was, for Hadrian, the tragic climax of their love life. Yourcenar credits J. A. Symonds with having discovered this "conscious revival by Hadrian of [the heroic] erotic tradition" ("Bibliographical Note" to *Hadrian*, 308). According to Symonds:

[Hadrian] must needs enact the part of Alexander, and realize, if only by a sort of makebelieve, a portion of his Greek ideal. Antinous, the beautiful servant, was to take the place of Ganymede, of Patroclus, of Hephæstion; never mind if Hadrian was a Roman and his friend a Bithynian, and if the love between them, as between an emperor of fifty and a boy of nineteen, had been less than heroic. (*Sketches and Studies* 202)

But if Symonds's Hadrian invokes the paradigm in order to glamorize his relationship with Antinous, Yourcenar's Hadrian does so in order to equalize it. He does so in order to turn him into what *we* think of as a friend. He does so, as Yourcenar has him put it, so as to oblige "the beloved to maintain also the difficult role of friend" (172), so as to invent "a new kind of intimacy in which the companion in pleasure would not cease to be the beloved and the friend" (177). In this respect, although she may not know it, Yourcenar is actually following in the footsteps of Stendhal, who, in an anomalous passage in *De l'amour*, complains: "Look what gentle Racine made of the heroic and time-honored friendship between Orestes and Pylades. Orestes addresses Pylades in the second person singular, while Pylades replies to him as *my lord*. And we are expected to find Racine our most moving author!" (*Love* 258). (The passage is anomalous inasmuch as it is the only reference in *De l'amour* to either same-sex love or—not incidentally—friendship.)

Both Yourcenar and Stendhal are on shaky ground here. The modern conception of friends as equals is quite out of place in a classical context. Hero/pal relationships were fundamentally asymmetrical. Like pederastic relationships, they were both dyadic and hierarchical.[16] A Patroclus or a Pylades was "subordinated—personally, socially, and narratologically" to an Achilles or an Orestes (Halperin 78). Just as, it might be said, Antinous is subordinated to Hadrian in Yourcenar's own account. And just as Ralph is inclined to be somewhat "imperious" with Laurie, who, having been Ralph's junior at school, finds he must resist "ancient habits of precedence" (*Charioteer* 200, 240). But in treating heroic comradeship as synonymous with nonhierarchical friendship, Yourcenar and Renault are attending to, and taking advantage of, the tendency of their readers to associate the two. As Halperin notes, theirs is not history's first misreading of the hero/pal paradigm, although in Yourcenar's case the misreading may well be deliberate. Even post-Homeric ancient Greeks could not get it right.

Classical Greeks, who, looking at the love of Achilles and Patroclus from the perspective of their own social and emotional institutions, tended naturally to assume that the relation between the heroes was a paederastic one. According to the Attic orator Aeschines, for example, Homer did not bother to describe the love-affair more explicitly because "he considered that the extraordinary degree of their good will towards one another would be self-explanatory to those among the audience who were cultivated people." (Halperin 86)

Halperin's primary reference in this passage is to the fact that, unlike modern gay relationships, hero/pal relationships, in their original form, were not sexual. If they had been, their structural asymmetry would have been even more pronounced. Classical sex, as Halperin notes, "is a deeply polarizing experience":

It effectively divides, classifies, and distributes its participants into distinct and radically opposed categories. Sex possesses this valence, apparently, because it is conceived to center essentially on, and to define itself around, an asymmetrical gesture, that of the penetration of the body of one person by the body—and, specifically, by the phallus—of another. Sex is not only polarizing, however; it is also hierarchical. For the insertive partner is construed as a sexual agent, whose phallic penetration of another person's body expresses sexual "activity," whereas the receptive partner is construed as a sexual patient, whose submission to phallic penetration expresses sexual "passivity." Sexual "activity," moreover, is thematized as domination: the relation between the "active" and the "passive" sexual partner is thought of as the same kind of relation as that obtaining between social superior and social inferior. "Active" and "passive" sexual roles are therefore necessarily isomorphic with superordinate and subordinate social status. (30)

To cite John Winkler's more succinct formulation: "what are significant in [classical] sexual activity are (i) men, (ii) penises that penetrate, and (iii) the articulation thereby of relative statuses through relations of dominance" (39). As Yourcenar and Renault are no doubt aware, this is also, to a certain extent, true of contemporary sex. According to conventional wisdom, sexual penetration is analogous to, and in some instances constitutive of, social subjection. Fucking and screwing are often exercises in, and figures for, domination. So if Yourcenar's Hadrian were to sodomize Antinous, most readers would feel that he was not being very friendly. Hence his discreet silence concerning his sex life with Antinous. And hence Yourcenar's burning of several pornographic drafts (*quelques descriptions assez obscènes*) of the novel ("Carnets de notes" in *Mémoires*, 341). Any polarizing sexual proclivities on Hadrian's part are simply too incompatible with his depolarizing erotic fantasies to be articulated.[17]

One Who Can Play for the Dancers, Yet Not Dance

Yourcenar would probably have burned the pornographic drafts even if there were no sexual polarization problem. Too many of her readers credit the dominant nonsexual paradigm of friendship. Too many readers assume that neither friends nor heroic comrades make love, including nonhierarchical love. Too many readers are apt to believe that if Yourcenar, as Halperin puts it, does "not bother to describe the [friendly] love-affair more explicitly," there must be nothing more to describe. (Aeschines would smile at this.) Yourcenar, however, wants her erotic message to reach these readers and so must play to their conventional conception of friendship as chaste by keeping her novel clean. But not too clean. She wants to convey the idea that sexual love should be more like, not exactly like, friendship. She wants lovers to continue making love and so never denies that Hadrian and Antinous do so.

Renault maintains a similar tactical silence in order to accommodate and expropriate conventional friendship. She lets us imagine that Alexander and Hephaestion do not sleep together all that much so as to enable us to think of them as familiar, equal friends. She lets us imagine them, to quote *The Nature of Alexander*, "in love, at a depth where the physical relationship becomes *almost* irrelevant" (159–60, emphasis added). Indeed, many readers, especially homosocial ones, cannot conceive of Renault's friendly homosexuals as at all sexual. Bernard Dick, for example, the homophobic author of *The Hellenism of Mary Renault*, invariably reads such characters as "sensual but unerotic" (5) and, in the course of doing so, unwittingly reveals the conventional constrictions with which Renault must contend. Despite his belief that "Socrates . . . represents the *mean* between homosexual friendship and loveless sodomy," Dick finds that Renault's historical fiction polices the purportedly Socratic distinction between *philia* and *eros* (50; emphasis added). Dick's classical erudition should lead him to realize the extent to which Renault is articulating just such a deconstructive "mean," but he is obstructed by the contemporary polarization of friendship and love. And Dick's reading of Renault's nonhistorical novel *Purposes of Love* (1939) suggests the extent to which many readers view modern friendship in terms of heroic comradeship, and heroic comradeship in terms of modern friendship:

One thinks of a Theocritean idyll where two shepherds find a sexless quiescence in each other's song. Thus to inquire whether or not a homosexual act ever transpired between Colonna and Vivian is as ludicrous and naïve as asking whether Achilles and Patroclus were lovers. The traditional classroom answer has always been, "Probably, but not in the *Iliad*," and one might give the same reply to those who have found more in Mary Renault's characters than she had chosen to disclose. (5)

Once again, remember what Aeschines had to say about the *Iliad*—that Homer does not describe the Achilles/Patroclus love-affair explicitly because its sexual nature is "self-explanatory to . . . cultivated people."[18]

Although Renault, like Yourcenar, has almost nothing to say about the heroic sex life of Alexander and Hephaestion, she does not hesitate to describe the pederastic one of Alexander and Bagoas. *The Persian Boy*, a love-slave's memoirs, would be truly "ludicrous and naïve" if she did not. Consequently, Renault must find a way for Bagoas to service Alexander sexually yet remain on somewhat friendly terms with him. She must, in other words, devise a solution for which Yourcenar, with her coolish catamite, has no particular need. Her solution is both clever and Freudian. According to Freud, "Where [men] love they do not desire and where they desire they cannot love" ("On the Universal Tendency to Debasement in the Sphere of Love," *Standard Edition* 11: 183). According to Renault, Bagoas experiences sexual pleasure, but not sexual desire, and can only experience sexual pleasure with someone he loves. The castration that deprived Bagoas of his manhood also deprived him of his sex drive. "Like a poet who can sing of battles though not a warrior, I could conjure the images of desire, without suffering the sharpness of its wounds. . . . I could make the music, its pauses and its cadenzas; . . . I was like one who can play for the dancers, yet not dance" (25–26). But although he has no sexual appetite, he has a sense of sexual taste: "With people like me, sex is a pleasure but not a need" (153). It is a sense, however, that can only be gratified when Bagoas loves his sexual partner. He experiences no pleasure with the cowardly (and therefore, to Bagoas's mind, unlovable) emperor Darius: "In all the time I was with him, he gave no sign of knowing a eunuch can feel anything" (29). He experiences pain with the friendly squire Ismenios: "When I caught my breath, Ismenios thought it was from rapture, and was happy" (242). Yet when Bagoas realizes that his beloved Alexander "really want[s] love from me," he experiences, for the very first time, "pleasure . . . as piercing as . . . pain" (137). Recovering from this erotic revelation, he finds that his "body echoe[s] like a harp-string after the note" (137).

The solution is clever in that it accommodates the conventional notion that friends do not even *want* to have sex together. Bagoas does not desire Alexander but, when called upon to service him, cannot help but enjoy himself. The solution is also clever in that it makes several arguments concerning love, pleasure, and desire. If to love someone is to truly know him or her, Renault suggests, it may be impossible for us to desire people we love. Perhaps we desire only people we do not know. Perhaps we cannot lust after people we both know and love. In other words, Renault does more than pay lip service to the conventional notion that friends do not even *want* to have sex. She suggests that although "friendly" lovers do not want to either, they can still offer one another erotic pleasure as satisfying as erotic desire. Bagoas remembers what desire is ("All this had been altered in me, yet not killed" [25]), but does not miss it. He is content to be a loving, pleasing pleasure-lover.

These suggestions have subversive, Foucauldian overtones—although Foucault, unlike Renault, sees no reason to renovate so quaint a notion as love. Foucault, too, has a utopian vision of "a different economy of bodies and pleasures" (*History of Sexuality* 159) and treats friendship, which he defines as "the sum total of all those things which enable [two people] to give pleasure to each other" ("De l'amitié" 5), as a liberating erotic paradigm. But some of Renault's more credulous readers may draw an inference that Foucault would never sanction. If Bagoas is the archetypical Renauldian subject, and if he only experiences sexual pleasure with the one man he ever knows and loves, then Renauldian subjects might expect to have unpleasant sex lives until they manage to find their one and only true love, should that day ever come. But Renauldian subjects need not draw this inference. Unlike Bagoas, who is a one-man eunuch, they need not be one-man women, one-woman men, one-man men, or one-woman women. They may love, and make love with, many people. Renault's real point is probably not that loveless sexual pleasure is a physical and psychical impossibility. Rather, it is probably that what she means by sexual love can be just as pleasurable as what some people call meaningless sex.

One of the problems Renault faces in depicting friendly homosexual lovers does not plague an analogous representation of a pair of friendly heterosexual lovers. In *The Bull from the Sea* (1962), Renault shows the relationship of Theseus and Hippolyta to be just as familiar and nonhierarchical as is that of Alexander and Hephaestion in *The Persian Boy*. Theseus, a king, sees Hippolyta as one as well ("she is more than queen. . . . There is a king's fate in her eyes" [101]), and professes to know her ("We learned as much of each other in battle as we did in bed" [122]). The polarization-depolarization paradox (one can know but not penetrate an equal; one can penetrate but not know a subaltern) still exists insofar as women are disempowered under patriarchy, but is resolved by the fact that Hippolyta, an Amazon queen, is as powerful as Theseus. However, the problem posed by the idea of two friends having sex no longer exists. Since straight-minded readers assume that men and women do have sex together, Renault need not pretend, for their sake, that Theseus and Hippolyta have no, or almost no, sex life. They learn about one another "in bed" and manage to conceive Hippolytus.

Given that friendship is a same-sex institution, that women are too "mysterious" and subordinate to be men's friends, why is Renault able to characterize this relationship as friendly? Because, it bears repeating, Hippolyta is an Amazon. She is as manly as women ever get.[19] Her friendly heterosexual love for Theseus occupies an anomalous, and indeed mythical, position within patriarchy. In a nonmythical and modern setting, their egalitarian romance, as Renault herself acknowledges, would seem both "silly" and "naive" ("Afterword," *Friendly Young Ladies* 281).[20] Hence, even readers who insist that same-sex friends are not and should not be lovers have little trouble imagining this, but *only* this, pair of cross-sex lovers as friends and even as heroic comrades. Bernard Dick, for example, who cannot conceive of Alexander and Hephaestion making love ("From the author's presentation, one has no other choice but to infer that Alexander and Hephaestion were far more concerned with pursuing the Greek ideal of *philia* or mutual love than sexual gratification" [104]), and who considers Theseus's love for Pirithous to be "Homeric" (73), believes that Theseus "has a relationship with Hippolyta which could only have been realized with a male companion, except for the heterosexual gratification that they experience after a day of high adventure. In a sense, he achieved the Greek goal of bisexuality with a female lover who was also a 'friend'" (78). Unfortunately, given the rarity of Amazon queens, Theseus was, as Renault, if not Dick, must know, probably the only Greek to have done so.[21]

Although Yourcenar, like Renault, invokes the Freudian segregation of love and desire in *Alexis*, in which the gay protagonist asserts that people "imagine they love because they do not perceive that they desire" (20), she does not do so in *Memoirs of Hadrian*. There, she tries to reconcile the polarization-depolarization paradox, to enable Hadrian to have sex with a socially inferior and therefore relatively unknowable boy he wants to know as a sexually impenetrable "friend," by relying on two common metaphors. Like Stein, Hadrian claims to be able to "know" lovers in a Biblically double sense: "human knowledge based on eroticism [affords] a more complete but also more specialized form of approach to the Other, [a] technique for getting to know what is not ourselves" (14). He also claims, like Gide and Firbank, but without their Wildean anti-essentialism, that lovers who reveal their bodies reveal themselves: "I know no decision which a man makes for simpler or more inevitable reasons, where the object chosen is weighed more exactly for its balance of sheer pleasure, or where the seeker after truth has a better chance to judge the naked human being" (12). Yourcenar herself considers these arguments fairly forceful. In *Les Yeux ouvertes* she urges readers to restore "the feeling that pleasure is a gateway to knowledge" (*Open Eyes* 54). And, in *Fires*, she makes the two claims simultaneously: "To possess is the same thing as to know: the Bible is always right. Love is a sorcerer: it knows the secrets; love is a dowser: it knows the sources. Indifference is one-eyed; hate is blind; side by side they stumble into the pit of disdain. Indifference is ignorant; love knows [*l'amour sait*]; it spells out the flesh. You must have pleasure from a creature to contemplate him naked. [*Il faut jouir d'un être pour avoir l'occasion de le contempler nu*]" (79–80; *Feux* 139).

These two attempted reconciliations fail, however, to alleviate Hadrian's suspicion that he does not, in fact, know Antinous very well—a suspicion that first arises when the boy's body is pulled from the muddy waters of the Nile. Hadrian realizes that he "shall never know anything [about Antinous's death] precisely because it would be of utmost importance to [him] to know all" (*Hadrian* 90). He also comes to recognize his ignorance at earlier moments in their love life: "But after all had I so well understood, on that morning, the living boy who sobbed at my side?" (205). He even reasons inductively that every beloved is a "fair stranger" (172). One of Arthur Goldhammer's translations of *Les Yeux ouverts* is startling when considered in the light of such pronouncements. Yourcenar describes Hadrian as "a man of innumerable carnal experiences who late in life is sunstruck by love" [*C'est l'homme aux innombrables expériences charnelles qui a eu tard le coup de soleil de l'amour* (74)], a line Goldhammer renders as: "Hadrian is a man of abundant carnal experience who late in life basks in the *sunshine* of love" (*Open Eyes* 51; emphasis added). Sunshine is not exactly sunstruck. Erotic clear-sightedness is not tantamount to erotic blindness. But while as between these two tropes it is Yourcenar's whose is the more Stendhalian—"sunstruck by love" is not so very different from "crystallization"—unlike Stendhal, Yourcenar is not suggesting that erotic blindness is a condition toward which one should aspire. Sunstroke connotes an unpleasantness that crystallization simply does not. Hadrian, thinking he never knew who Antinous really was, is not, as Stendhal would have him, as happy as can be. He is, on the contrary, quite miserable. For Yourcenar, a lover's bliss depends upon a true knowledge of the beloved that is not always easily obtained.

Hadrian, sunstruck by love, does not obtain it—which may be why he comes to feel so ill at ease with Yourcenar's egalitarian reading of the hero/pal paradigm. He senses that Antinous and he were not really friends, much as he wishes they had been, because they never really knew each other. Friends, Hadrian feels, know one another "better than anyone" (*Elle m'a connu mieux que personne*; [*Mémoires* 96]).[22] Their "two minds [are] closely intermingled" (*Hadrian* 82)—an intermingling unlikely to occur when the relationship is complicated by a "thousand approximate notions of title, function, and name" (7). Hadrian recognizes, in retrospect, that his relationship with Antinous was not the equal marriage of true minds he believes that of Achilles and Patroclus to have been. "I was beginning to realize that our observance of that heroic code which Greece had built around the attachment of a mature man for a younger companion is often no more for us than hypocrisy and pretence" (178). Hadrian feels that although Arrian's comforting analogy provides a picture of his life as he should have wished it to be, it does not provide a very accurate picture. He feels, in fact, that it masks the truth of his relationship with Antinous: "I was grateful to him for ranking that love, which he had witnessed, with the famous mutual attachments of antiquity; from time to time we spoke of it, but although no lie was uttered I frequently had the impression of a certain falsity in our words; the truth was being covered beneath the sublime" (223).

In "Patrocle ou le Destin" ("Patroclus, or Destiny") one of the narratives in *Feux*, Yourcenar composes another variation on the theme of the bereaved hero obsessed with knowing, and with not having known, his comrade. Her Achilles begrudges Hector the murder of Patroclus because he feels that "only he, himself, should have torn away the last veils that thought, gesture, the very fact of being alive, placed between them, in order to discover Patroclus in the sublime nudity of his death" (*Fires* 29). This passage recalls *Memoirs of Hadrian* inasmuch as it reiterates the figuration of the known beloved as the nude beloved, and inasmuch as it designates knowledge of one's comrade as "sublime." But it differs from the later text in two respects. First, it does not equate the hero/pal paradigm with contemporary, cognizant friendship. Achilles had not known Patroclus all that well. Second, it intimates that true knowledge of the beloved begins with his death, a notion Hadrian would find laughable. These differences demonstrate, of course, that the two narratives are not meant to make the same erotic argument.[23] They demonstrate that "Patrocle ou le Destin" does not claim, as *Memoirs of Hadrian* does, that lovers should be more like friends.

But the differences also demonstrate that Yourcenar finds our conventional conceptions of both friendship and heroic comradeship to be deconstructible. She finds, if not that friendship is really as hierarchical as she probably knows heroic comradeship to have been, at least that friends really know one another as incompletely as Achilles knew Patroclus. More generally, she may even find, if not that no relationship is unaffected by power differentials, at least that no subject can ever fully know an other. Yet Yourcenar also finds that conventional conceptions, faulty or not, are the only available means of disseminating her utopian erotic theory— that, as Barthes puts it, "it is necessary to posit a paradigm in or- der to produce a meaning and then to divert, to alter it" (*Barthes by Barthes* 92). She finds that friendship and heroic comradeship *as we know them* are the only epistemological categories at all close to what she considers love. So to the question, "Do many men to- day really want a lover who is also a traveling companion and a comrade in time of danger?" Yourcenar might well reply, "What else could they want?"

Renault's utopian contestations seem more successful than Yourcenar's, but no more so than Barthes's. When Antinous dies, Hadrian deifies him. He crystallizes, and has his subjects crystal- lize, the beloved he tried but failed to know as a friend. When Alexander dies, Bagoas writes a clear-sighted account Hephaes- tion alone could improve upon. To some extent, Yourcenar's con- servative pessimism and Renault's subversive optimism are func- tions of their nationalities. Whereas Continental writers tend to take a dark view of love, British writers prefer to look on the bright side. Continental adulterers kill themselves; British lovers get married. They are also functions of the fact that Continental writers find it hard to resist Continental erotics. Renault rejects

Stendhalian crystallization with a happy, patriotic zeal Yourcenar
never quite matches. Yourcenar claims she would jettison "love à
la française" yet chastizes Alexis for "react[ing] against a whole
century of romantic exaggeration" ("Preface," *Alexis* xii), for
"put[ting] love aside [and limiting himself] to trite encounters,
through a vague fear of . . . suffering" (53). Dismal love, it would
appear, is better than no love at all. Barthes, as will be seen, has a
similar handicap. Like Alexis, Barthes would cast conventional
love aside, would disburden sexuality of its erotic baggage. However, like Yourcenar, who remains somewhat Stendhalian, Barthes,
who remains Wertheresque, can do no such thing.

And neither can Renault. Barthes tries but fails to free sexuality
of love. Renault tries but fails to free love of sexuality. At first
glance, this would not appear to be the case. The lover, according
to Renault, has no sexual desire for the well-known beloved. Sexuality, according to Foucault, is culture's response to its interrogation of desire. Without desire, there can be no such interrogation,
and, hence, no sexuality. A woman who does not desire other
women is not a lesbian, even if she enjoys having sex with them,
because sexual pleasure, unlike desire, is indiscriminate. It is, to
use a term of which Barthes is fond, unisexual. However, Renault's
utopian eroticism, like Barthes's, can never free us from the prison
house of sexuality. The world of the Renauldian lover is not really
devoid of desire. In it, desire still exists and is still interrogated—
elsewhere. Consequently, the sexuality of the Renauldian lover is
also activated—elsewhere. It is activated, that is, by—and only
by—the "fair strangers" she wants to have but does not yet love.

CHAPTER 5

Barthes's Love-Tricks

—I think I'll be falling in love with you.
What a drag. What should I do?
—Give me your address.

Roland Barthes, *Incidents*

Like many post-structural feminists, I find the late work of Roland Barthes—in particular his dazzling deconstructions of doxa, of what passes for common sense—nearly irresistible.[1] Consequently, when Barthes takes up the crucial work of sexual liberation—which for him means freeing sexuality from the stranglehold of common sense—I expect, as usual, to be won over. If anyone could disarm us of our most cherished, and most oppressive, sexual stereotypes, it would be someone as disarming as Barthes. To a certain extent, I am won over. I am convinced that sexuality must be rendered unintelligible. I am convinced that romantic love has by now an "alien strength" that can and should be mustered in order to achieve this unintelligibility. And I am convinced that a truly liberated sexuality must be "unisexual" and "promiscuous" in the least meaningful senses of those terms. However, when I trouble to scrutinize Barthes's deconstruction of sexuality, like Naomi Schor, who sees his "discourse of sexual indifference / pure difference [as] the latest ruse of phallocentrism" (57), I find it to be disturbingly incomplete. Barthes adheres to cultural stereotypes of femininity.[2] He dismantles only a number of related stereotypes that pertain to his own gay male sexuality. And he deploys a number of figures that ground sexuality in, as well as release it from, gay male meaning. Barthes's deconstructive project need not be quite so partial. Luckily, those of us who are, or who want to be, less phallocentric than Barthes—and are, or want to be, less conventionally gay than Barthes—are in a fairly good position to try to see it through to the end.

Werther Is Not Perverse

Barthes recognizes that romantic love has been suppressed by the discursive practices that have produced sexuality.[3] We have undergone an unfortunate "historical reversal [in that] it is no longer the sexual which is indecent, it is the *sentimental*—censured in the name of what is in fact only *another morality*" (*Lover's Discourse* 177; hereafter cited as *LD*). This suppression, this censure, calls for countervailing articulations of lovers' discourses. Barthes's *A Lover's Discourse: Fragments* (*Fragments d'un discours amoureux*, 1977) is one such articulation, or "affirmation" (*LD* 1). But as affirmations go, it is quite discouraging—especially, perhaps, for Barthes's feminist readers. Barthes's lover, or rather his simulation of the lover as a subject in discourse, "is not loved" (*Grain of the Voice* 300).[4] His "preeminent intertext," as Domna Stanton puts it, is *The Sorrows of Young Werther*, "the paradigmatic discourse of impossible possession of the Other" ("Mater" 69). Like Werther, he is an anxious, forlorn fellow who finds his lonely love life "unbearable" and who knows he has "no likelihood of being *really* fulfilled" (*LD* 140, 55). And like Werther, he is indeed a phallic "fellow": "The lover might be defined as a child getting an erection: such was the young Eros" (*LD* 105).

Why is love, for Barthes, so unhappy, so Wertheresque? Some critics feel that it is because *A Lover's Discourse* simulates a specifically gay male eroticism—even though its figures actually "permutate 'he' and 'she,' hetero and homosexual love," in an attempt to inscribe "an imaginary of sexual indifference" (Heath 105). Philip Thody, for example, the obtuse author of the aptly titled *Roland Barthes: A Conservative Estimate*, explains "the frequency with which the themes of jealousy, loneliness and desertion recur in *Fragments d'un discours amoureux* by invoking the essential im-

permanency which writers such as Proust and Genet have depicted as characterising homosexual relationships" (154). Such esti-
mates are, of course, nauseatingly familiar. Contemporary doxa is
constantly predicating gay love as essentially impermanent and
nongay love as essentially eternal. However, *A Lover's Discourse* exempts itself from this regrettable predication. Like Proust, of
whom Thody is a stereotypically inattentive reader (one who reads
along and not against the stereotype),[5] Barthes sees *all* romantic
love—heterosexual as well as homosexual—as impermanent. Even
so, the unhappiness of the Barthesian lover *is* gay in ways that are
completely unrelated to any sadness attributable to the unavoid-
able impermanence of his erotic attachments.

Barthes displaces onto the male lover a number of stereotypes
associated with the male homosexual. One such stereotype is that
of sexual inversion. Barthes, emulating Socrates, Schlegel, and
Kierkegaard, repeatedly argues that unfulfilled, unfulfillable love
feminizes men.[6] "If a lover manages to 'love,'" he claims, "it is
precisely insofar as he feminizes himself" (*LD* 126). In part, this is
because the discourse of erotic absence has always been carried on
by women: "It follows that in any man who utters the other's absence *something feminine* is declared" (*LD* 14).[7] This is also because falling in love is akin to being raped: "every lover who falls
in love at first sight has something of a Sabine Woman (or of
some other celebrated victim of ravishment)" (*LD* 188). This figuration of the lover, whether gay or nongay, as "always implicitly
feminized" (*LD* 189) is clearly meant to help eradicate the cultural myth that encodes gay men as would-be women (e.g., as
"femmes"). Barthes even insists upon the displacement: "A man is
not feminized because he is inverted but because he is in love"
(*LD* 14). In other words, if the narrator of *A la recherche du temps
perdu* is "really" a woman, it is because he is in love with Alber-
tine, and not because, as several Proust scholars have argued, Al-
bertine is "really" a man.[8]

Another gay male stereotype displaced onto the lover is the figure of the son with an arrested development, the mother-obsessed
man who has never had to come to terms with the father. Not

only, as Lawrence Kritzman observes, does Barthes emasculate the lover "in order to . . . question the association of sexual inversion with feminization" (111), he also turns him into a perennial mama's boy. All his figures of erotic absence are appeals to the mother.[9] The figure "catastrophe," for example, involves a genitalized vision of "oneself abandoned by the Mother" (*LD* 48). In the "fadeout," the lover invokes "the other, the Mother, but [finds] merely a shade" (*LD* 113). The "embrace" marks "the return to the mother" (*LD* 104). And "I-love-you" expresses "the (maternal, amorous) dyad" (*LD* 148). But the lover is not, or at least is not simply, a sexually indifferent Lacanian subject who, as Stanton claims, merely wants to "recapture the originary bliss in/with the Mother, before the fall into the symbolic, the paternal" ("Mater" 59). He is also, as Barthes acknowledges, "the Proustian child" (REF: homosexuality) who only ever asks "that his mother sleep in his room" and who gets his wish by having for a father a man, as Wilde might say, of no importance: "by a reversal, by the Father's capricious decision, conceding him the Mother" (*LD* 150). The lover's father, like the father in *Roland Barthes by Roland Barthes* (*Roland Barthes par Roland Barthes*, 1975), and like the father in *A la recherche*, is a problematic absence that, as psychoanalytic discourse would have it, structures his gay son's erotic bent. With "no father to kill," the lover, like "Barthes," can't help but experience a "great Oedipal frustration!" (*Barthes by Barthes* 45).[10] He can't help but wonder "what would . . . have been if he had really known his father and by some misfortune had loved him too!" (*Barthes by Barthes* 125). (That "misfortune" is rather sly: it implies a paradoxical devaluation of the normal male sexual development nonabsent fathers are presumed to foster.) In short, he can't help but (not) love Albert(ine).

These two stereotypes—the femme and the mama's boy—occasionally conspire with one another in Barthes's erotic texts. The young Proustian narrator, just before he gets the mother for the night, "correctly identifies himself with the 'mistress' sent away by her lover's concierge" (*LD* 150). Franz Schubert, two years after he "loses his mother at fifteen," writes "his first great song, *Gret-*

chen at the Spinning Wheel, [which] utters the tumult of absence, the hallucination of the return" ("Romantic Song" 289). In both of these examples, Barthes reiterates the cultural myth of the mama's boy who, naturally enough, becomes, in a sense, a man's man (the sissy who grows up to be a femme). But the combination of the stereotypes also results in a uniquely Barthesian figure: the "maternal Son" (Stanton, "Mater" 66). This figure, unlike its cognate, the mama's boy, marks the lover's double identification as both mother and son. He is simultaneously the "male child in . . . relation to the beloved maternal Other, [and] the Mother in relation to the beloved Other/man" (Stanton, "Mater" 69–70). He is the man who can say of his beloved: "we mother each other reciprocally" (*LD* 224). However, even the "maternal Son" has a notorious gay counterpart: the "aunt" (or *tante*). The aunt, too, is a man who both mothers and is mothered. Barthes is all too familiar with this stereotypical approximation of the "maternal Son," this commonplace version of his paradoxical figure. He was an aunt himself. And he tends to associate the unintelligibility of his "erotic perversion" with the closeted discourse—discourse "the public face of [which] is somehow sanded down and rendered quite insignificant" (*Barthes by Barthes* 86–87)—of Céline and Flora, those two uncommonly close Proustian aunts.

All this lover-ly gayness—the lover as femme, as mama's boy, as aunt—is unhappy precisely because it is stereotypical. For Barthes, all stereotypes are insidiously meaningful: they halt the liberating play of *signifiance.* Stereotypes are also ideological: they belong to doxa (to consensus: the natural, the obvious, the "it goes without saying"). Sexual stereotypes are no exception. A stereotype like femme, for example, reduces homosexuality to inversion and induces gay men to misconstrue themselves—gay men who are, Barthes insists, "repressed, refracted, blinded as to their true sexuality, *because they are unwilling to let go of a stereotype*" (*Barthes by Barthes* 90). It is for this reason that Barthes displaces sad gay stereotypes onto the lover: he wants to clear a stereotype-free utopian space for a truly gay, or "happy," sexuality.

For Barthes, sexuality should not mean a thing. He dreams of a

"*matte* fall of sexuality outside discourse" and feels that true eroticism requires that one "abolish—in oneself, between oneself and
others—*adjectives*" (*Barthes by Barthes* 165, 43). Sexuality should be
featureless and indescribable. It should be unpredicatable by stereotypes, by adjectives. He believes, moreover, that "a happy sexuality" will arise only when "meaning and sex become the object
of a free play [and] achieve a state of infinite expansion," when
"meaning [is] dispers[ed] and sex [is] taken into no typology"
(*Barthes by Barthes* 133, 69). (Hence his identification of *signifiance*, the play of signifiers, with *jouissance*, the bliss of "coming.")[11]
But Barthes also believes that one cannot simply "disperse" the
stereotypes, the adjectives, that predicate sexuality. For Barthes,
sexual stereotypes are sticky: to be displaced, they must be placed
elsewhere. One must "make sure that [a stereotype] doesn't *stick*"
(*Barthes by Barthes* 162). Most of us, he realizes, are far too uncomfortable with senselessness (with *signifiance*) to discard altogether the labels that enable us to comprehend one another. If we
are not to think of a gay man as a femme, we must be allowed to,
and be made to, think of someone else as one. In theory, that
someone else could be almost anyone. He could be, for example,
the man who drinks *fraisette*: "All of a sudden, the Woman in
Charlus surfaced: not when he was cruising soldiers and coach-
men, but when, at the Verdurins', he asked for a strawberry li-
queur—asked, in a shrill voice, for some *fraisette*" (*Barthes by
Barthes* 95–96). However, the lover is a more practical choice than
the *fraisette* guzzler insofar as prior texts (by Socrates, Schlegel,
Kierkegaard, etc.) have already feminized him. The displaced gay
stereotype fits best where others have already made space for it.

If the sticky gay stereotypes displaced onto the lover are not to
reattach themselves to the gay man, now happy at last, the Barthesian lover must not be readable as gay. However, Barthes is too
scrupulous to allow him to be readable as straight. Like Proust, he
sees "being in love [as] a unisex situation [in that] exactly the
same *tonality* can be found in a man who loves a woman or a
man, and a woman who loves a man or a woman" (*Grain of the
Voice* 293). And like Proust, he wants to construct "a lover's dis-

course [that] is [no] more related to homosexuality than it is to heterosexuality" (*Grain of the Voice* 300). But unfortunately for the attempted displacement of gay male stereotypes, Barthes is unable to do so—even though, as noted above, his figures "permutate 'he' and 'she,' hetero and homosexual love." The very stereotypes from which he wants to liberate male homosexuality cannot help but further signify the gayness of the unisexual (i.e., quite possibly homosexual) lover. In other words, by describing his sexually ambivalent lover as an invert, Barthes is unwittingly characterizing him as queer.

A successful displacement of gay male stereotypes onto the lover would also require that love and sexuality remain conceptually distinct. And Barthes does indeed discriminate between these two erotic categories.[12] He equates "being in love [with] a distancing of sexuality" (*Grain of the Voice* 298), an unequivocal formulation based upon a fairly uncomplicated view of love as essentially significant and sexuality as potentially insignificant. Unlike the happy homosexual, the lover, Barthes insists, is in the very "crucible of meaning," not "*atopos*, but . . . classified" (*LD* 67, 35). He is "someone quite banal, with a well-thumbed dossier" (*Grain of the Voice* 281). His unhappiness derives "from the stereotype," and his "delirium [is] tamed and banalized by literature" (*LD* 35, 177). However, this uncomplicated view gets rather complicated. In many ways, Barthes insists, both the lover and the beloved are quite as unclassifiable as the happy homosexual. The lover, who "sees everyone around him as 'pigeonholed'" (*LD* 45), is himself "*de trop*." As a "maternal Son," he is "an atopical subject—undivided: I am my own child" (*LD* 99). And the beloved, best designated as "such" [*tel*], escapes predication, "the death of classification," altogether. He, too, "is virtually *de trop*": "*As he is*, the loved being no longer receives any meaning . . . he is no more than a text without a context" (*LD* 65, 220–21). He "cannot be imprisoned in any stereotype"; even *I-love-you*—"ultimately the most worn-down of stereotypes"—"plays against the signs . . . at the extreme limit of language, where language itself . . . recognizes that it is without backing or guarantee, working without a net" (*LD*

34, 151, 154). These more or less tentative assertions are subsumed by a sweeping claim later made in *Camera Lucida* (*La Chambre claire*, 1980): "the frivolous insignificance of language [is] the very space of love" (72).

Ironically, Barthes exempts love, like sexuality, from meaning, and thereby jeopardizes the welcome displacement of the stereotypes, in what may well be an attempt to valorize gay love. Barthes asserts that love is unisexual in order, in part, to show that homosexual love has "exactly the same *tonality*" as heterosexual love. By "unisexual," he means that romantic love, like utopian sexuality, has nothing to do with gender. That it, too, is "neuter."[13] "Neuter," for Barthes, signifies *signifiance*.[14] "The neuter . . . is what *confuses* meaning, the norm, normality" (*Sade* 109). It represents "the ideal state of sociality [in which] countless meanings . . . explode, crepitate, burst out without ever assuming the definitive form of a sign grimly weighted by its signified" (*Barthes by Barthes* 98). Love, like sexuality, by transcending the binarism male/female, transcends the integrity of meaning in language.[15] Unfortunately, romantic love in its conventional sense is far from neuter. It usually concerns the ideal union of two people who complement one another as male and female. It usually has, in other words, *everything* to do with gender. By claiming otherwise, Barthes is being paradoxical, if not disingenuous—a paradoxicality or disingenuousness that is resoundingly clear in his essay "The Romantic Song" ("Le Chant romantique," 1977). Barthes characterizes the romantic song (or Lied), in which he hears "the pure expression" (291) of the lover's emotion, as catalyzed by what Kritzman calls "the need to (re)discover the dream of omnipotence in a romance of union represented as a conflict-free relation liberated from the laws of gender overdetermination" (106). The Lied, Barthes claims, "does not take into account the sexual marks of the voice, for the same lied can be sung by a man or a woman, no vocal 'family,' nothing but a human subject,—*unisexual*, one might say precisely insofar as it is *amorous*: for love—passion, romantic love—is no respecter of sexes or of social roles" ("Romantic Song" 287). Nothing could be further from what most people would agree to be the truth, from the doxa. The Lied, especially when it takes love as its subject, "precisely insofar as it is *amorous*," is just as gendered as the opera. Contrary to what Barthes would have us believe, women do not perform Schubert's *Die schöne Müllerin*, a first-person account of a man's love for a woman, and men do not perform Schumann's *Frauenliebe und Leben*, a first-person account of a woman's love for a man. In other words, Schubert may have written "Gretchen at the Spinning Wheel," but he certainly never sang it.

Barthes also exempts love, like homosexuality, from meaning because he finds them both "perverse." A perversion, for Barthes, approaches *signifiance* ("generates a blissful surplus of meaning" [Kritzman 110]), not because it transcends binarisms like male/female, but because it is generally incomprehensible. Homosexuality is perverse insofar as it is excluded from everyday, popular language: "I cannot get into my writing the *enchantment* (pure image) of a seduction . . . except by relays so complicated that [it] will lose all its publicity, and hence all its joy" (*Barthes by Barthes* 86). Love is similarly excluded from popular or public discourse. The lover is an epistemological orphan who is misunderstood by contemporary philosophy, who is "discredited by modern opinion," and whose perverse discourse is seen as "stupid" (*LD* 175, 177). A perversion also approaches *signifiance* because it is excessive. Homosexuality is perverse insofar as "it produces a *more* . . . —and in this *more* is where we find the difference (and consequently, the Text of life, life-as-text)" (*Barthes by Barthes* 64). It is also perverse insofar as it is nonprocreative: it "exerts itself for nothing" (*Grain of the Voice* 232). Love, too, is excessive, "produces a *more*"; it participates in "a perverse economy of dispersion, of waste, of frenzy (*furor wertherinus*)" (*LD* 85).

The equivocation as to whether love is significant (stereotypical)—a banal dossier in the crucible of meaning—or insignificant (neuter and perverse)—a contextless text that cannot be pigeonholed—leads Barthes to equivocate as to love's role within sexuality. On the one hand, he finds love perverse enough to liberate sexuality beyond any possibility of recuperation.[16] In an all-too-

thorough estrangement of the category (erotic sentimentality may
be more familiar to contemporary subjects than he would like to
believe), Barthes states that the sentimentality of love has an
"alien," and therefore transgressive, strength that sexual freedom
fighters would do well to deploy.[17] The reintroduction into the
liberated politico-sexual field of even "*a touch of sentimentality . . .*
would . . . be the *ultimate* transgression . . . the transgression of
transgression itself . . . [the return of] *love . . . but in another place*"
(*Barthes by Barthes* 65–66).[18] When one's "sexual and sensual relationship" is with someone one loves, "eroticism itself is a kind of
access to a transcendence of sexuality" (*Grain of the Voice* 298).
On the other hand, Barthes finds love stereotypical enough to act
as a drag anchor on sexuality's propensity to float free. "Erotiza-
tion is a production of the erotic: light, diffuse, mercurial; which
circulates without coagulating; a multiple and mobile flirtation
links the subject to what passes, pretends to cling, then lets go for
something else (and then, sometimes, this variable landscape is
severed, sliced through by a sudden immobility: love)" (*Barthes by
Barthes* 62). Werther, in fact, "is not perverse, he is in love: he
creates meaning, always and everywhere, out of nothing" (*LD* 67).

A Virtual Love

Barthes wants to have his cake and eat it too. He wants a happy, insignificant sexuality that is further exempted from meaning
by an admixture of romantic love, but he also wants one that is
unscathed by love's perilous significance, a significance *A Lover's
Discourse* itself reconstitutes. And he suggests that one might attain this improbable sexuality by restricting one's erotic life to
"cruising" [*la drague*].[19] Cruising, for Barthes, represents the perpetual, and fruitless, search for love. "In homosexual milieux, . . .
where cruising is quite extensive, one can cruise for years at a time
. . . with in fact the invincible idea that one will find *someone with
whom to be in love*" (*Grain of the Voice* 299). The cruiser is like the
Flying Dutchman, who "cannot stop wandering (loving)," who is
afflicted "with a compulsion to . . . say 'I love you' in one port of

call after another" (*LD* 102). However, and this is crucial, no one can give this phrase back to him, "no one can assume the impossible reply (of an insupportable fulfillment)," and so his wandering continues (*LD* 102). The advantage of cruising, at least in theory, is that by soliciting, but only soliciting, love, one repeatedly avoids repetition and therefore escapes erotic stereotypology. "Cruising implies a temporality that accentuates the meeting, the 'first time.' As if the first meeting possessed an unheard-of privilege: that of being withdrawn from all repetition. Repetition is a baleful theme for me—stereotype, the same old thing, naturalness as repetition. Cruising is anti-natural, anti-repetition. Cruising is an act that repeats itself, but its catch is absolutely fresh" (*Grain of the Voice* 231). Cruising, supposedly, constantly reiterates the *coup de foudre* while forestalling its ugly and predictable aftermath—the "downfall which would envelop . . . the glamorous encounter that first revealed [lovers] to each other" (*LD* 198). When I cruise, "I see daylight again . . . because I abandon that love altogether and set out again, trying to reiterate, with others, the encounter whose dazzlement remains with me: for it is of the order of the 'first pleasure' and I cannot rest until it recurs: I affirm the affirmation, I begin again, without repeating" (*LD* 198).

Unfortunately, cruising is an inapt metaphor for the improbable sexuality Barthes envisions. For one thing, most readers dissociate cruising and love. Although Barthesian cruising represents the perpetual and fruitless search for love, conventional cruising represents the perpetual, and intermittently fruitful, search for *sex*. (Note the use of the term "conventional"—I neither deny that many people, like Barthes, cruise for love nor assert that every cruiser distinguishes between love and lust.) And by claiming that the cruiser is looking for anything more than a good time, Barthes is contravening a stereotype that is simply too young to be renovated. People have searched for sex for millennia, but have only called it "cruising" since the 1960's.

Another reason why the metaphor is inapt is that even a Barthesian cruiser can hardly be said to avoid repetition and escape stereotypology. He is, Barthes realizes, pigeonholed.[20] His

beloveds are not "such" [*tel*]—they reduplicate one another. "Is
the lover," Barthes asks, "merely a choosier cruiser, who spends
his life looking for 'his type'" (*LD* 34)? And by repeatedly saying "I
love you" to one charmer after another, the cruiser is merely acting. He is rehearsing a scene it is all too obvious someone else has
already scripted. He is the libertine with the stale come-on, the
roué to whom no self-respecting ingenue will give the time of day.
As even Barthes knows, this cruiser is a character who cannot help
but signify the significance of his signature line, of his "I love
you." "The ideal," Barthes writes, "would of course be to erase
[the signs which display the stereotype's 'wear'] while keeping the
frozen word from returning to a state of nature: but to do this, the
stereotyped discourse must be caught up in a *mimesis* (novel or
theater): it is then the characters themselves who function as quotation marks" (*Barthes by Barthes* 89). The cruiser himself, in other words, functions as a set of quotation marks around his characteristic, and stereotypical, catchphrase. No wonder every time
he says "I love you," his bored, if not nauseated, audience fails to
respond "I love you, too."[21]

Cruising is also an inapposite trope for a happy sexuality because, at least as portrayed by Barthes, it is an essentially unhappy
(unfulfilled, unfulfillable) activity. The cruiser, like the lover, is
fated never to be loved. He is only ever alone. He *is*, in fact, the
Barthesian lover, even though he purports never to utter that lover's discourse. The cruiser may not actually enact the *coup de
foudre*'s "sequel"—"the long train of sufferings, wounds, anxieties,
distresses, resentments, despairs, embarassments, and deceptions"
(*LD* 197–98)—but he is no happier than the lover who does. And
at least the lover gets to act out his inevitable unhappiness.
Barthes's cruiser is a thoroughly suppressed lover.

Indeed, "Barthes's" own experience as a cruiser (as reflected in
Incidents [1987], a posthumous compilation of autobiographical
fragments, some of which Barthes intended to publish) fails to
warrant his association of cruising with a blissfully insignificant
commingling of love and sexuality. (This rather indelicate leap
into Barthes's "life" is justified, if not demanded, by Barthes's own
pervasive, but all-too-delicate, self-referentiality.) Barthes writes:

I hang around at home (I have some toast and feta cheese), then, telling myself that I have to break the habit of *planning* my pleasures (or my distractions), I go out again and go to see the new porno flic at the Dragon: as always—and perhaps even more than usual—deplorable. I don't dare cruise my neighbor, although he seems available (idiotic fear of being turned down). Descent to the back room [*la chambre noire*]; afterwards, I always regret this sordid episode where I invariably expose my loneliness. (104–5)

In this passage, "Barthes" himself touches on the three problems outlined above. The cruise that nearly occurs at the Dragon would have been a search for sex, and not a search for love. There is no glamorous *coup de foudre* where Barthes's "available" neighbor is concerned. (And there is certainly no *coup de foudre* in *la chambre noire*—no love at first sight when you can't see a thing.) Barthes could hardly have turned to a strange man, or boy, in a dimly lit porn palace and murmured "I love you." He would have been out of line. And even if he had, the utterance would not have escaped stereotypology. It would have been a premeditated, prescripted attempt to say something unpremeditated, unprescripted. ("Telling myself that I have to break the habit of *planning* my pleasures. . . . ") The declaration would have been *studiedly* spontaneous, which is as unstereotypical as stereotypes ever get.[22] Finally, when Barthes cruises the back room rather than his neighbor, he is left desolate. He "exposes his loneliness," but not because he doesn't get what he wants (unadulterated sex—why else is the episode "sordid"?). Every back room habitué can get what he wants. In "Barthes's" more or less real world, even cruisers who get lucky are unhappy.

Barthes also associates the "trick" with the blissfully insignificant commingling of love and sexuality. However, contrary to popular belief, to doxa, the Barthesian trick is not simply the person for whom one cruises. The Barthesian trick involves "more than cruising, [but] less than love" ("Preface" 295). Unlike the cruiser, the trick actually seems to utter the lover's discourse—at least until matters take their inevitable turn for the worse. (The term "trick" can refer to either party to a trick.) "The trick is . . . homogeneous to the amorous progression; it is a virtual love, deliberately stopped short on each side, by contract; a submission to the cultural code which identifies cruising with Don Juanism" ("Preface" 294). He seems to say more than just "I love you," but not so much as to get himself into trouble (into significance). He has "a way of not getting stuck in desire, though without evading it," as well as a way of hoodwinking the "harpy [that usually] presides over the erotic contract, leaving each party within a chilly solitude" ("Preface" 295). What does this really mean? That, although Barthes does not say so, the trick is a cruiser to whom a beloved responds, "I love you, too—for now." The Barthesian trick involves "more than cruising" insofar as its amorous impulse is not unidirectional. One can escape the desperate solitude of the lover, not via the equally desperate solitude of the cruiser, but via the cheerful gregariousness of the trick, who can love and be loved by several people at once, "for a while, anyway," who can "bathe in an atmosphere of [multiple] love[s], of generalized flirtation" (*Grain of the Voice* 296).

This cheerful gregariousness is what Barthes finds so blissfully insignificant about the trick. The cruiser, whose transient loves are ever unreciprocated and unfulfilled, is firmly inscribed within two stereotypes. He is inscribed within the Wertheresque stereotype of the lonely lover as well as the stereotype of the lonely homosexual. The trick, however, whose transient love is ever reciprocated and fulfilled, escapes both of these stereotypes. This is why Barthes, who never disclaims the gayness of cruising (and who would believe him if he did?), is so bold as to disclaim the gayness as well as the significance of the trick. People who "trick" neither "'are' [nor] 'aren't'" homosexual ("Preface" 291). They refuse "to proclaim [themselves] something . . . at the behest of a vengeful Other, to enter into his discourse, to argue with him, to seek from him a scrap of identity; 'You are . . . ' 'Yes, I am . . . '" ("Preface" 291). Rather, they are " . . . *nothing*, or, more precisely, [they are] *something* [that is] provisional, revocable, insignificant, inessential, in a word irrelevant" ("Preface" 291–92). They reflect, in Kritzman's view, "the essence of the [Barthesian] neuter, which is unquestionably an entity without essence beyond the plenitude of being" (111).

Barthes's bold disclaimer is, in fact, somewhat compelling. Whereas the femme, the mama's boy, and the aunt are sexual *identities*, the trick, like cruising, is a sexual *activity*—one, moreover, in which any "personage," to use Foucault's term, regardless of her identity, should be able to engage. This, however, is not the case. Barthes's disclaimer may be compelling, but it also strains credulity. The trick is no less gay than cruising. The cultural encoding of the trick as gay is no weaker than the analogous encoding of cruising. There are, it is true, discursive communities in which nongay cruising and tricking do occur. Female prostitutes turn male tricks, and teenage boys cruise teenage girls. However, when a writer like Barthes deploys the two terms in such a way as to make clear that he is not referring to erotic transactions of a commercial or bilaterally pubescent nature, he can only be understood to denote gay male eroticism—even though, no doubt, he cannot help but connote the nongay transactions as well. And the very gregariousness with which Barthes credits the trick, and which he finds exempts it from meaning, invokes a gay stereotype as powerful as, if not more powerful than, the stereotype of the lonely homosexual: the *promiscuous* homosexual. The doxa that constantly predicates gay love as essentially impermanent also predicates it as essentially multiple. (Obviously, the two predications reinforce one another.) Hence, as with cruising, the trick may well be too singularly meaningful to signify erotic insignificance. It may well be too gay-identified to stand for Barthes's happy, unisexual sexuality.

And it may well be too *unhappy* to stand for it. As with cruising, which leaves the cruiser, like the lover, desolate, the trick may be a far from cheerful affair. For one thing, Barthes is unsure as to whether gregariousness is felicitous. He regrets the fact that erotic isolation is now unfashionable—that Werther has been displaced by Warren Beatty.[23] "The human subject has changed," Barthes writes, none too happily: "interiority, intimacy, solitude have lost their value, the individual has become increasingly gregarious" ("Loving Schumann" 293). Barthes is also unsure as to whether erotic fulfillment makes one truly happy. "Barthes," for example, finds that when one's beloved responds "I love you, too," one is reduced, not unlike the less fortunate lover, to tears. "But if by some miracle the jubilatory answer should be given, what might it be? What is the *taste* of fulfillment? Heine: '*Doch wenn du sprichst: Ich liebe dich!* / *So muss ich weinen bitterlich:*' I stagger, I fall, *I weep bitterly*" (*Barthes by Barthes* 114). And these are not tears of joy.[24]

But even if erotic fulfillment is happier than Heine would have "Barthes" believe, the trick is still a problematic figuration of the blissfully insignificant commingling of love and sexuality. For many gay men, as well as for many prostitutes and their customers, the trick does not even begin to approximate "a virtual love, deliberately stopped short on each side, by contract." It does not even begin to forestall love's "chilly solitude." It does not even begin, that is, to represent erotic fulfillment. As "Barthes" himself knows all too well, most real tricks would never respond "I love you too—for now." In other words, the reason even Barthesian cruisers, who are looking for love and not sex, rarely, if ever, utter "I love you," even to people who seem "available," is that nine out of ten tricks, who are looking for sex and not love, would not know what to say. They would be dumbstruck. Such, at least, is the fate of Olivier G., a young Tadzio-like trick Barthes invites into his home. (Although Barthes does not specifically call Olivier a "trick," there is no other erotic category—lover, friend, spouse, hustler—to which he can be said to belong.)

Yesterday, Sunday, Olivier G. came to lunch; I had given to waiting for him, to greeting him, the attention that usually shows that I am in love. But, already during lunch, his shyness or his distance made me self-conscious; no euphoric intercourse, far from it. I asked him to come join me on the bed during my nap; he came very nicely, sat on the edge, read a picture-book; his body was very far away, if I stretched out my arm to him, he didn't budge, withdrawn: no obligingness; in fact he soon retired to the other room. A kind of despair took hold of me, I wanted to cry. I inferred from the evidence that I had to give up boys, because they had no desire for me, and because I am either too scrupulous or too clumsy to impose my own; I also inferred, as an inescapable fact, proven by all my attempts at flirtation, that I have a sad life, that, in the end, I'm bored, and that I have to erase this interest, or this hope, from my life. (If I take my friends one by one—except for those who are no longer young—each time it has been a failure: A., R., J.-L. P., Saül T., Michel D.—R.L., too brief, B.M. and B.H., no desire, etc.) All I'll have left will be hustlers. (But what then will I do when I'm out? I always notice young men, desire them immediately, fall in love with them. What will the world-stage be for me?)—I played a piano piece for O., at his request, knowing then that I had renounced him; he had his very beautiful eyes, and his sweet face, softened by his long hair: a delicate but inaccessible and enigmatic creature, at once sweet and distant. Then I sent him on his way, saying that I had to work, knowing that it was over, and that something beyond him was over: the love of *a* boy [*l'amour d'un garçon*]. (*Incidents* 115–16)

Admittedly, young Olivier does not seem to be in the mood for sex, let alone love. He has no desire for Barthes, who fails to impose his own. But the passage is less concerned with Olivier's sexual disinterest than with his amorous aversion. "Barthes" is lovesick, not horny. And Olivier, as one may well imagine, is at a loss for words. Everything Barthes does says "I love you," and everything Olivier does says "I do *not* love you"—or at least does *not* say "I love you, too—for now." They have "no euphoric intercourse," and hence the whole unpleasant incident is, for "Barthes," more of a Barthesian cruise than a Barthesian trick.

What does Barthes mean by the obscure and indeterminate phrase "the love of *a* boy?"[25] Perhaps he simply means that he will no longer love this one boy—that he will get over Olivier and proceed to love one boy after another until one (or more than one) of them does the trick and loves him in return. Or perhaps he means that he will never again love any one boy in particular—that from now on he will only love all boys in general. The suggestion that Barthes must continue to love as he always has ("I always notice young men [and] fall in love with them") supports the former alternative, while the claim that "something beyond [Olivier] was over" supports the latter. But whichever alternative is meant, both are promiscuous. Loving boys simultaneously—that is, loving the Platonic idea of (all of) them—is as promiscuous as, if not more promiscuous than, loving (many of) them seriatim. Both, that is, insofar as doxa predicates homosexuality as promiscuous and promiscuity as homosexual, are stereo-typically gay. And Barthes is not at all troubled by this promiscuous gayness of the happy eroticism (or eroticisms) he recommends to himself.

This is not surprising. Barthes is not particularly troubled by the promiscuous gayness of the cruising and tricking he recommends to all his readers. Barthes, who knows that promiscuity is a gay stereotype, who realizes that sexuality is not exempt from meaning if it is gay, and who abjures all stereotypes (whether gay or not), treats gay promiscuity as sui generis. Whereas certain gay stereotypes—the femme, the mama's boy, the aunt—are so nause-ating, so significant, as to require displacement onto the figure of the lover, the stereotype of the promiscuous homosexual, for Barthes, is not. It may be significant (what stereotype isn't?), but it is also insignificant. Promiscuity is "perverse." Like homosexuality itself, it is excessive, it "produces a more." Like love itself, pro-miscuity participates in "a perverse economy of dispersion." Hence, although both cruising and the trick, which invoke the stereotype of the promiscuous homosexual, may be too homosex-ual, too gay, to stand for Barthes's happy, meaningless, unisexual commingling of love and sexuality, they are also sufficiently pro-miscuous, sufficiently perverse, to do so.

There may well be another reason why Barthes is more inclined to displace the stereotypes of the femme, the mama's boy, and the aunt onto the lover than he is to displace the stereotype of the promiscuous homosexual. (Like Werther, Barthes's lover has only one beloved.) The femme, the mama's boy, and the aunt are all feminized males. The femme (the invert) has a female soul trapped in a male body, the mama's boy never reaches normal manhood, and the aunt is a mothered mother. According to phal-locentric discourse, such emasculations are disgusting. The pro-miscuous male homosexual, however, is not feminized at all. He is all man. Even though there are plenty of predicates for female profligates (slut, whore, harlot, tramp), none attach themselves to promiscuous gay men. Except, of course, in camp discourse. Pro-miscuity, moreover, is seen (again, by phallocentric discourse) as a male prerogative, which is why the predicates for male profligates (playboy, rake, libertine, lothario) tend, unlike their feminine counterparts, to be rather complimentary. Barthes, despite his purported contempt for all stereotypes, is loath to displace a stereotype that, from a certain gay male (i.e., phallocentric) perspective, does not seem all that negative. Barthes would like to believe that his deconstructive enterprise is indiscriminate: he thinks that "he systematically goes where there is . . . a stereotype [and] makes sure that . . . it doesn't *stick*. . . . it is a pure language tactic, which is deployed *in the air*, without any strategic horizon" (*Barthes by Barthes* 162). But in fact it is not. It is, in this instance, as in others, phallocentric.[26]

Whence the phallocentrism inherent in Barthes's complacent and confusing suggestion that a happy unisexual sexuality is really a happy *gay male* unisexual sexuality? Why does a man who wants to invent a world of neutral gender make that world phallic (cruisy and tricky)? Barthes offers one answer—"I must always choose between masculine and feminine, for the neuter and the dual are forbidden me" ("Inaugural Lecture" 460)—but it is evasive. If Barthes could have "chosen" to make his happy sexuality, like his lover, stereotypically feminine, why didn't he? Because, to cite one of Barthes's own axiomatic admissions: "*in what he writes, each protects his own sexuality*" (*Barthes by Barthes* 156). Each writer, that is, protects not the imaginary sexuality he might like to have, but the actual sexuality he does, in fact, already have. Barthes, of course, disproves this rule insofar as he fails to protect the feminine (and therefore undesirable) stereotypes that adhere to his homosexuality, displacing them, or at least trying to displace them, onto the unfashionable figure of the lover. However, he proves the rule insofar as he fails to relinquish, to write off, his identity as a manly gay man who cruises for tricks. This failure is, of course, quite startling in view of the fact that this identity has never made Barthes particularly happy ("I have a sad life") and will never fully comport with the insignificant sexuality for which he yearns. But it is not at all startling when one considers that cruising for tricks is such a butch (and therefore desirable) thing for Barthes to do. I have to wonder whether Barthes himself detected the irony in all this, for, by inscribing these phallocentric figures into his utopian eroticism, is Barthes not, indeed, "blinded as to [his] true sexuality, *because [he is] unwilling to let go of a stereotype*"?

An Atmosphere of Generalized Flirtation

As it turns out, there is a better figure for Barthes's utopian eroticism than either cruising or the trick—"flirtation" [*le flirt*]. Flirtation has many of the advantages of Barthes's figures and few of the disadvantages. People who flirt, like Barthesian men who cruise for tricks, invoke love without uttering the lover's discourse and provoke desire without getting caught in it. Their love and desire are truly virtual and evanescent. Flirtation, too, is perverse—multiple, excessive, and promiscuous. (We have a different word for nonperverse flirtation: courtship.) However, unlike Barthes's figures, flirtation nearly escapes stereotypology. "The flirt" is, of course, a stereotype, but flirtation does not connote the perpetual quest for one's type. Flirts flit. They are erratic as well as erotic. Nor does flirtation connote male homosexuality (even though it is promiscuous). Women flirt [*faire la coquette*] and men flirt [*conter fleurette*]. Gays flirt and straights flirt. Gays and straights even flirt with one another. Flirtation, in other words, is a remarkably insignificant and unisexual erotic practice and, as such, is a wonderful trope for the insignificant and unisexual eroticism Barthes envisions.[27]

But insignificance and unisexuality are not the only qualities that distinguish flirtation from Barthesian cruising and tricking. Unlike them, flirtation is also fun. Whereas cruising for tricks, at least for Barthes, is sad and desolate, as sad and desolate as love itself, flirting, like any good "perversion, quite simply, *makes happy*" (*Barthes by Barthes* 64). The flirt, unlike Barthesian men who cruise for tricks, never says "I love you" to people too dumbstruck to reply "I love you, too." Rather, s/he tells them, to quote this chapter's quintessentially flirtatious epigraph: "I think I *will be* falling in love with you" [*Je sens que je vais être amoureux de toi*]

(*Incidents* 42; emphasis added in translation). S/he never suggests "Your place or mine." Rather, s/he responds, to quote the epigraph once again: "Give me your address." The flirt, in other words, neither proffers nor emplaces love/sex. S/he defers and displaces it—until an unspecified future moment for which, although it may never occur, it is well worth waiting, for which in fact it is exhilarating to wait. Until, that is, a point in time analogous to that at which Barthes's utopian eroticism itself will, perhaps, arrive. And it is this delectably delayed bliss, this preorgasmic pleasure, that enables flirtation to represent, as well as any trope can, the delectably delayed bliss of a Barthesian commingling of love and sexuality.

Barthes's failure to deploy this insignificant, unisexual, and blissful trope is, not unlike his purported "affirmation" of love, discouraging. Relatively few people can identify with a cruisy and tricky utopian eroticism, but nearly everyone—women, men, gays, and straights—could identify with a flirtatious one. And it is particularly discouraging in light of the fact that flirtation is by no means alien to Barthes's image repertoire. Barthes knows that tricking involves flirting (that it can occur, as he puts it, in "an atmosphere . . . of generalized flirtation") and sees himself as an indefatigable flirt (Olivier represents only one of many unsuccessful "attempts at flirtation"). Such pronouncements, such flirtations with the trope of flirtation, raise an interesting, and complicated, question—one which I will pose but, flirt that I am, not answer (at least not here and not now): What makes Barthes, a feminist and deconstructive theorist, deploy problematic, phallocentric, and homocentric figurations when it should be easy for him to deploy a relatively unproblematic, nonphallocentric, and nonhomocentric one with which he is familiar? Yet even if flirtation *were* alien to Barthes's image repertoire, his failure to formulate a flirtatious eroticism would still raise two intriguing questions. First, if Barthes were a less closeted writer (he is "outed" by, and does not quite "come out" in, *Incidents*), if his autobiographical texts "protected his sexuality" in a more conventional (say, Gidean, as opposed to Proustian) way, would he still protect, and privilege, his homosexuality, or at least the butch aspect of his homosexuality, in his theoretical writings? (Caution no. 1: This distinction between Barthesian theory and autobiography is somewhat spurious. Caution no. 2: Barthes's French readers, for whom the homosexuality of a writer who, to cite one gay signifier among many, sees himself as Proust, goes without saying, find him far less closeted than do his American readers.) In other words, if there were no need for critics to bring Barthes out, would there be a need for me to take him to task in this fashion? The second question concerns the extent to which Barthes's homocentrism and phallocentrism are interrelated. Must Barthes, a gay (i.e., socially peripheral) subject, deploy phallic (i.e., symbolically central) figures in order to center himself discursively? In other words, is it enough to say, as Stanton does, that Barthes, like the rest of us, can't help but write within "a symbolic order that is paternal to the core" ("Mater" 61)? Is it not, perhaps, also true that he can't help but avail himself of the core paternal symbol, the phallus, in order to write anything about, to "protect," his own marginalized sexuality? Once again, this is neither the time nor the place to address these propositions.

Afterword

"I never wanted it to come out this way," said Escheal.
"Ah," said the countess, standing up; "the greatest
delusion of all. . . . "

Susan Fromberg Schaeffer, *Love*

It is, of course, hypocritical of me to disparage Barthes for pro-
tecting his sexuality when I've managed, with far less finesse, to
protect mine. I've protected my phallocentrism by focusing on
mannish lesbians, my femininity by focusing on womanish gay
men, my Eurocentrism by ignoring American writers, and my
postmodernity by trying to be queer. I've also protected aspects of
my sexuality from which I have little critical distance and of which
you, my attentive reader, are no doubt well aware. Nor could I
have done otherwise. If, like Barthes, I'm a gay writer who protects his sexuality, I am also, like Barthes, a gay reader who "reads
resistantly for inscriptions of his condition [and searches] for signs
of himself" (Koestenbaum 176–77). You may wish to do so as
well, to situate *your* self in a love story, to ask "what has love to do
with *my* sexuality?" If we are at all unlike, the answer will probably
surprise me.

REFERENCE MATTER

Notes

⌖

Introduction

1. See Gay 44; Polhemus 1.

2. See Miller, *Heroine's Text* 27, 56, 78, 98, 123–33; Gay 46, 77, 97; Polhemus 3, 79–136; Boone 191–96; Fiedler 62–73; Edwards 39, 58; DuPlessis 66.

3. See Singer 2: 6, 58, 166, 256, 289–95, 411–18, 435–42, 468–82.

4. Compare Tanner and Boone. See Gay 419.

5. See Boone 143: "the sex war becomes a central issue and image in the counter-traditional reevaluation of romantic and marital companionship."

6. See Boone 11.

7. Cf. Barthes, *Lover's Discourse* 226: "the story of the two halves trying to join themselves back together [is] a matter of supplements, not complements."

8. Both Tanner (72) and Polhemus (189) read the deaths of Maggie and Tom as a love-death.

9. These studies include Joseph A. Boone, *Tradition Counter Tradition: Love and the Form of Fiction*; Maria DiBattista, *First Love: The Affections of Modern Fiction*; Rachel Blau DuPlessis, *Writing Beyond the Ending: Narrative Strategies of Twentieth-Century Women Writers*; Lee R. Edwards, *Psyche As Hero: Female Heroism and Fictional Form*; Nancy K. Miller, *The Heroine's Text: Readings in the French and English Novel, 1722–1782*; Robert M. Polhemus, *Erotic Faith: Being in*

Love from Jane Austen to D. H. Lawrence; and Tony Tanner, *Adultery in the Novel: Contract and Transgression.*

10. DuPlessis defines "reparenting" as "a triangular plot of nurturance offered to an emergent daughter by a parental couple" (91).

11. For discussions of homoeroticism in Melville, see Martin 67–94; Sedgwick 91–130; Boone 241–66. See also Boone 24: "Gay and lesbian fiction forms another noncanonical tradition that may seem missing . . . from my counter-traditions. . . . Were this book's argument extended further into the twentieth century, the increasingly vocal role played by gay and lesbian writers, or by texts with homosexual themes, in attacking the dominant sexual ideology would necessarily form an important countercurrent."

12. See Chauncey 116; Foucault, *History of Sexuality* 37–38.

13. Literary erotics is not exclusively novelistic, of course, and the tropes of romantic love, it should be noted, often register differently in different literary genres. Complementary merger, for example, signifies differently in lyric poetry, with its aristocratic, Petrarchan heritage, than it does in the novel, with its bourgeois, Richardsonian one.

14. For a description of Freud's remarks on love, see Singer 3: 97–158.

15. See Kopelson 22: "the sad story of these two gay hedonists' paradoxical relationship to truth is the story of their metaphors, their metaphysics, of the ejaculation."

Chapter 1

1. See Weeks, *Sex, Politics* 22; Harvey 939, 947.

2. See Dellamora, *Masculine Desire* 21: "While the circle of Cambridge friends with whom Byron shared his sexual interest in males is too small to indicate the existence of a subculture, the printing of a text like *Don Leon* implies the existence of another such network, probably a number of them, and of contacts with potentially sympathetic members of other social groupings."

3. Quoted in Crompton 347. The references are to notorious scandals involving William Beckford, M.P. for Wells, the Hon. William Courtenay, afterwards Viscount Courtenay and Earl of Devon, and the Hon. Percy Jocelyn, bishop of Clogher.

4. My usage of the term "gay" in this text is frequently anachronistic insofar as the persons under consideration never referred to

themselves as "gay," but is nevertheless appropriate insofar as, like contemporary "gays" (and unlike contemporary "homosexuals") they *identified* themselves as a distinct "sexual" minority. See Weeks, *Sex, Politics* 111.

5. *Teleny: Or, The Reverse of the Medal: A Physiological Romance* is believed to be the work of Wilde and several of his friends, with Wilde serving as either primary author or general editor and coordinator.

6. For example, just as the "buggery" statute (as enforced) concerned homosexual sodomy and just as the Labouchère Amendment (1885) concerned homosexual "gross indecency," Victorian sexology continued to focus on homosexual sexual activity even after it had succeeded in turning the sodomitical "actor" into the homosexual "personage" (Foucault, *History of Sexuality* 43). Such, in part, were the structural constraints of a discipline devoted to identifying with increased specificity various forms of sexual behavior. When Krafft-Ebing's 1886 *Psychopathia Sexualis* was first translated into English in 1892, readers were warned that the newly nominated anomaly of "homo-sexuality" "is limited to the sexual life, and does not more deeply and seriously affect character and mental personality" (240). (This warning, which would seem to deny that the "homosexual" is a "personage" at all, attests to the fact that nineteenth-century sexology was no less dialogical, or polyvocal, than nineteenth-century literature.) Sexologists even problematized deviant sexual behavior as the most critical symptom of a pathological sexual "inversion" that connoted "a broad range of deviant gender behavior" (Chauncey 116), a problematization that enabled Havelock Ellis to distinguish between heterosexual cross-dressers and homosexual inverts.

7. See Foucault, *History of Sexuality* 101. See Dollimore, "Dominant and Deviant" 180–81.

8. On the other hand, early-twentieth-century lesbians, who confronted a dominant ideology that saw women as inherently passionless, had to *sexualize* the female homosexual. See Newton.

9. See Craft 84: the "topos of self-recognition via Platonic texts is . . . a staple in the cultural construction of nineteenth-century male homosexual subjectivity." Craft argues that an elegiac text such as Tennyson's *In Memoriam*, like Platonic texts, also helped embed "homosexuality" within an "ideal" spiritual register (it is "a virtual copy-text for the recognition and articulation of a homosexual desire

whose subjective effects were almost palpable in their intensity but whose distantiated object had always already been exiled to a realm beyond touch if not beyond the desire for touching" [98]).

10. Karl Heinrich Ulrichs based a cult of "Uranism" on Pausanias's praise of Uranian, or "heavenly," pederasty in Plato's *Symposium*. J. A. Symonds, in *A Problem in Greek Ethics* (1901), encouraged the view that "Dorian" love has nothing "sensual and lustful" about it (*Male Love* 30). And Edward Carpenter, in *The Intermediate Sex*, argued that "Uranian" men enjoy love "in one of its most perfect forms—a form in which . . . the sensuous element, though present, is exquisitely subordinated to the spiritual" (*Selected Writings* 198).

11. See Sedgwick 138: "The 'Hellenic ideal,' insofar as its reintegrative power is supposed to involve a healing of the culturewide ruptures involved in male homosexual panic, necessarily has that panic so deeply at the heart of its occasions, frameworks, demands, and evocations that it becomes not only inextricable from but even a propellant of the cognitive and ethical compartmentalizations of homophobic prohibition." See Sedgwick, *passim*, for distinctions between minoritizing and universalizing figurations of homosexuality.

12. Those straight minds need not have been more attuned to Continental than to British literature. Even though nineteenth-century Continental literature typically figures love as adulterous, whereas nineteenth-century British literature typically figures it as marital (and somewhat less typically as incestuous), the latter does evince "a sympathy and understanding with the adulterous violator that works to undermine [the law]" (Tanner 14).

13. See Polhemus 186–87 on how the problem of representing characters "making love without actually doing so" animates and disrupts many Victorian texts.

14. In part, ingrained preterition made "gay" sex inarticulable. The rhetoric of (and epistemology represented by) "the Love that dare not speak its name" (Fone 196 [from Lord Alfred Douglas's "Two Loves"]) was the product of centuries of bespeaking sodomitical conduct in terms of an unspeakable erotic negative: *nefandam libidinem*, "that sin which should be neither named nor committed" (Boswell 349 [from a legal document dated 533] and 380 [from a 1227 letter from Pope Honorious III]); the "detestable and abominable sin, amongst Christians not to be named," "things fearful to name,"

"the obscene sound of the unbeseeming words" (Bray 61 [from Edward Coke's *Institutes*] and 62 [from William Bradford's *Plimouth Plantation* and Guillaume Du Bartas's *Divine Weeks*]). By Wilde's day, such descriptions were commonplace and reflected a dominant ideology that enjoined homosexuality to "go without saying."

15. For contemporaneous interpretations of Isolde's death as orgasmic, see Gay 266–67.

16. Erskine describes their halcyon days in glowing, loving terms: "I was a year or two older than he was, but we were immense friends, and did all our work and all our play together. There was, of course, a good deal more play than work, but I cannot say that I am sorry for that. . . . I was absurdly devoted to him. . . . He certainly was wonderfully handsome. . . . I think he was the most splendid creature I ever saw" (Wilde, *Portrait* [1889] 144, 159, 139, 141–42).

17. See Dijkstra 396: Wilde's *Salomé* made Salomé "a household word for pernicious sexual perversity." Cf. Gilman 53: "if Salome is perverted, her perversion certainly has nothing to do with the representation of homosexuality on stage, but rather with the representation of a sexual hysteria and the source of her hysteria." See Chauncey 117: "The major current in Victorian sexual ideology declared that women were passionless and asexual, the passive objects of male sexual desire." For accounts of powerful countercurrents to the Victorian belief in female passionlessness, see Marcus and Poovey.

18. See Sedgwick, "The Beast in the Closet: James and the Writing of Homosexual Panic," in *Epistemology of the Closet,* for an account of homoeroticism and homosexual panic in nineteenth-century bachelor narratives.

19. All citations from *The Portrait of Mr. W.H.* are to the 1893 edition unless otherwise noted.

20. See Dellamora, "Representation" 79.

21. The Erskine/narrator relationship, like the Hughes/Shakespeare and Graham/Erskine relationships, is homoerotically charged. See W. A. Cohen 235.

22. See Lambert 134. Symonds treats Antinous in an essay in *Sketches in Italy and Greece* (1898) and in *A Problem in Greek Ethics.*

23. See Lambert, *passim.* Yourcenar's *Memoirs of Hadrian* is one such history.

24. See Winckelmann 1: 219–20. See Pater's "A Study of Diony-

sus" (1876) and "Denys l'Auxerrois" (1886). (In *Masculine Desire*, Richard Dellamora argues that these two works by Pater should be read as analyses of homophobia.)

25. See Symonds, *Male Love* 5: "In another but less prevalent Saga the introduction of paiderastia is ascribed to Orpheus."

26. "Phobic enchantment" is Peter Stallybrass and Allon White's term for the simultaneous repugnance and fascination attendant upon self-delineation by a dominant culture whose political imperative to reject and eliminate a debased and debasing other "conflicts powerfully and unpredictably with a desire for this Other" (4).

27. See Bataille, *Trial* 202: according to court records, Gilles de Rais was convicted of "committing and maliciously perpetrating the crime and unnatural vice of sodomy on children of both sexes."

28. Wilde misremembers his Dante. Malebolge is the circle of hell to which the fraudulent and malicious are condemned. Sodomites are condemned to circle 7, round 3 (the violent against nature), and murderers are condemned to circle 7, round 1 (the violent against neighbors).

29. See MacDonald 84; Bartel. Magazine articles on the subject began appearing in the early 1880's, and by 1893 newspapers were issuing regular reports on the current suicide "epidemic" and regular warnings that matters would get worse; see Gates 152. Rumors of "suicide clubs," of small groups of people who planned to kill themselves simultaneously, circulated widely and were taken very seriously; see Stokes 130. More and more young, urban would-be bohemians shot themselves in the head, committing and attempting suicides that were labelled "Ibsene," and more and more aesthetes, quoting *Hedda Gabler*, rhapsodized about "this beautiful act." There was even a short-lived aesthetic suicide "cult"; see Anderson 369, 242, 245.

30. See Hyde 136.

31. Although it managed to avoid the epidemic of "Wertherism" that swept Europe in the late eighteenth and early nineteenth centuries, England does not seem to have become wholly immune to the *Werther* virus until the twentieth century. This may be because of the potency of the initial infection, which occurred on the heels of Thomas Chatterton's legendary suicide. No fewer than seven English translations of *Werther* appeared between 1779 and 1809. Shortly after a new translation appeared in 1854, Wertherism reemerged as a distinctive feature of the enormously popular sensation novels of the

1860's. The 1890's were believed to have been characterized by a "new" Wertherism. See Long 172.

32. See Anderson 242.

33. See Gates 131.

34. See Showalter.

35. The *Westminster Gazette*, May 27, 1895, wrote of Wilde's disgrace that "in view of recent events, Nordau's summing up of his case against Oscar Wilde as the typical English 'decadent' comes with all the force of a fulfilled prophecy." (Max Nordau was the notorious author of *Degeneration* [1895].) The suicide "craze" of the 1890's was widely held to be indicative of the new generation's degeneracy. See Anderson 243–44.

36. From the 1850's and 1860's on, advocates of psychological medicine believed that suicides were nearly always mentally ill. See Anderson 385; MacDonald 85.

37. Weeks, "Inverts" 205.

38. In the novel's original version, Teleny's final, explicatory words are "Your mother . . . debts" (181). A later version recasts his suicidal motive by making his dying declaration "Bryancourt . . . letter" (174; ellipses in original for both quotes). For some readers, then, Teleny's death may not have been quite so pointless.

39. See E. Cohen 810.

40. See Sedgwick 87–90.

Chapter 2

1. *Si le grain ne meurt* had been published privately in 1920 but, like *Cardinal Pirelli*, was first released commercially in 1926.

2. See Dollimore, "Different Desires" 54–55: when Gide published "the controversial commercial edition of *If It Die*, which . . . contained, for that time, astonishingly explicit accounts of his homosexuality, [he was] savagely castigated." Brentano's rejected *Cardinal Pirelli* for publication in the United States on "religious and moral grounds" and feared that the "outspokenness of the book regarding the life of the Cardinal" would alienate its bookstore clientele (C. J. Herold to Firbank, June 18, 1925, quoted in Benkovitz 274–76).

3. See Ellmann 4.

4. See Lucey 180: "*dénuement* . . . might apply as much to a homoerotic gaze as to a peeling off of worldly goods." See Pollard 346: for Gide, the veil is "a symbol of puritan restraint." See Apter, "Ho-

motextual Counter-Codes" 79: Gide casts off clothes "like the tenets of middle-class morality."

5. See Lucey 186.

6. See *Cardinal Pirelli* 305 (ellipsis in original):

> "A lover; what? His Eminence . . . ??"
> The duchess tittered.
> "Why not? I expect he has a little woman to whom he takes off his clothes," she murmured, turning to admire the wondrous *Madonna of the Mule-mill* attributed to Murillo.

7. See *Cardinal Pirelli* 294:

> "I trust the choir-boys, Dame, are all in health?"
> "Ah, Don Alvaro, no sir!" . . .
> "To-morrow, all well, I'll take them some melons."
> "Ah, Don, Don!!"
> "And, perhaps, a cucumber," the Cardinal added.

8. See Brophy 566 for a creative interpretation that reflects Firbank's own initial ambivalence: "Stripped, by the ardence of his pursuit and the jutting bits of the monuments he dodges and clambers over, of all his clothes except his mitre."

9. This is Firbank's variation on the Wilde epigram: "I have nothing to declare except my genius" (Harris 75). See Brophy 566. Pirelli has forgotten that he had also packed "a flask of Napolean brandy, to be 'declared'" (334).

10. Either the *Index Librorum Prohibitorum* or the *Index Expurgatorius.*

11. The phrase is an adaption of Dante's "selva oscura" (dark wood).

12. See Dollimore, *Sexual Dissidence* 3–35 for an extended comparison of Gidean essentialism and Wildean anti-essentialism. As Dollimore demonstrates, "for Gide transgression is in the name of a desire and identity rooted in the natural, the sincere, and the authentic; Wilde's transgressive aesthetic is the reverse: insincerity, inauthenticity, and unnaturalness become the liberating attributes of decentred identity and desire" (14).

13. In a second letter to Valéry, also written in 1891, Gide states: "since Wilde, I hardly exist anymore" (Mallet 92).

14. Compare: "But with me . . . Wilde had now thrown aside his mask. It was the man himself I saw at last" (*If It Die* 279–80). Com-

pare also: "I don't know which of us was more of an actor; but a sincere actor, after all, for each one was acting out his own character" ("Notes on Oscar Wilde," quoted in Delay 291).

15. See Brophy *passim*.

16. According to Firbank's own discrepant accounts, *The Artificial Princess* was written in either 1906 or 1910 (Brophy 105).

17. André Walter's dream recalls Saint-Preux's nightmare vision of Julie's "impenetrable veil" in Rousseau's *La Nouvelle Héloise*: "I recognized her although her face was covered with a veil. I gave a shriek, I rushed forward to put aside the veil, I could not reach it, I stretched both my arms. I tormented myself, but touched nothing. 'Friend be calm,' she said to me in a faint voice. 'The terrible veil covers me. No hand can put it aside'" (365).

18. It may be that Firbank fashioned Pirelli's "fabulous mitre" after one of Lytton Strachey's. The Cardinal Manning section of *Eminent Victorians* (1918) concludes: "The Cardinal's memory is a dim thing to-day. And he who descends into the crypt of that Cathedral which Manning never lived to see, will observe, in the quiet niche with the sepulchral monument, that the dust lies thick on *the strange, the incongruous, the almost impossible object* which, with its elaboration of dependent tassels, hangs down from the dim vault like some forlorn and forgotten trophy—the Hat" (130; emphasis added).

19. According to Gide, the pederastic subject should be at least three years older than his beloved, who should be between 13 and 22; see Pollard 16, 29.

20. See Lucey 188: for Gide, "first came the pastoral stage where sex was 'face à face' . . . then came consumerism, dandyism, colonialism, decadence, differentiation, and sodomy"; see also Dollimore, *Sexual Dissidence*, 340: "the precondition for [Gidean] pastoral sublimity is the loss of history."

21. Douglas has already identified himself to Gide as such: "I hope you are like me. I have a horror of women. I only like boys" (*If It Die* 279).

22. "I suddenly fell in love—yes, positively in love!—with a small boy a little older than myself. . . . He was dressed as an imp or a clown, that is, his slender figure was perfectly moulded in black tights covered with steel spangles" (*If It Die* 70).

23. Earlier that year, Firbank had written his mother that he had seen in Cézanne's studio a drawing of child to whom he could pray

(letter to Lady Harriette Jane Garrett Firbank, Sept. 6, 1920, quoted in Benkovitz 277).

24. See Benkovitz 241.

25. Nina Hamnett, undated document written at request of Richard Buckle, quoted in Benkovitz 242.

26. Firbank to Carl Van Vechten, Dec. 16, 1924, quoted in Benkovitz 267.

27. Jean Delay, Gide's "psychobiographer," takes vigorous exception to Gide's self-conception. According to Delay, Gide "desired boys he did not love" (474). He even omits Gide's reference to love in this passage from *If It Die* in order to sustain the thesis that "Love had no part in that fundamental experience" (395). Brigid Brophy, one of Firbank's biographers, also maintains that her subject "excluded love from his life" (518).

28. Compare Firbank's "True Love" (1903), in which the consumptive protagonist takes "a bunch of blue and white violets" his mistress has dropped, kisses it and whispers, "She and me" (9).

29. See Pollard 46: Gide was an early advocate of Schopenhauer's conception of love as the mutual attraction of opposites.

30. Cf. Lucey 182: politics simply has a way of "writing itself into [*If It Die*] even as it is being effaced."

31. The "M." referred to in this passage is probably Marc Allégret; see O'Brien 265.

32. See Pollard 230.

33. One anti-amorous lyric ("I am disgusted with Love. / I find it exceedingly disappointing, / Mine is a nature that cries for more ethereal things, / Banal passions fail to stir me. / I am disgusted with Love," or some variation thereof) recurs in nonpederastic contexts with notable frequency: once in *The Artificial Princess* (277) and twice in *Vainglory* (90, 151–52).

34. This incapacity helps explain Gide's odd identification with the hero of Stendhal's *Armance*, who, although heterosexual, is at the same loss for words: "when I am surrounded by fishermen's sons and I watch them swimming, I involuntarily think of Octave" ("Voyage en Bretagne" [1889], quoted in Pollard 210).

35. Not every literary pederast is quite so power-crazed. As Charles Nantwich, a character in Hollinghurst's *The Swimming-Pool Library*, remarks: "being senior I had power, which I could use over [the younger boys] & then luxuriously abdicate in making my feelings clear" (131).

36. See *Cardinal Pirelli* 338:

"Oh, tral-a-la, sir." Laughing like some wild spirit, the lad leapt (Don Venturesome, Don Venturesome, his Eminence trembled) from the ledge of A Virtuous Wife and Mother (Sarmento, *née* Tizzi-Azza) to the urn of Ivy, the American marchioness.

"You'd not do that if you were fond of me, boy!" The Cardinal's cheek had paled.

"But I *am* fond of you, sir! Very. Caring without caring: don't you know?"

37. See Freud, "On Narcissism: An Introduction" (1914), *Standard Edition* 14: 73–102; "The Libido Theory and Narcissism" (1916), *Standard Edition* 16: 412–30; "On Transformations of Instinct as Exemplified in Anal Erotism" (1916), *Standard Edition* 17: 125–34.

38. Isidore Sadger, for example, believed that the road to homosexuality passes over narcissism. For Sandor Ferenczi, narcissism was the sole distinguishing feature of homosexual object choice: "Homosexuals are only more strongly fixed than other people in the narcissistic stage; the genital organ similar to their own remains throughout life as an essential condition for their love" (298). Felix Boehm based a nosology of homosexuality on whether a narcissistic stage is achieved, regressed to, or reactivated.

39. See Hocquenghem 66–67.

40. See Warner 201–2: "the equation between homosexuality and narcissism in psychoanalysis [is] designed for a heterosexist self-understanding [that] disguises from itself its own ego erotics [its own narcissism]."

41. Gide does not appear to have read Freud until 1921. He was, however, well aware of the figuration. See Pollard 88–109.

42. See Irigaray, "Any Theory of the Subject Has Already Been Appropriated by the 'Masculine,'" in *Speculum*. See also Warner 190; "the modern system of sex and gender would not be possible without a disposition to interpret the difference between genders as the difference between self and Other."

43. It may well be easier for pederasts to resist this notion than it is for homosexuals. See Sedgwick 159–60: "The *homo-* in the emerging concept of the homosexual seems to have the potential to perform a definitive de-differentiation—setting up a permanent avenue of potential slippage—between two sets of relations that had previously been seen as relatively distinct: identification and desire. It is

with *homo*-style homosexuality, and *not* with inversion, pederasty, or sodomy (least of all, of course, with cross-gender sexuality) that an erotic discourse comes into existence that makes available a continuing possibility for symbolizing slippages between identification and desire. . . . Initiating, along with the stigma of narcissism, the utopic modern vision of a strictly egalitarian bond guaranteed by the exclusion of any consequential difference, the new calculus of homo/hetero . . . owes its sleekly utilitarian feel to the linguistically unappealable classification of anyone who shares one's gender as being 'the same' as oneself, and anyone who does not share one's gender as being one's Other."

44. "I am disgusted with Love. . . . Mine is a nature that cries for more *ethereal* things" (*Vainglory* 90; emphasis added). "I am disgusted with Love. . . . Mine is a nature that craves for more *elusive* things" (*The Artificial Princess* 277; emphasis added).

45. Conversation with Léon Pierre-Quint, quoted in Pollard 394: "Jealousy is a feeling which is only experienced violently in a strong heterosexual love: it is the hatred of the male for the male. In other love jealousy is of a quite different nature, and I think it is much more rare."

Chapter 3

1. *Orlando*'s closet has been unlocked quite recently; see Glendinning and Knopp.

2. I somewhat shamelessly—but not, I think, unrigorously—conflate the terms "living," "being," and "identity" in this chapter. In doing so, I am merely accepting and reflecting (although not necessarily condoning) the refusal of Woolf and Stein to draw distinctions among these terms—naive or inspired as that refusal may seem to some.

3. Chodorow asserts that pre-Oedipal issues persist in daughters and not sons because gender identification with the mother makes total separation impossible.

4. Cf. DuPlessis 167: Woolf's " 'I' rejected; 'we' substituted" represents a turn toward "the communal protagonist," for which "the fluid ego boundaries of the preoedipal bond are one source."

5. See Abel 415: "Lily Briscoe's (unfulfilled) desire in *To the Lighthouse* to merge with . . . Mrs. Ramsay demonstrates" that Cicero's description of friendship "as a mingling of souls . . . characterizes the

dynamics of female friendship more accurately than male"; and see Kahane 74: Woolf "repeatedly . . . seeks the subject-self in and through perceptual objects, and indicates the genesis of that quest in a desire for unity with a mother conceived as the source of plenitude, for a merger which destroys otherness and absence, though it necessarily destroys the self as well." See also Rosenman.

6. See Kahane 78.

7. See Chessman 54–76 for a related analysis of the "doubleness inherent in and essential to [Stein's conception of] identity" (56).

8. Woolf's remark is a reference to a letter obviously meant for Sackville-West but addressed to "Miss Virginia Woolf."

9. Weil is referring primarily to the exchange: "'You're a woman, Shel!' she cried. 'You're a man, Orlando!' he cried" (*Orlando* 227).

10. According to Souhami (119) Stein believed that to call someone by the wrong name is to deny their identity.

11. See Woolf, *To the Lighthouse* 300: "to feel simply that's a table, that's a chair, and yet at the same time, it's a miracle, it's an ecstasy." Cf. DuPlessis 61, 97; for DuPlessis, who reads words like "life" and "being" vocationally and not ontologically, *To the Lighthouse* and *Orlando* combine romance and "quest" narratives.

12. See Glendinning 203.

13. See Chessman 65: for Stein, "dialogue [is] a metaphor for a certain form of relationship, where two 'ones' may be distinguished, yet where the boundaries may also become confused and even disappear."

14. See Souhami 96.

15. See DuPlessis: "*Orlando* shows that one can have the erotic without the intense and repressive form of gender polarization upon which the romance plot has traditionally been built" (61) and "The bond Clarissa and Sally make is, like the party, a network of pleasurable connections; the bond between Miss Kilman and Elizabeth is, like heterosexual thralldom, another form of bullying. If lesbianism is a nondominant form of the erotic, Woolf valorizes it; if it is yet another version of power and dominance, she satirizes it" (59).

16. See Souhami *passim*.

17. Note that Girard reduces the subject-Other-object triad to the subject-other dyad anyway: "the desiring subject wants to become his mediator" (54). Note, too, that an Althusserian account of trian-

gulated desire would, drawing on Lacan, denominate the three parties "subject," "Subject," and "other."

18. Cf. Herrmann 6: Woolf recognizes "the other not as an object but as 'an/other' subject."

19. This did not prevent Sackville-West from being "horribly, murderously jealous" herself, when the occasion demanded it (Glendinning 147, quoting a letter of Nov. 5, 1925, to Harold Nicolson).

20. On the other hand, Woolf could tolerate male infidelity, having learned quite early from her sexually abusive half-brothers that men change partners at will. See DeSalvo.

21. The quote was related to Dydo by Leon Katz in an interview.

22. The Stein-Bookstaver affair lasted from 1901 to 1903, while Stein was attending medical school. Stein's more successful rival was Mabel Haynes. For a detailed commentary on the affair, see Leon Katz's introduction to *Fernhurst, Q.E.D. and Other Early Writings.* See also Souhami 54–57.

23. Hemingway's memory is probably faulty. It is quite unlikely, for example, that Stein thought of Natalie Barney, one of her more promiscuous friends, as "repulsive" and "vicious." See Souhami 160.

24. See Nicolson 202: *Orlando* is "the longest and most charming love letter in literature."

25. In the manuscript and first typescript (Dydo 11).

26. Cf. Tanner 363: any "crisis in marriage is . . . , not by metaphor but by identity, a crisis in language."

27. See Polhemus 154: Victorians considered the heart "the official organ of love." Cf. Barthes, *S/Z*: " 'Heart' can only designate the sexual organ" (116); "the 'heart' designates the very thing removed from the castrato" (170).

28. Cf. Polhemus. *Lady Chatterley's Lover*, published in the same year as *Orlando*, concludes with an enheartened phallus: the line "John Thomas says good night to Lady Jane, a little droopingly, but with a hopeful heart" represents a "cock [that] may sometimes droop, but [that] talks and . . . even possesses a Victorian heart" (280).

29. Note, too, that the manuscript of *The Autobiography* tells a similar story. There, the passage continues "When we return to Paris this autumn I will read it" (Collection of American Literature, Beinecke Rare Book and Manuscript Library, Yale University; hereafter cited as YCAL)—a line crossed out in red by Toklas. Stein wants to displace Toklas's present full knowledge of the manuscript to a future

moment that may never arrive, whereas Toklas is unwilling to acknowledge, or to have Stein acknowledge for her, that she aspires to such full knowledge.

30. One of the more amusing sections of *The Autobiography* manuscript reveals what typing Stein's texts may have *actually* done to Toklas. The original version of the line "It [*The Making of Americans*] was over a thousand pages long and I was typewriting it" (113) reads: "It was over a thousand pages long and I was typewriting it *and I enjoyed every minute of it*" (YCAL; emphasis added). Toklas's red redaction of this final clause suggests that she found the unreaderly task quite unpleasurable.

31. According to Max White (as quoted in Souhami 267), who refused to collaborate with her, Toklas does prevaricate in *What Is Remembered*: "All she can do is lie and deny it and contradict herself." However, given the many congruities of *What Is Remembered* and *The Autobiography*, it is hard to believe, as White does, that Toklas simply "couldn't remember her memories."

32. Cf. Tanner 13: the adulterous woman is "a paradoxical presence of negativity within the social structure, her virtual nonbeing offering a constant implicit threat to the being of society."

Chapter 4

1. Most historical novels eroticize the past. See Polhemus 56: "Scott's most popular 'conception' as a novelist was to marry history . . . to the love story. Fusing private romantic experience with epic matter of the Scots and other peoples, he created and institutionalized 'the historical novel.'"

2. The bracketed material supplements Goldhammer's translation. Yourcenar's original response is: "Non, je suis loin d'être doué de ces qualités exceptionnelles et l'autre non plus, probablement; rendons-nous compte de ce qui est; aimons ce qui est" (*Yeux ouvertes* 76).

3. Nancy K. Miller sees this dissent as essentially feminist, if not lesbian. The Princess of Clèves's celebrated "refusal of love," for example, belongs to a novelistic tradition that abjures "an ideal of love, suffering, and conformity to female plot" and that may well require "an outside to heterosexual economies" (*Subject to Change* 10).

4. See Gay 55: "Romantic love naturally participates in this enthusiastic vision, at once a foundation and demonstration of its force."

5. When Orlando becomes female, she finds that "the obscurity, which divides the sexes . . . was removed" and that "at last . . . she knew Sasha as she was" (*Orlando* 147). In the Preface to *Alexis* (1929), Yourcenar explains her failure to compose a response from Monique that would "give us a less idealized but more complete image of this young woman" by claiming: "Nothing is more secret than a woman's existence" (xiii). If Yourcenar really believes this to be true, it would help explain why she, like Renault, prefers male subjects.

6. Although Renault was born in London and lived in South Africa, her contestation of crystallization is not extraordinary. Many British novelists, including Dickens, wrestle with this Continental figure; see Polhemus 45, 148.

7. See, e.g., Edwards 210: "The coalescence between Janie and Phoebe replaces in [Zora Neale Hurston's *Their Eyes Were Watching God*], as Sula and Nel's does in [Toni] Morrison's [*Sula*], the older model of relationship through complementarity and contrast manifest even in Janie's most successful relationship to a man."

8. See Boone 59–60: companionate marriage in Anglo-American literature tends to be hierarchical: "equal but not equal"; see also Edwards 298–99 n.1: although "friendships may include both sexes and need not exclude heterosexuality, [it is] difficult to represent an ideal mutuality in terms of a structure as ingrown with hierarchical assumption as marriage has been within our culture."

9. Although Yourcenar and Renault—like Woolf, who can't find "the line between friendship and perversion" (*Letters* 4: 200 [Aug. 15, 1930]), and Sedgwick, who can't find the line between homosociality and homosexuality—detect the structural instability of this paradigm, they assume their readers do not.

10. Both Yourcenar and Renault are averse to contemporary identity politics and appreciate the fact that premodern characters like Zeno cannot be construed as essentially homosexual. See Renault's "Afterword" to *The Friendly Young Ladies* 283: "Congregated homosexuals are really not conducive to a goodnatured 'Vive la différence!' Certainly they will not bring back the tolerant individualism of Macedon or Athens, where they would have attracted as much amazement as demonstrations of persons willing to drink wine. Distinguished homosexuals like Solon, Epaminondas or Plato would have withdrawn the hem of their garments; Alexander and his friends would have dined out on the joke. Greeks asked what a man was

good for; and the Greeks were right. People who do not consider themselves to be, primarily, human beings among their fellow-humans, deserve to be discriminated against, and ought not to make a meal of it."

11. See Halperin 55.

12. The terms *erastes* and *eromenos* refer to the senior and junior partners in a pederastic relationship.

13. See also Renault, *Nature of Alexander* 160.

14. See Halperin 11. My description of the "hero/pal" paradigm is taken from Halperin.

15. See Halperin 79: "it is not too much to say that death is to [heroic] friendship what marriage is to romance."

16. See Halperin 77–78.

17. See Boone 372 n.47: "The problem of presenting sexual passion within an equal comradeship without threatening its dynamic is one from which" a number of counter-traditional novelists shy away.

18. Renault, no doubt, would reject Dick's sexless reading of *Purposes of Love*. See her "Afterword" to *The Friendly Young Ladies* 283: "I have sometimes been asked whether I would have written [*The Friendly Young Ladies*] more explicitly in a more permissive decade. No. . . . If characters have come to life, one should know how they will make love; if not it doesn't matter. Inch-by-inch physical descriptions are the ketchup of the literary cuisine, only required by the insipid dish or by the diner without a palate." In *The Charioteer*, Renault argues that Ralph's sexual love for Laurie is preferable to Andrew's asexual attachment.

19. Renault's heterosexual solution is rather contemporary. Nineteenth-century novels about companionate marriage tend to castrate men, and not to phallicize women. This is true, for example, of Rochester in *Jane Eyre*, Casaubon in *Middlemarch*, and Knightly in *Emma*. See Edwards 102: "the diminution of male energies restores parity between the male and female characters . . . even as it expresses a kind of vengeance that the authors exercise on behalf of their women characters against their male counterparts."

20. Renault makes this acknowledgment in a self-critique of the happy, friendly, and sexual conjunction of Leonora and Joe in her Afterword to *The Friendly Young Ladies* 281: "On re-reading this forty-year-old novel for the first time in about twenty years, what struck me most was the silliness of the ending. Leo and Joe have both

been credited with reasonably good intelligence. He at least, the brighter of the two, would surely have had sense enough . . . to steer them clear of such inevitable disaster. Sexual harmony apart, one cannot contemplate without a shudder their domestic life. . . . Of course, more doomed and irresponsible unions happen in real life every day; but it is naive to present them as happy endings."

21. In addition to these related reconciliations of the polarization-depolarization problem, both Yourcenar and Renault also rely on a trope that could be called "transracination." In *Coup de Grâce*, Erick points out that whereas Conrad "was Balt with some Russian ancestry; I was Prussian with French and Baltic blood in my veins, so we cut across two neighboring nationalities" (10). In *The Persian Boy*, Renault argues that the overtly sexual relationship of Alexander and Bagoas, which, although never heroic, is not altogether unfriendly, inverts their diacritically related racial statuses. It turns Alexander, the Greek master of a Persian slave, into a Persian, and Bagoas, the Persian slave of a Greek master, into a Greek. Bagoas, in whom "all that was Persian [has rotted] away" (115), claims to have made a Persian of Alexander (157), who himself admits to having been "Persianized" (304). (In *The Nature of Alexander*, Renault calls Alexander "*déraciné*" [11].) This inversion unsettles, although it does not demolish, the reader's certainty that Alexander is the dominant partner in this friendly pederastic affair.

22. The woman Hadrian is referring to here is Plotina, the wife of Trajan. Plotina is Hadrian's "sole friend among women" (*Hadrian* 166). Yourcenar also notes with approval that their relationship was reputed to have been an "'amorous friendship,' to quote verbatim from one of the ancient chronicles" (*Open Eyes* 226).

23. Yourcenar notes that *Fires* is "the product of a love crisis" ("Preface" ix). *Memoirs of Hadrian*, on the other hand, is the product of "the perpetual search for, or presence of, love" ("Reflections," *Hadrian* 325).

Chapter 5

1. Many feminists are "seduced" by Barthes's valorization of the body and its pleasures, and in particular of *jouissance*, and by his marginal stance: "even at his most doctrinaire, Barthes's voice is never strident; [his] is a voice whose grain reveals vulnerability [and that aligns itself] with the excluded of the bourgeois social order, with all those who resist ordering" (Schor 48).

2. See Hermann 16–18. See also Schor 49: "Barthes's discourse of indifferentiation ends up re-essentializing woman and/or denying her specificity altogether."

3. See Ungar 115.

4. Notwithstanding its titular ambiguity, *Fragments d'un discours amoureux* concerns a single lover constituted by multiple discourses, not a single discourse constituted by multiple lovers.

5. Peter Gay, who finds that "Proust made his homosexuals, male or female, *singularly* joyless" (200; emphasis added), is another such reader.

6. See Smyth 272: "The wandering or interruption of the binary couple also occurs, more or less benignly, as a (more or less provisional, temporary, staged) reversal of roles or positions, as in Kierkegaard's description of courtship and the 'feminization' of the philosophical knight, or even, perhaps, in certain of Socrates' more harmonious relationships, in which he assumes the role of the beloved. . . . Schlegel's *Lucinde* may be said to participate in a comparable utopia in that it offers a scene of *coitus*, in which masculine and feminine positions are reversed."

7. As Stephen Heath notes, such pronouncements prove that the Barthesian lover is male: "can the notion of 'subjects in whom there is something feminine' be anything other than a *masculine* conception?" (105).

8. See Rivers 2–8.

9. See Stanton, "Mater" 69: "the suffering and anguish associated with maternal absence permeates most of the figures and phrases of love in *Fragments*"; and see Kritzman 112: "[Barthes] stages the lover's discourse as a catastrophic theatrical event characterized by the nostalgia for a lost maternal plenitude manifested as the projection of nothingness."

10. The quotation marks around "Barthes" are meant to problematize the identification of Barthes as the subject of his autobiographical texts. But cf. Stanton, "Mater" 60, who sees the Barthesian father as "an unproblematic absence."

11. See Beaver 116.

12. See Kritzman 111: "in *A Lover's Discourse* . . . Barthes conceptualizes the discourse of love as separate from sexuality."

13. See Kritzman 106–7, 109: for Barthes, "passionate romantic love . . . reflects the desire for a primary relationship of narcissistic wholeness in which the other and the one are the same without at-

tributes recognizable as either specifically masculine or feminine";
similarly, his "idea of a 'happy sexuality' can only become possible
when sexual difference is disavowed."

14. Barthes upholds Blanchot's association of the neuter and *signifiance* in *Writing Degree Zero; Sade, Fourier, Loyola; The Pleasure of
the Text;* and *Roland Barthes by Roland Barthes.*

15. See Kritzman 110: Barthes "coupl[es] the erotic and semiotic in
the figure of the neuter [in order to produce] a radical signifying
practice that challenges both closure in gender (i.e., the institution of
heterosexuality) and in language."

16. See Culler 112–13: "To bring back the sentimentality of ordi-
nary love, [Barthes] suggests, is a transgression of transgression, a vi-
olation of the orthodoxy that values radical transgression."

17. See *Lover's Discourse* 84: "the transgressive force of love-as-
passion: the assumption of sentimentality as alien strength."

18. Barthes's reference is to Vico's spiral, along which the past re-
turns—elsewhere; see *Grain of the Voice* 282.

19. A literal translation of *la drague* (from *draguer*) might be "trol-
ling." Barthes, however, is aware of, and deploys, the nautical con-
notation of its English equivalent. "Woman is faithful (she waits),
man is fickle (he sails away, he cruises [*il navigue, il drague*])" (*LD* 14;
Fragments 20).

20. "The system is a whole in which everyone has his place (even
if it is not a good place); husbands and wives, lovers, trios, marginal
figures as well (drugs, cruising), nicely installed in their marginality:
everyone except me" (*LD* 45).

21. See *Pleasure of the Text* 43: "The stereotype is this nauseating
impossibility of dying."

22. For Barthes, spontaneity is "the great dream: paradise, power,
delight" (*LD* 63).

23. See Heath 104: "The lover is a solitude, modestly marginal.
Barthes will affirm, take up that solitude—its discourse, its imaginary—as *value.*"

24. As Barthes is no doubt aware, the speaker of these lines by
Heine is male, as is the subject of *Dichterliebe,* the song cycle in
which they are set to music by Schumann. The full text is: "When I
look into your eyes, all my sorrow and pain disappear; but when I
kiss your lips, I regain my health totally. When I lean upon your
breast, I get a feeling of heavenly pleasure; but when you say 'I love
you,' I have to weep bitterly" (my translation).

25. In looking for any such meaning, I am disregarding Barthes's suggestion that *Incidents* (or some projected book very much like it) "report[s] a thousand 'incidents' but . . . refuse[s] ever to draw a line of meaning from them" (*Barthes by Barthes* 151).

26. Cf. Bersani 220: the process by which "the phallocentrism of gay cruising becomes diversity and pluralism [and] representation is displaced from the concrete practice of fellatio and sodomy to the melancholy charms of erotic memories and the cerebral tensions of courtship" is part of "what might be called a frenzied epic of displacements in the discourse on sexuality and on AIDS."

27. The unisexuality of flirtation is fairly modern. In the nineteenth and early twentieth centuries, flirtation was seen as an effeminate practice typical of women and gay men; see Kaye.

Works Cited

Abel, Elizabeth. "(E)Merging Identities: The Dynamics of Female Friendship in Contemporary Fiction by Women." *Signs* 6, no. 3 (Spring 1981): 413–35.

Anderson, Olive. *Suicide in Victorian and Edwardian England.* Oxford: Clarendon, 1987.

Apter, Emily S. *André Gide and the Codes of Homotextuality.* Saratoga, Calif.: ANMA Libri, 1987.

———. "Homotextual Counter-Codes: André Gide and the Poetics of Engagement." *Michigan Romance Studies* 6 (1986): 75–87.

Arnold, Matthew. *Poetry and Criticism of Matthew Arnold.* Riverside Edition. Ed. A. Dwight Culler. Boston: Houghton Mifflin, 1961.

Bartel, Roland. "Suicide in Eighteenth-Century England: The Myth of a Reputation." *Huntington Library Quarterly* 23 (1960): 145–58.

Barthes, Roland. *Camera Lucida: Reflections on Photography.* Trans. Richard Howard. New York: Hill & Wang, 1981.

———. *Elements of Semiology.* New York: Hill & Wang, 1985.

———. *Fragments d'un discours amoureux.* Paris: Seuil, 1977.

———. *The Grain of the Voice: Interviews 1962–1980.* Trans. Linda Coverdale. New York: Hill & Wang, 1985.

———. "Inaugural Lecture, Collège de France." In *A Barthes Reader.* Ed. Susan Sontag. Trans. Richard Howard. New York: Hill & Wang, 1982.

———. *Incidents.* Paris: Seuil, 1987.

————. *A Lover's Discourse: Fragments.* Trans. Richard Howard. New York: Hill & Wang, 1978.

————. "Loving Schumann." In *The Responsibility of Forms.* Trans. Richard Howard. New York: Hill & Wang, 1985.

————. *The Pleasure of the Text.* Trans. Richard Miller. New York: Hill & Wang, 1975.

————. "Preface to Renaud Camus's *Tricks.*" In *The Rustle of Language.* Trans. Richard Howard. New York: Hill & Wang, 1986.

————. *Roland Barthes by Roland Barthes.* Trans. Richard Howard. New York: Hill & Wang, 1977.

————. *Roland Barthes par Roland Barthes.* Paris: Seuil, 1975.

————. "The Romantic Song." In *The Responsibility of Forms.* Trans. Richard Howard. New York: Hill & Wang, 1985.

————. *Sade, Fourier, Loyola.* Trans. Richard Miller. New York: Hill & Wang, 1976.

————. *S/Z.* Trans. Richard Miller. New York: Hill & Wang, 1974.

Bataille, Georges. *Literature and Evil.* Trans. Alastair Hamilton. New York: Urizen, 1981.

————. *The Trial of Gilles de Rais.* Trans. Richard Robinson. Los Angeles: Amok, 1991.

Beaver, Harold. "Homosexual Signs (In Memory of Roland Barthes)." *Critical Inquiry* 8, no. 1 (Autumn 1981): 99–119.

Benkovitz, Miriam. *Ronald Firbank: A Biography.* New York: Knopf, 1969.

Berry, Ellen E. "On Reading Gertrude Stein." *Genders* 5 (Summer 1989): 1–20.

Bersani, Leo. "Is the Rectum a Grave?" *October* 43 (Winter 1987): 197–222.

Boehm, Felix. "Beträge zur Psychologie der Homosexualität IV: Über zwei Typen von Männlichen Homosexuellen." *Internationale Zeitschrift für Psychoanalyse* 19 (1933): 499–503.

Boone, Joseph Allen. *Tradition Counter Tradition: Love and the Form of Fiction.* Chicago: University of Chicago Press, 1987.

Bossard, Abbot Eugène. *Gilles de Rais, Maréchal de France.* 8 vols. Paris, 1886.

Boswell, John. *Christianity, Social Tolerance and Homosexuality: Gay People in Western Europe from the Christian Era to the Fourteenth Century.* Chicago: University of Chicago Press, 1980.

Bray, Alan. *Homosexuality in Renaissance England*. London: Gay Men's Press, 1982.

Brontë, Emily. *Wuthering Heights*. Norton Critical Edition. New York: W. W. Norton, 1972.

Brophy, Brigid. *Prancing Novelist: A Defence of Fiction in the Form of a Critical Biography in Praise of Ronald Firbank*. New York: Harper & Row, 1973.

Byron, George Gordon. *Byron's Letters and Journals*. 12 vols. Ed. Leslie A. Marchand. Cambridge, Mass.: Harvard University Press, 1973–82.

Carpenter, Edward. *Selected Writings*. Vol. 1: *Sex*. London: Gay Men's Press, 1984.

Chauncey, George. "From Sexual Inversion to Homosexuality: Medicine and the Changing Conceptualization of Female Deviance." *Salmagundi* 58–59 (Fall–Winter 1982–83): 114–46.

Chessman, Harriet Scott. *The Public Is Invited to Dance: Representation, the Body, and Dialogue in Gertrude Stein*. Stanford, Calif.: Stanford University Press, 1989.

Chodorow, Nancy. *The Reproduction of Mothering: Psychoanalysis and the Sociology of Gender*. Berkeley: University of California Press, 1978.

Cohen, Ed. "Writing Gone Wilde: Homoerotic Desire in the Closet of Representation." *PMLA* 102, no. 5 (1987): 801–13.

Cohen, William A. "Willie and Wilde: Reading *The Portrait of Mr. W.H.*" *SAQ* 88, no. 1 (Winter 1989): 219–45.

Coleridge, Samuel Taylor. *Shakespearean Criticism*, vol 2. Ed. Thomas Middleton Raysor. London: Dent, 1960.

Craft, Christopher. "'Descend and Touch and Enter': Tennyson's Strange Manner of Address." *Genders* 1 (Spring 1988): 83–101.

Crompton, Louis. *Byron and Greek Love: Homophobia in 19th-Century England*. Berkeley: University of California Press, 1985.

Culler, Jonathan. *Roland Barthes*. New York: Oxford University Press, 1983.

Delay, Jean. *The Youth of André Gide*. Trans. June Guicharnaud. Chicago: University of Chicago Press, 1963.

Dellamora, Richard. *Masculine Desire: The Sexual Politics of Victorian Aestheticism*. Chapel Hill: University of North Carolina Press, 1990.

————. "Representation and Homophobia in *The Picture of Dorian Gray.*" *Victorian Newsletter* 73 (Spring 1988): 78–81.

Derrida, Jacques. "The Purveyor of Truth." Trans. Alan Bass. In John P. Muller and William J. Richardson, eds., *The Purloined Poe: Lacan, Derrida and Psychoanalytic Reading.* Baltimore: Johns Hopkins University Press, 1988.

DeSalvo, Louise A. *Virginia Woolf: The Impact of Childhood Sexual Abuse on Her Life and Work.* Boston: Beacon, 1989.

DiBattista, Maria. *First Love: The Affections of Modern Fiction.* Chicago: University of Chicago Press, 1991.

Dick, Bernard. *The Hellenism of Mary Renault.* Carbondale: Southern Illinois University Press, 1972.

Dijkstra, Bram. *Idols of Perversity: Fantasies of Feminine Evil in Fin-de-Siècle Culture.* New York: Oxford University Press, 1986.

Dollimore, Jonathan. "Different Desires: Subjectivity and Trangression in Wilde and Gide." *Textual Practice* 1, no. 1 (1987): 48–67.

————. "The Dominant and the Deviant: A Violent Dialectic." *Critical Quarterly* 28, nos. 1–2 (Spring–Summer 1986): 179–92.

————. *Sexual Dissidence: Augustine to Wilde, Freud to Foucault.* Oxford: Clarendon Press, 1991.

DuPlessis, Rachel Blau. *Writing Beyond the Ending: Narrative Strategies of Twentieth-Century Women Writers.* Bloomington: Indiana University Press, 1985.

Dydo, Ulla E. "*Stanzas in Meditation*: The Other Autobiography." *Chicago Review* 35, no. 2 (1985): 4–20.

Edelman, Lee. "Homographesis." *Yale Journal of Criticism* 3, no. 1 (Fall 1989): 189–207.

Edwards, Lee R. *Psyche as Hero: Female Heroism and Fictional Form.* Middletown, Conn.: Wesleyan University Press, 1984.

Eliot, George. *The Mill on the Floss.* Riverside Edition. Ed. Gordon S. Haight. Boston: Houghton Mifflin, 1961.

Ellmann, Richard. *Oscar Wilde: A Collection of Critical Essays.* Englewood Cliffs, N.J.: Prentice-Hall, 1969.

Fassler, Barbara. "Theories of Homosexuality as Sources of Bloomsbury's Androgyny." *Signs* 5, no. 2 (Winter 1979): 237–51.

Ferenczi, Sandor. "The Nosology of Male Homosexuality (Homoerotism)." In *Sex in Psychoanalysis.* Trans. Ernest Jones. Boston: Gorham, 1916.

Fiedler, Leslie. *Love and Death in the American Novel*. New York: Stein & Day, 1966.

Firbank, Ronald. *The Artificial Princess*. In *Five Novels*. New York: New Directions, 1981.

———. *Concerning the Eccentricities of Cardinal Pirelli*. In *Five Novels*. New York: New Directions, 1981.

———. *The Princess Zoubaroff*. In *The Complete Ronald Firbank*. London: Duckworth, 1961.

———. "True Love." In *Complete Short Stories*. Ed. Steven Moore. Elmwood Park, Ill.: Dalkey Archive, 1990.

———. *Vainglory*. New York: Brentano's, 1925.

———. *Valmouth*. In *Five Novels*. New York: New Directions, 1981.

Fone, Byron R. S. *Hidden Heritage: History and the Gay Imagination*. New York: Irvington, 1981.

Foucault, Michel. "De l'amitié comme mode de vie: un entretien avec un lecteur quinquagenaire." *Le Gai Pied* 25 (Apr. 1981): 38–39.

———. *Discipline and Punish: The Birth of the Prison*. Trans. Alan Sheridan. New York: Vintage, 1979.

———. *The History of Sexuality*. Vol. 1: *An Introduction*. Trans. Robert Hurley. New York: Vintage, 1980.

Freud, Sigmund. *The Standard Edition of the Complete Psychological Works of Sigmund Freud*. 24 vols. Trans. James Strachey. London: Hogarth, 1973–74.

Gates, Barbara T. *Victorian Suicide: Mad Crimes and Sad Histories*. Princeton, N.J.: Princeton University Press, 1988.

Gay, Peter. *The Bourgeois Experience: Victoria to Freud*. Vol. 2: *The Tender Passion*. New York: Oxford University Press, 1986.

Genet, Jean. *The Thief's Journal*. Trans. Bernard Frechtman. New York: Grove, 1982.

Gide, André. *Amyntas*. Paris: Gallimard, 1925.

———. *Amyntas*. Trans. Richard Howard. New York: Ecco, 1988.

———. *Les Cahiers et les Poésies avec des fragments inédits du Journal d'André Walter*. In *Oeuvres Complètes*. Paris: Gallimard, 1986.

———. *If It Die*. Trans. Dorothy Bussy. New York: Vintage, 1963.

———. *The Immoralist*. Trans. Richard Howard. New York: Knopf, 1970.

———. *L'Immoraliste*. In *Romans, recits, et sôties*. Paris: Gallimard, 1958.

————. *Journal 1889–1939*. Paris: Gallimard, 1960.

————. *The Notebooks of André Walter*. Trans. Wade Baskin. New York: Philosophical Library, 1968.

————. *Si le grain ne meurt*. Paris: Gallimard, 1955.

————. *Le Traité du Narcisse*. In *Romans, récits et sôties*. Paris: Gallimard, 1958.

Gilman, Sander L. "Strauss, the Pervert, and Avant Garde Opera of the Fin de Siècle." *New German Critique* 43 (1988): 35–68.

Girard, René. *Deceit, Desire, and the Novel: Self and Other in Literary Structure*. Trans. Yvonne Freccero. Baltimore, Md.: Johns Hopkins University Press, 1988.

Glendinning, Victoria. *Vita: The Life of V. Sackville-West*. New York: Knopf, 1983.

Goethe, Johann Wolfgang von. *The Sorrows of Young Werther*. Trans. Victor Lange. New York: Holt, Rinehart & Winston, 1949.

Halperin, David. *One Hundred Years of Homosexuality and Other Essays on Greek Love*. New York: Routledge, 1990.

Harris, Frank. *Oscar Wilde: His Life and Confessions*. New York: Harris, 1918.

Harvey, A. D. "Prosecutions for Sodomy in England at the Beginning of the Nineteenth Century." *Historical Journal* 21, no. 4 (Dec. 1978): 939–48.

Heath, Stephen. "Barthes on Love." *SubStance* 37/38 (1983): 100–106.

Heilbrun, Carolyn G. *Toward a Recognition of Androgyny*. New York: Harper Colophon, 1973.

Hemingway, Ernest. *A Moveable Feast*. New York: Scribner's, 1964.

Hermann, Claudine. *Les Voleuses de langue*. Paris: des femmes, 1976.

Herrmann, Anne. *The Dialogic and Difference: "An/Other Woman" in Virginia Woolf and Christa Wolf*. New York: Columbia University Press, 1989.

Hocquenghem, Guy. *Homosexual Desire*. Trans. Daniella Dangoor. London: Allison & Busby, 1978.

Hollinghurst, Alan. *The Swimming-Pool Library*. New York: Vintage, 1989.

Huysmans, Joris-Karl. *Là-bas*. Paris: Tresse & Stock, 1896.

Hyde, H. Montgomery. *The Love That Dared Not Speak Its Name: A Candid History of Homosexuality in Britain*. Boston: Little Brown, 1970.

Irigaray, Luce. *Speculum of the Other Woman.* Trans. Gillian C. Gill. Ithaca, N.Y.: Cornell University Press, 1985.

Kahane, Claire. "The Nuptials of Metaphor: Self and Other in Virginia Woolf." *Literature and Society* 30 (1980): 72–82.

Kant, Immanuel. *Lectures on Ethics.* Trans. Louis Infield. New York: Harper & Row, 1963.

Kaye, Richard. *Suspended Desires: Flirtation in the Victorian and Edwardian Novel.* Ph.D. diss., Princeton University, 1994.

Keats, John. *Complete Poems.* Ed. Jack Stillinger. Cambridge, Mass.: Harvard University Press, 1982.

Knopp, Sherron E. "'If I Saw You Would You Kiss Me?': Sapphism and the Subversiveness of Virginia Woolf's *Orlando.*" *PMLA* 103, no. 1 (Jan. 1988): 24–34.

Koestenbaum, Wayne. "Wilde's Hard Labor and the Birth of Gay Reading." In Joseph A. Boone and Michael Cadden, eds., *Engendering Men: The Question of Male Feminist Criticism.* New York: Routledge, 1990.

Kopelson, Kevin. "Wilde, Barthes, and the Orgasmics of Truth." *Genders* 7 (Mar. 1990): 22–31.

Krafft-Ebing, Richard von. *Psychopathia Sexualis.* Trans. Franklin S. Klaf. New York: Bell, 1965. Orig. pub. 1886.

Kristeva, Julia. *Desire in Language: A Semiotic Approach to Literature and Art.* Trans. Thomas Gora, Alice Jardine, and Leon S. Roudiez. New York: Columbia University Press, 1980.

———. *Tales of Love.* Trans. Leon S. Roudiez. New York: Columbia University Press, 1987.

Kritzman, Lawrence D. "The Discourse of Desire and the Question of Gender." In Steven Ungar and Betty R. McGraw, eds., *Signs in Culture: Roland Barthes Today.* Iowa City: University of Iowa Press, 1989.

Lacan, Jacques. "The subversion of the subject and the dialectic of desire in the Freudian unconscious." In *Écrits: A Selection.* Trans. Alan Sheridan. New York: Norton, 1977.

Lambert, Royston. *Beloved and God: The Story of Hadrian and Antinous.* Secaucus, N.J.: Meadowland, 1988.

Lejeune, Philippe. "Autobiography in the Third Person." Trans. Annette and Edward Tomarken. *New Literary History* 9, no. 1 (Autumn 1977): 26–50.

Long, O. W. "English Translations of Goethe's *Werther*." *Journal of English and Germanic Philology* 14 (1915): 169–203.

Love, Jean. "*Orlando* and Its Genesis: Venturing and Experimenting in Art, Love, and Sex." In Ralph Freedman, ed., *Virginia Woolf: Revaluation and Continuity*. Berkeley: University of California Press, 1980.

Lucey, Michael. "The Consequences of Being Explicit: Watching Sex in Gide's *Si le grain ne meurt*." *Yale Journal of Criticism* 4, no. 1 (Fall 1990): 174–92.

Lucie-Smith, Edward. *The Dark Pageant*. London: Gay Men's Press, 1986.

Ludlam, Charles. *Bluebeard*. In *The Complete Plays of Charles Ludlam*. New York: Harper & Row, 1989.

MacDonald, Michael. "The Secularization of Suicide in England 1660–1880." *Past & Present* 111 (May 1986): 50–100.

Mallet, Robert, ed. *Self-Portraits: The Gide/Valéry Letters*. Trans. June Guicharnaud. Chicago: University of Chicago Press, 1966.

Mann, Thomas. *Essays*. Trans. H. T. Lowe-Porter. New York: Vintage, 1957.

Marcus, Steven. *The Other Victorians: A Study of Sexuality and Pornography in Mid-Nineteenth-Century England*. New York: New American Library, 1977.

Martin, Robert K. *Hero, Captain, and Stranger: Male Friendship, Social Critique, and Literary Form in the Sea Novels of Merman Melville*. Chapel Hill: University of North Carolina Press, 1986.

Mason, Stuart. *Bibliography of Oscar Wilde*. London: 1914.

Merrill, Cynthia. "Mirrored Image: Gertude Stein and Autobiography." *Pacific Coast Philology* 20, nos. 1–2 (Nov. 1985): 11–17.

Miller, Nancy K. *The Heroine's Text: Readings in the French and English Novel 1722–1782*. New York: Columbia University Press, 1980.
———. *Subject to Change: Reading Feminist Writing*. New York: Columbia University Press, 1988.

Moglen, Helen. *Charlotte Brontë: The Self Conceived*. New York: 1976.

Newton, Esther. "The Mythic Mannish Lesbian: Radclyffe Hall and the New Woman." *Signs* 9, no. 4 (Summer 1984): 557–75.

Nicolson, Nigel. *Portrait of a Marriage*. New York: Atheneum, 1973.

O'Brien, Justin. *Portrait of André Gide: A Critical Biography*. New York: Knopf, 1953.

Plato. "The Symposium." In *Collected Dialogues of Plato*. Ed. Edith

Hamilton and Huntington Cairns. Trans. Michael Joyce. New York: Pantheon, 1961.

Polhemus, Robert M. *Erotic Faith: Being in Love from Jane Austen to D. H. Lawrence.* Chicago: University of Chicago Press, 1990.

Pollard, Patrick. *André Gide: Homosexual Moralist.* New Haven, Conn.: Yale University Press, 1991.

Poovey, Mary. *Uneven Developments: The Ideological Work of Gender in Mid-Victorian England.* Chicago: University of Chicago Press, 1988.

Renault, Mary. *The Bull from the Sea.* New York: Pantheon, 1962.

———. *The Charioteer.* New York: Pantheon, 1959.

———. *The Friendly Young Ladies.* New York: Pantheon, 1984.

———. *The Nature of Alexander.* New York: Pantheon, 1975.

———. *The Persian Boy.* New York: Vintage, 1988.

Rivers, J. R. *Proust and the Art of Love: The Aesthetics of Sexuality in the Life, Times, and Art of Marcel Proust.* New York: Columbia University Press, 1980.

Rosenman, Ellen Bayuk. *The Invisible Presence: Virginia Woolf and the Mother-Daughter Relationship.* Baton Rouge: Louisiana State University Press, 1986.

Rougemont, Denis de. *Love in the Western World.* Trans. Montgomery Belgion. New York: Harper & Row, 1974.

Rousseau, Jean Jacques. *Julie, or The New Eloise.* Trans. Judith H. Mc-Dowell. University Park: Pennsylvania State University Press, 1968.

Sadger, Isidore. "Ein Fall von Multipler Perversionem mit hysterischen Absenzen." *Jahrbuch für Psychoanalytische und Psychopathologische Forschungen* 2 (1910): 59–133.

Schopenhauer, Arthur. "The Metaphysics of the Love of the Sexes." In *The World as Will and Idea,* vol. 3. Trans. R. B. Haldane and J. Kemp. London: Routledge, 1948.

Schor, Naomi. "Dreaming Dissymmetry: Barthes, Foucault, and Sexual Difference." In Elizabeth Weed, ed., *Coming to Terms: Feminism, Theory, Politics.* New York: Routledge, 1989.

Sedgwick, Eve Kosofsky. *Epistemology of the Closet.* Berkeley: University of California Press, 1990.

Shaw, George Bernard. *Saint Joan.* In *Bernard Shaw: Selected Plays.* New York: Dodd Mead, 1981.

Shelley, Percy Bysshe. *The Poetical Works of Shelley.* Cambridge Edition. Ed. Newell F. Ford. Boston: Houghton Mifflin, 1974.

Showalter, Elaine. *The Female Malady: Women, Madness, and English Culture, 1830–1980.* New York: Pantheon, 1985.

Silverman, David, and Brian Torode. *The Material World.* London: Routledge, 1980.

Silverman, Kaja. *The Subject of Semiotics.* New York: Oxford University Press, 1983.

Singer, Irving. *The Nature of Love.* Vol. 2: *Courtly and Romantic.* Vol. 3: *The Modern World.* Chicago: University of Chicago Press, 1984, 1987.

Smyth, John Vignaux. *A Question of Eros: Irony in Sterne, Kierkegaard, and Barthes.* Tallahasee: Florida State University Press, 1986.

Souhami, Diana. *Gertrude and Alice.* Hammersmith, London: Pandora, 1991.

Stallybrass, Peter, and Allon White. *The Politics and Poetics of Transgression.* Ithaca, N.Y.: Cornell University Press, 1986.

Stanton, Domna. "Autogynography: Is the Subject Different?" *New York Literary Forum* 12–13 (1984): 5–22.

———. "The Mater of the Text: Barthesian Displacement and Its Limits." *L'Esprit Créature* 25, no. 2 (Summer 1985): 57–72.

Stein, Gertrude. "Ada." In *Geography and Plays.* New York: Something Else, 1968.

———. *The Autobiography of Alice B. Toklas.* New York: Vintage, 1961.

———. *Fernhurst, Q.E.D. and Other Early Writings.* New York: Liveright, 1971.

Stendhal. *De l'amour.* Paris: Garnier-Flammarion, 1965. Orig. pub. 1882.

———. *Love.* Trans. Gilbert and Suzanne Sale. Harmondsworth: Penguin, 1975.

Stimpson, Catharine. "Zero Degree Deviancy: The Lesbian Novel in English." *Critical Inquiry* 8, no. 2 (Winter 1981): 363–79.

Stokes, John. *In the Nineties.* Chicago: University of Chicago Press, 1989.

Stone, Lawrence. *The Family, Sex, and Marriage in England, 1500–1800.* New York: Harper & Row, 1977.

Strachey, Lytton. *Eminent Victorians.* San Diego: Harcourt Brace Jovanovich, n.d.; orig. pub. 1918.

Symonds, J. A. *Male Love: A Problem in Greek Ethics and Other Writings.* New York: Pagan, 1983; orig. pub. 1901.

————. *Sketches and Studies in Italy and Greece.* London: John Murray, 1927. Orig. pub. 1898.

Tanner, Tony. *Adultery in the Novel: Contract and Transgression.* Baltimore, Md.: Johns Hopkins University Press, 1979.

Thody, Philip. *Roland Barthes: A Conservative Estimate.* Atlantic Highlands, N.J.: Humanities, 1977.

Toklas, Alice B. *What Is Remembered.* New York: Holt, Rhinehart & Winston, 1963.

Ungar, Steven. *Roland Barthes: The Professor of Desire.* Lincoln: University of Nebraska Press, 1983.

Vidal, Gore. "A Good Man and a Perfect Play." Review of Richard Ellmann, *Oscar Wilde. TLS* (Oct. 2–8, 1987).

Warner, Michael. "Homo-Narcissism: or, Heterosexuality." In Joseph A. Boone and Michael Cadden, eds., *Engendering Men: The Question of Male Feminist Criticism.* New York: Routledge, 1990.

Weeks, Jeffrey. "Inverts, Perverts, and Mary-Annes: Male Prostitution and the Regulation of Homosexuality in England in the Nineteenth and Early Twentieth Centuries." In Martin Bauml Duberman, Martha Vicinus, and George Chauncey, eds., *Hidden From History: Reclaiming the Gay and Lesbian Past.* New York: New American Library, 1989.

————. *Sex, Politics and Society: The Regulation of Sexuality Since 1800.* London: Longman, 1981.

Weil, Kari. "The Aesthetics of Androgyny in Balzac and Woolf, or the Difference of Difference." *Critical Matrix: Princeton Working Papers in Women's Studies* 1, no. 6 (1985): 1–24.

Wilde, Oscar. *The Complete Illustrated Stories, Plays and Poems of Oscar Wilde.* London: Chancellor, 1986.

————. "The Critic as Artist." In *The Artist as Critic: Critical Writings of Oscar Wilde.* Ed. Richard Ellmann. Chicago: University of Chicago Press, 1968.

————. *De Profundis and Other Writings.* Middlesex, Eng.: Penguin, 1987.

————. *The Letters of Oscar Wilde.* Ed. Rupert Hart-Davis. London: Rupert Hart-Davis, 1962.

————. *The Picture of Dorian Gray.* Harmondsworth: Penguin, 1949.

————. *The Portrait of Mr. W.H.* [1889]. In *Complete Shorter Fiction.* Ed. Isobel Murray. London: W. H. Allen, 1979.

———. *The Portrait of Mr. W.H.* [1893]. In *The Artist as Critic: Critical Writings of Oscar Wilde*. Ed. Richard Ellmann. Chicago: University of Chicago Press, 1968.

———. *Teleny*. San Francisco: Gay Sunshine, 1984.

Winckelmann, Johann Joachim. *History of Ancient Art*. 4 vols. Trans. G. Henry Lodge. New York: Ungar, 1968.

Winkler, John J. *The Constraints of Desire: The Anthropology of Sex and Gender in Ancient Greece*. New York: Routledge, 1990.

Woolf, Virginia. *The Diary of Virginia Woolf*. 5 vols. Ed. Anne Olivier Bell. New York: Harcourt Brace Jovanovich, 1977–84.

———. *The Letters of Virginia Woolf*. 6 vols. Ed. Nigel Nicolson. New York: Harcourt Brace Jovanovich, 1975–80.

———. *Moments of Being*. Ed. Jeanne Schulkind. New York: Harcourt Brace Jovanovich, 1976.

———. *Mrs. Dalloway*. New York: Harcourt Brace, 1948.

———. *Night and Day*. New York: Harcourt Brace, 1948.

———. "On Being Ill." In *Collected Essays*, vol. 4. Ed. Leonard Woolf. New York: Harcourt Brace, 1967.

———. *Orlando: A Biography*. London: Hogarth, 1978.

———. *A Room of One's Own*. New York: Harcourt Brace Jovanovich, 1981.

———. *To the Lighthouse*. New York: Harcourt Brace, 1954.

———. *The Voyage Out*. San Diego: Harcourt Brace Jovanovich, n.d.

———. *The Waves*. New York: Harcourt Brace, 1950.

———. *A Writer's Diary*. New York: Harcourt Brace Jovanovich, 1954.

Yaeger, Patricia. "Towards a Female Sublime." In Linda S. Kauffman, ed., *Gender and Theory: Dialogues in Feminist Criticism*. Oxford: Basil Blackwell, 1989.

Yourcenar, Marguerite. *Alexis*. Trans. Walter Kaiser. New York: Farrar Straus Giroux, 1984.

———. *Coup de Grâce*. Trans. Grace Frick. New York: Farrar Straus Giroux, 1957.

———. *Feux*. Paris: Gallimard, 1974.

———. *Fires*. Trans. Dori Katz. New York: Farrar Straus Giroux, 1981.

———. *Mémoires d'Hadrien*. Paris: Gallimard, 1974.

————. *Memoirs of Hadrian.* Trans. Grace Frick. New York: Modern Library, 1984.

————. *With Open Eyes: Conversations with Matthieu Galey.* Trans. Arthur Goldhammer. Boston: Beacon, 1984.

————. *Les Yeux ouvertes: Entretiens avec Matthieu Galey.* Paris: Editions du Centurion, 1980.

Index

ᔓ

In this index "f" after a number indicates a separate reference on the next page, and "ff" indicates separate references on the next two pages. A continuous discussion over two or more pages is indicated by a span of numbers. *Passim* is used for a cluster of references in close but not consecutive sequence.

Library of Congress Cataloging-in-Publication Data

Kopelson, Kevin.
   Love's Litany : the writing of modern homoerotics / Kevin Kopelson
     p.   cm.
   Includes bibliographical references and index.
   ISBN 0-8047-2299-4 — ISBN 0-8047-2345-1 (pbk.)
   1. Homosexuality and literature—Great Britain—History—20th
century. 2. Homosexuality and literature—Great Britain—
History—19th century. 3. Erotic literature, English—History and
criticism—Theory, etc. 4. Erotic literature, French—History and
criticism—Theory, etc. 5. Gays' writings, English—History and
criticism—Theory, etc. 6. Gays' writings, French—History and
criticism—Theory, etc. 7. Lesbians in literature. 8. Gay men in
literature. 9. Love in literature. I. Title.
PR468.H65K66 1994
820.9′353—dc20

                                                       93-39677
                                                       CIP